FIRST FRUITS

First Fruits

THE LEWELLINGS AND THE BIRTH OF THE PACIFIC COAST FRUIT INDUSTRY

Linda Ziedrich

Oregon State University Press Corvallis

Cataloging-in-publication information is available from the Library of Congress.
ISBN 978-1-962645-30-0 paper; ISBN 978-1-962645-31-7 ebook

∞This paper meets the requirements of ANSI/NISO Z39.48-1992 (Permanence of Paper).

First published in 2025 by Oregon State University Press
Printed in the United States of America

Oregon State University Press
121 The Valley Library
Corvallis OR 97331-4501
541-737-3166 • fax 541-737-3170
www.osupress.oregonstate.edu

Oregon State University Press in Corvallis, Oregon, is located within the traditional homelands of the Mary's River or Ampinefu Band of Kalapuya. Following the Willamette Valley Treaty of 1855, Kalapuya people were forcibly removed to reservations in Western Oregon. Today, living descendants of these people are a part of the Confederated Tribes of Grand Ronde Community of Oregon (grandronde.org) and the Confederated Tribes of the Siletz Indians (ctsi.nsn.us).

[The apple tree] migrates with man, like the dog and horse and cow: first, perchance from Greece to Italy, thence to England: thence to America; and our Western emigrant is still marching steadily toward the setting sun with the seeds of the apple in his pocket, or perhaps a few young trees strapped to his load. At least a million apple-trees are thus set farther westward this year than any cultivated ones grew last year. . . for when man migrates, he carries with him not only his birds, quadrupeds, insects, vegetables, and his very sword, but his orchard also.

—Henry David Thoreau, "Wild Apples"

Contents

Henderson's Marriages and Children

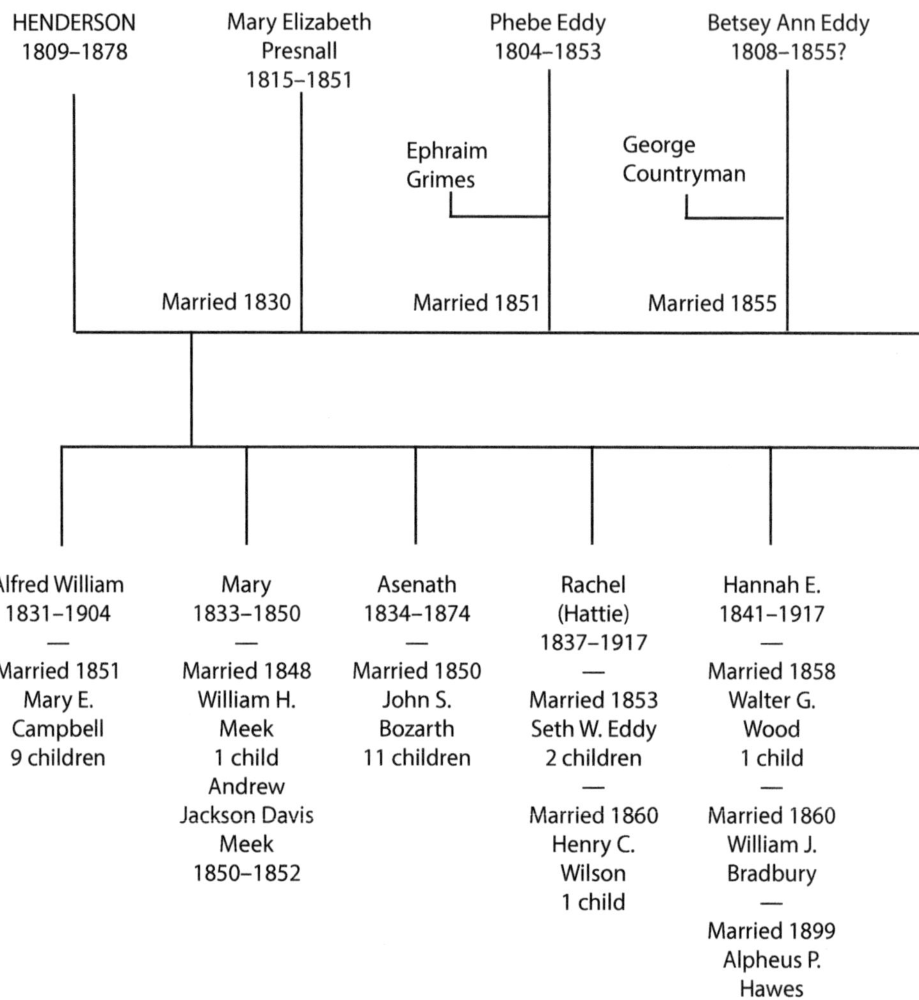

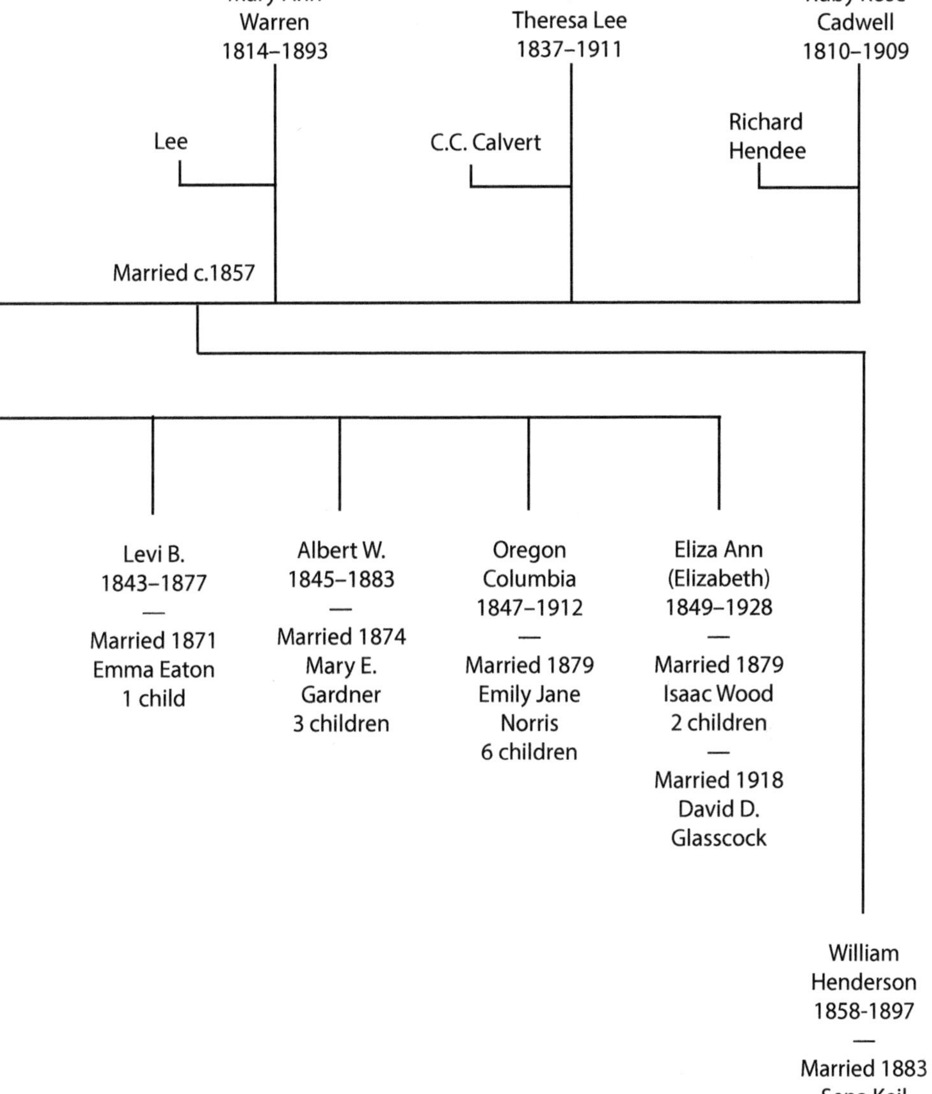
Mary Ann
Warren
1814–1893
?
Theresa Lee
1837–1911
Ruby Rose
Cadwell
1810–1909
Lee
C.C. Calvert
Richard
Hendee
Married c.1857
Levi B.
1843–1877
—
Married 1871
Emma Eaton
1 child
Albert W.
1845–1883
—
Married 1874
Mary E.
Gardner
3 children
Oregon
Columbia
1847–1912
—
Married 1879
Emily Jane
Norris
6 children
Eliza Ann
(Elizabeth)
1849–1928
—
Married 1879
Isaac Wood
2 children
—
Married 1918
David D.
Glasscock
William
Henderson
1858-1897
—
Married 1883
Sena Keil
4 children

Meshack and Jane's Children

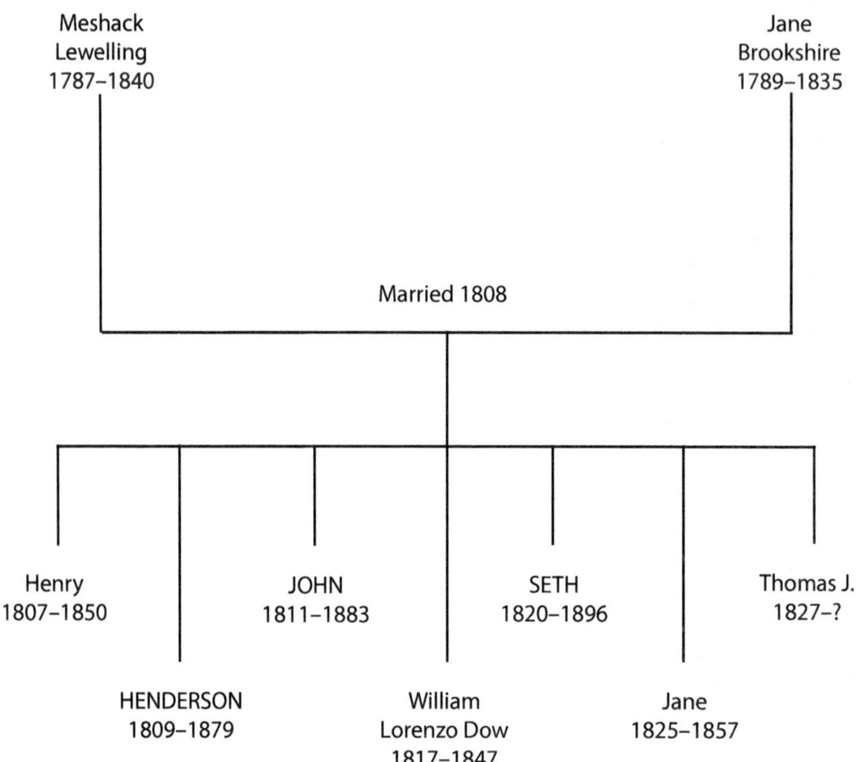

John and Elvy's Children

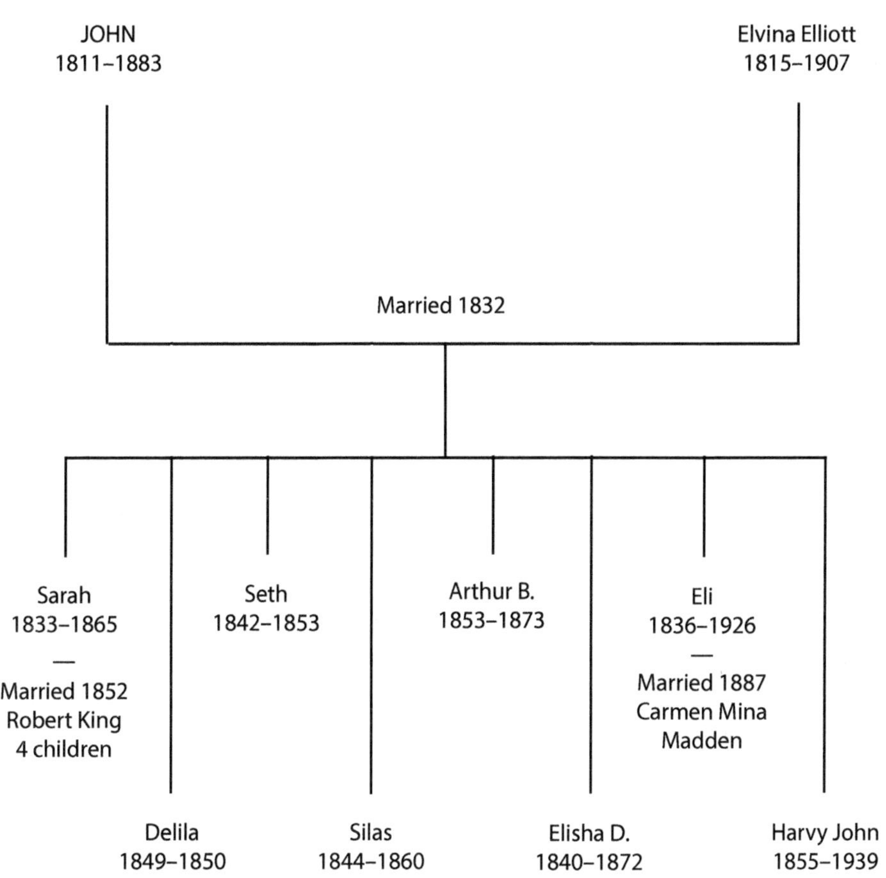

Seth's Marriages and Children

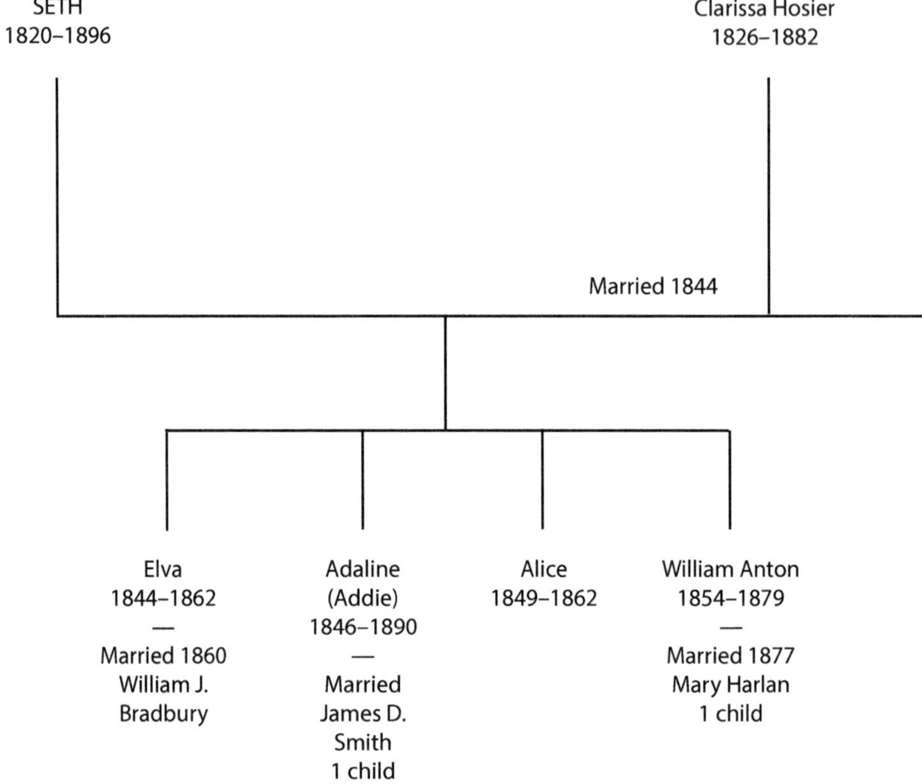

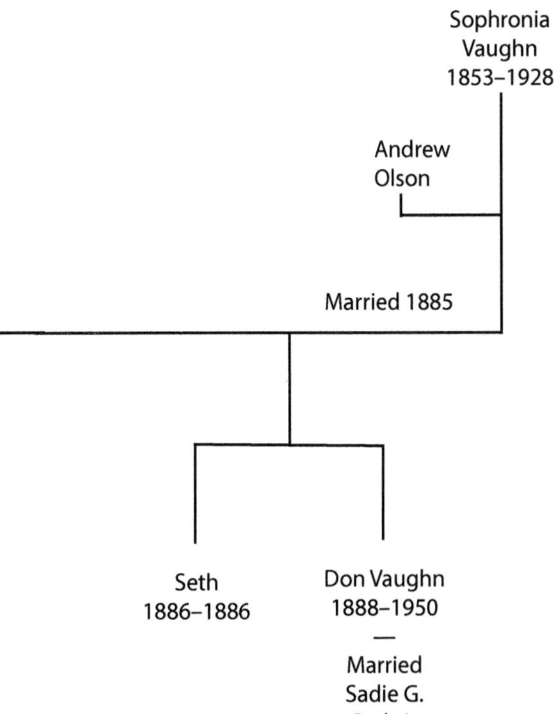

Sophronia
Vaughn
1853–1928
Andrew
Olson
Married 1885
Seth
1886–1886
Don Vaughn
1888–1950
—
Married
Sadie G.
Guthrie

Introduction

> There is no doubt but that health, comfort, sociability, temperance, and good morals, generally, would be promoted, by making a choice fruit garden near our dwelling.
>
> G. W. N., *New England Farmer*, November 1858

The brothers Henderson, John, and Seth Lewelling were principal founders of the Pacific coast fruit industry. From their orchards and nurseries in Oregon and California, they sold plants and fruit up and down the West Coast and eventually in Eastern cities as well. Theirs is a story of clearing land, planting, grafting, searching for superior varieties, and sometimes breeding their own. But the Lewellings weren't simply horticultural pioneers. Their lives reflect the history of westward expansion, including the infectious urge to conquer the continent, the epidemics of often deadly diseases, the displacement and killing of the native peoples, the battles over slavery, the rapid advancements in transportation, and the anti-Chinese hysteria. To examine the Lewellings in their social milieu is to reappraise this history—while yearning to taste those intriguing old varieties of cherries, pears, and apples.

The brothers' story has been told many times, but always in snatches, incompletely and usually inaccurately. In Iowa, the story centers on Henderson, the bold Underground Railroad agent whose house, with its trap door to a basement hidey-hole, is now a museum. In the Oregon telling, Henderson was the man with the traveling nursery who brought apple trees from Iowa on the Overland Trail; two children's picture books offer riffs on this theme. But sometimes, especially in California, the pioneer with the wagonload of grafted trees was Henderson's brother John, or even their friend William Meek. Although Fruitvale, in Oakland, was once Henderson's farm and nursery, his horticultural contributions are mostly forgotten in California; there he is remembered, when he is remembered at all, as a fool and a failure, a man who abandoned his wife while attempting to establish a utopian free-love colony in Honduras. Even in Oregon, Henderson's younger brother Seth, a breeder who named two cherries for the anti-slavery cause and another for his Chinese foreman, is sometimes identified as Henderson's son and sometimes conflated with Henderson himself, as if the two brothers were one and the same. In short, the Lewelling story needs sorting out.

The full story of the Lewelling brothers takes us from one coast to the other, with two long stops along the way and trips back and forth. When the brothers were young, the Lewellings moved from North Carolina to Indiana. Later, Henderson and John moved from Indiana to Iowa before all three traversed the Overland Trail, with Henderson heading to Oregon and Seth and John to California. In addition to these journeys by foot, horse, and wagon, Henderson and John traveled to and from the Eastern states by steamship, Henderson via the Isthmus of Panama and John via Nicaragua. Later Henderson voyaged to Central America again, in his own sailing ship. The Lewellings' story covers a lot of ground.

Their tale spans a long time, too, from the early nineteenth century to near its end (Henderson was born in 1809, and Seth died in 1896). Major historical events seemed often to affect the Lewellings personally. Henderson befriended Marcus Whitman shortly before the missionary and his family were killed. All three Lewellings took part in California's gold rush, and Henderson also prospected in Idaho. The brothers experienced the splintering of Quakerism and the birth of a new quasi-religion, Spiritualism. They witnessed the coming of the railroad, and they pioneered its use for shipping fruit by rail to Eastern cities. They experienced economic booms and busts, mass immigration from China and Europe, and the corruption and inequity of the Gilded Age. The brothers were repeatedly pulled into politics. Collectively, they participated not only in the Underground Railroad and abolitionist agitation but also in the development of the Liberty Party, the Grange, the Farmers' Alliance, and the Populist Party. Examining the details of their story compels us to take a fresh look at a long span of American history.

The Lewellings were in many ways typical of the westering emigrants. Like so many others, they repeatedly pulled up roots to homestead in newly opened territories, though each move required an amount of labor almost unimaginable in an era of highways, chainsaws, and tractors.

While Indians were driven west by war, trickery, starvation, and forced marches, the Lewelling brothers, like other emigrants, were driven by their own curiosity, imagination, and ambition. Like other emigrants, too, they profited from the U.S. government's low-cost distribution of "virgin" land, killed the native fauna without compunction, and cut down forests to plant fields, orchards, and pastures. Like so many others, they lost loved ones along the way and eventually much of their wealth. In examining their motivations, we gain insight into the whole wild westering movement.

In other ways, the Lewellings diverge from the conventional image of westering migrants. Henderson may have had a restless and impulsive nature, but none of the Lewellings were individualists. They believed in cooperation. They worked together as partners at times, and they supported each other in various ways throughout their lives. Their cooperation within the family served as a model for collaborations with neighbors and acquaintances in the wider communities in which they lived. These collaborations were essential in establishing thriving farms, orchards, and towns in climes unlike any the brothers or their associates had known before. Their concern for the common good made them champions of education; although none had had much schooling, all three helped found schools. And their sense of social responsibility turned Seth and John, along with Henderson's son Alfred, into respected civic leaders. Their commitment to equality spurred them to toil for democracy.

The Lewellings' story compels us to consider the role of the Religious Society of Friends in both westward expansion and the country's trajectory toward the Civil War. The brothers were not unusual among emigrants in having grown up Quaker. With their "plain" speech and drab clothing, the Friends were still partially stuck in the seventeenth century as they floundered through a series of schisms in the first half of the nineteenth century. And yet the Friends systematically moved westward, establishing new meetings (congregations) that were sponsored by older ones. They also established towns, industries, children's schools (which became models for public schools), and high schools that developed into prestigious liberal-arts colleges.

The Friends called themselves "the peculiar people," and they were indeed atypical in some ways. Most notably, they valued equality and peace to an extent that most Americans did not. To the Friends, equality wasn't just for landed white men; it extended—at least in limited ways—to women, Indians, and Black people. By the nineteenth century, American Friends were united against slavery and working toward its end.

The Lewelling family so thoroughly absorbed Quaker values that they took it as their duty not just to speak out against enslavement but to actively help bring slaves to freedom. The family joined a group of radical Friends—most, like themselves, from the North Carolina Piedmont—who doggedly broke laws to hide fugitives from slavery and to move them secretly toward places of freedom. The anti-slavery Friends found themselves at one extreme of a struggle that was tearing the country, and Quakerdom, apart.

Paradoxically, however, in their journeys to the West Coast the Lewellings walked or rode right out of their Quaker lives. They broke a Friends' rule by settling on land the native inhabitants still considered their own. They made homes where slavery didn't exist but Black people were unwelcome. The Lewellings gave up their *thees* and *thous* and broad-brimmed hats, accepted wine as a temperance beverage, and let themselves enjoy music and dancing, pleasures forbidden to Friends.

What aspects of Quakerism, then, stayed with the Lewellings? Although the brothers and their wives rejected the Friends' insularity and formalism, the Lewellings held to the primary Quaker values of honesty, equality, and pacifism. They were by all accounts gentle and kind. Quaker values supported the brothers' cooperative ventures, led Seth to give provocative names to his cherry cultivars, and prompted the Lewellings' involvement with various avant-garde social movements, from temperance to vegetarianism, feminism, Spiritualism, and, at least in Henderson's case, communalism and free love. Considering the Lewellings helps us see the connections among these movements and their special appeal for people with Quaker roots.

Quakerism also influenced the Lewellings' choice of profession. Horticulture had been a favorite Quaker métier since at least the eighteenth century. The Lewellings' story reveals the role of Quaker nurserymen in promoting orchards, especially grafted orchards, as symbols of comfort, prosperity, and rectitude and in ensuring that no family would have to live without delicious, beautiful fruit. Their story also demonstrates how the apple, despite its susceptibility to pests and disease, has remained the most cherished of American fruits.

If we disregard religion, politics, and social movements, the Lewelling story still fascinates as horticultural history. We must wonder at the speed at which the brothers grafted, grew, and distributed millions of fruit trees up and down the Pacific coast. Impressive, too, are the ways they adapted to changing conditions, including Iowa's cold, Oregon's wet springs, California's long summer droughts, and advances in trade and transportation. The brothers replaced barrels with boxes for packing fruit, for example, switched fruits and varieties in their orchards to suit their climates and markets, and developed their own superior cultivars. Their engagement in horticultural societies and fairs recalls for us a time when everyone cared about farming. And John's experience as a St. Helena "winegrower" illuminates how that little town, and the whole Napa Valley, became a center of excellence in wine making.

The Lewellings' story is about—all at once—westward expansion, social reform, egalitarian politics, and fruit culture. I hope my telling will promote recognition of the brothers' fruits: those they brought west, those they developed, those that are famous, and those long forgotten. I hope, too, that it will foster appreciation for unorthodox strains of thought that may seem fatuous today but that acted as a check on nineteenth-century greed and bigotry. Most of all, I hope the book will show how the Lewellings' cooperative spirit, and especially their dedication to one another, fostered their success both in farming and in life.

A note on the spelling of the name *Lewelling:* the Lewelling ancestor who immigrated from Wales spelled his last name *Llewellyn.* Meshack, the brothers' father and probably the great-grandson of that Welsh immigrant, spelled the family name *Lewelling.* At about age forty, Henderson changed the spelling of his name to *Luelling.* Whether he was motivated by a Quakerish commitment to plainness, by the reformist principles of Noah Webster, or by some creative urge, no one knows. But he used the *Luelling* spelling, for the most part, throughout the rest of his life. His younger brother Seth followed suit, although late in life, beginning soon after Henderson's death, Seth resumed spelling his name *Lewelling.* Their brother John always used the *Lewelling* spelling.

Others have sometimes overlooked these personal preferences. Contemporary newspapers often got the spelling wrong. Some of Henderson's descendants changed *Luelling* to *Llewellyn.*

For simplicity, I've used *Lewelling* to refer to the three brothers together and to John at any time in his life. I've used *Luelling* for Henderson and Seth and their children during the years they used this spelling. This inconsistency, although perhaps bothersome to some modern readers, reflects the nonchalant attitude toward spelling that prevailed in the nineteenth century. In his diaries Seth called his wife, Clarissa, Clarrissa, and even Claryssa ("Clarrissa and the Girls is gone to Spelling School," he wrote in 1859). Consistent spelling became more important as literacy increased but was never as obligatory as today.

Chapter 1 Leaving Carolina

> We ourselves must mark out the course of action and follow the path that will cause our progeny to feel proud of us as ancestors.
>
> –Enos Mendenhall to his nephew, 1873

In 1822, Meshack Lewelling and Jane Brookshire, a Quaker couple in Randolph County, North Carolina, packed up the family's essential possessions in a horse-drawn wagon or two. With six children ranging in age from two to fifteen, they began a long walk to Indiana, a distance of about five hundred miles. The younger children probably rode part of the way, perched on top of the household goods, but for the most part the family was on foot. For at least five weeks, they traveled on rough dirt roads. Their choice of routes probably took them over the Blue Ridge Mountains on Daniel Boone's Wilderness Road, through the Cumberland Gap, and across the ridges and ravines of the Cumberland Plateau to Mount Vernon, Kentucky. From there they headed north, through heavily forested lowlands, to the Ohio River. They may have crossed the river by ferry at Cincinnati, before continuing north to the little Quaker village of Richmond, Indiana, where they probably rested at a relative's cabin before moving on to the wilderness of Henry County. For some of the children, the trip must have been a grand adventure. thirteen-year-old Henderson, in particular, would later grow restless for more such expeditions.

The Lewellings were not the only Americans moving west over the Appalachians. The Quakers of North Carolina, especially, were leaving in droves. At least four hundred Quaker families—as many as two thousand individuals—had left the Carolina Piedmont for Indiana by 1835.

It may be hard to imagine such a move as anything but a flight of desperation—from famine, war, or some terrible oppression. But, twenty-three years before the term *manifest destiny* was coined, Americans were already undergoing a national fever for westering, for expanding their

The Lewellings' probable route from North Carolina to Indiana. Map by Rebecca Waterhouse.

young society into the wilderness. The Quakers were no exception. The westering fever would take the next generation of Lewellings all the way to the Pacific coast.

Quakers in Carolina

Today few people associate the Friends with North Carolina, but it was once a Quaker stronghold. In the seventeenth century North Carolina was certainly a happier place for Quakers than Massachusetts, where Puritans cut off Friends' ears, bored their tongues, and whipped, branded, and even hanged Quakers. "Sufferings," as the Friends called them, were milder but still substantial in Virginia, which banned Quakers from entering from 1660 on and penalized those already in the colony. Quakers suffered less in North Carolina, though church taxes were an ongoing bother and demands for military service at least an occasional nuisance. But the colony's charter permitted freedom of religion, and Quakers were welcomed for their industriousness. Friends were among the earliest settlers in North Carolina; the first arrived about 1665. Quaker evangelists, traveling on Indian trails, preached wherever a group could be assembled. They must have been eloquent indeed, because the Friends' numbers grew quickly, through conversion, or "convincement," as well as through immigration and natural increase.

Early Quakers in the colony readily assumed political leadership. In the late 1600s Friends dominated the North Carolina Assembly and some courts; for a year, from 1694 to 1695, the colony even had a Quaker governor. But in 1704 Parliament began requiring public officials to take an oath of office, and Friends sacrificed their posts rather than comply: taking an oath would imply they weren't always truthful, as their creed required them to be. By 1709 they were outnumbered by other denominations in the colony, but they still had outsize influence. Although they no longer ran for political office, they frequently took petitions to the government. This became the usual Quaker approach to politics.

The earliest Friends in North Carolina, like those in Virginia, settled along the coast. In the 1740s, Quakers began migrating to the Piedmont—the wide plateau on the eastern edge of the Appalachian Mountains—by the Great Wagon Road from Pennsylvania. Other waves came from Rhode Island, Virginia, and Nantucket. The Friends came to dominate the population in five Piedmont counties—Guilford, Randolph, Alamance, Orange, and Chatham.

Although the journey to Indiana was Meshack's first and only emigrant experience, he was just a generation removed from the last migration in his family. His father, William F. Lewelling, had been born in Virginia. But William wasn't Quaker at all; he was Anglican. Meshack and his family were, apparently, converts to the Society of Friends. This perhaps helps explain both their zealotry and Henderson's, John's, and Seth's later disillusionment with the sect. However deep their passion for Quaker causes—for promoting temperance, avoiding war, and ending slavery—the Lewellings weren't "birthright" Friends. Quaker values would prove fundamental to their identities, but Quakerism itself would not.

Life hadn't been bad for the Lewellings in North Carolina. Meshack owned 480 acres, 130 of them purchased for him by his father, in an area that had once been home to the Uwharrie (or Keyauwee) Indians. The Lewellings and their neighbors farmed primarily for their own subsistence. They kept pigs and cattle, which they usually let roam, to feed on fallen nuts and fruits, as well as green vegetation in the woods. The families grew grain, mostly corn; flax, hemp, and cotton for clothes and rope; indigo for dye; herbs for cooking and medicines; and abundant vegetables and melons. They gathered wild foods—grapes, strawberries, persimmons, and chestnuts—and made sugar from maple sap. The farmers' main cash crop was tobacco.

Every family planted an orchard, with pear, cherry, peach, and, especially, apple trees. Families pressed most of their apples into cider, and they may even have distilled some of the cider, because even for Quakers *temperance* meant moderate consumption of alcohol, not prohibition of it. They also dried apples, cooked them into pies and dumplings, fermented them into vinegar, and stored them for the winter. A family needed plenty of apple trees, at least six per person, according to the rule of thumb. The bad apples and pomace were treats for the livestock.

As young Quakers, the Lewelling children were taught not only religion, reading, writing, and arithmetic—they probably attended a school for these subjects, sponsored by the Back Creek Monthly Meeting—but also practical arts. Dance, music, and even frivolous conversation were forbidden, but natural history was a properly "innocent" form of recreation that might contribute to success in farming and even lead to a socially useful career as a physician, pharmacist, botanist, nurseryman, or orchardist. The farm and the woods around must have been an ideal environment for such an education.

While Jane Brookshire Lewelling tended the children and the garden, cooked and preserved food, made soap and candles, and spun, wove, and sewed, Meshack practiced at least one trade. He was a doctor, of the backwoods sort, carrying his medicines in his horse's saddlebags. He may have put in a short stint at a small, proprietary medical school, but he had more likely apprenticed with a local physician or even taught himself. This doesn't mean he was simply an herbalist or a quack; when he died, his estate included at least seven medical books, including two on surgery. Still, medicine at the time wasn't a particularly prestigious or lucrative occupation unless a person had a medical degree from a European university. Meshack probably traded his doctoring services for food and other farm goods. He must not have profited enough from this work to encourage his children to go into the trade. As far as we know, none of them did.

Meshack was also a grafter—that is, he grafted fruit trees. Grafting was still a rare craft in America; until recently seedling trees had satisfied most families. Plums and even peaches often grow close to true from seed. Apples generally do not; each seedling tree, like every human being, is unique. Although all named apple varieties, from America, Europe, and beyond, have started from seed, most seedling apple trees produce small, astringent, or sour fruit. These apples can make acceptably good cider, but a mix of selected apple varieties, together contributing tannic ("bitter"), tart ("sharp"), and sweet tastes, make even tastier cider. And apples of named varieties—that is, from grafted trees—are usually better for eating than fruit from seedling trees. As the anti-alcohol movement grew stronger and more extreme, cider lost its status as a temperance beverage (partially because it was often fortified, for long keeping, with corn whiskey). Americans, and especially Quakers, wanted apples they could enjoy eating, raw or cooked, from mid-summer through spring. And so they were coming to prefer to plant an assortment of grafted varieties in their orchards. For someone who knew only seedling apple trees, an orchard where every tree produced large, sweet fruit must have been a thing of wonder and delight.

Grafting is a simple but seemingly magical art. You cut a short, pencil-thin piece of branch from the tree you want to clone; this is your scion. You will graft it to a host plant, the rootstock. This could be a tree already established in an orchard, or it could be a young tree uprooted during its winter dormancy. Today rootstocks are themselves cloned, and selected for size and other virtues other than fruit. But before the twentieth century, scions were grafted to seedling trees (or, as I'll later explain, to pieces of root). Once you have your scion and your rootstock, you cut both the base of the scion and the top of the rootstock at a shallow, matching angle. You bind the two together so that the two cambium layers are touching, and if all goes well they grow together. You have created a whip graft. There are other kinds of grafts involving scions, such as whip-and-tongue and cleft, but they are all similar. You can also graft a tiny vegetative bud to your rootstock.

In Meshack's time, grafting wasn't a new technology. The ancient Greeks had practiced it, and the Romans had taken it to Britain. Thereafter, the craft was largely neglected until the late eighteenth century, when the wealthy rediscovered it in horticultural journals. But some Britons, especially monks, had kept right on grafting through the centuries. In Wales, among more than one hundred regional apple varieties is the Anglesey Pig Snout (or *trwyn mochyn*), said to date from the 1600s. The craft of grafting could have been passed down in Meshack's family all the way from his great-grandfather Llewellyn, an immigrant to the colonies from Wales.

It's more likely, however, that Meshack learned grafting from Quaker farmers in his neighborhood. Anne Jessop, a Quaker minister from Guilford County—neighbor to Randolph County, and with it the heart of North Carolina's Quaker District—had traveled to England, Ireland, and Scotland in 1790. Two years later, she returned with many kinds of apple, pear, and grape cuttings and vegetable, flower, and alfalfa seeds. Anne hired a man named Abijah Pinson to help her graft the apple and pear cuttings onto seedling trees. Abijah subsequently established a nursery at Westfield, North Carolina—a community formed by Quakers from Guilford County—and between them Anne and Abijah distributed the British varieties widely, even through the Yearly Meeting. North Carolina Quakers would take about twenty of these varieties with them on their migrations into Ohio, Indiana, Illinois, and Missouri from 1820 to 1826.

Meshack probably grafted Anne Jessop's varieties onto his own seedling trees. We can guess that he also grafted trees for his neighbors, because he spent enough time grafting to teach his children the craft. Henderson, his brother Seth later said, learned to graft as soon as he was old enough to whittle.

Meshack may have brought little grafted fruit trees on the trip to Indiana, packed in soil or moss or something else to keep their roots cool and damp. Or he may have brought only seeds. Even in the latter case, he would have been able to graft his favorite varieties onto his seedling trees, because when the family arrived in Indiana other people—fellow Quakers, especially—were already establishing nurseries in the Midwest.

Land Hunger

There were irksome things about North Carolina. One was a shortage of good land. The Quakers' grandparents had faced the same problem.

American expansionism didn't start with the trek over the Appalachian Mountains. Despite the persecutions they suffered elsewhere, the Quakers had come to North Carolina not for religious reasons but for land—inexpensive land for themselves and their numerous offspring. It was probably for land that Meshack's father, William, had come to North Carolina from Virginia. And a hunger for soil was a primary reason that Meshack, his family, and other Quakers would leave North Carolina for Indiana.

Britain's Proclamation of 1763, issued at the end of the French and Indian War, had declared all lands west of the Appalachian Divide to be off limits to colonial settlement. The goal was to prevent further strife between indigenous people and colonists, but the ban only increased the allure of the land west of the mountains.

By 1807, reports of Indiana's deep, black soil had reached ready ears in North Carolina. According to tradition, parents needed to provide land on which each of their sons could sustain their own families (daughters were expected to acquire their wealth through marriage). Meshack and Jane already had five sons; another was yet to come, and after Jane's death, Meshack would have three boys more by a second wife. By 1822, good land was scarce in the Piedmont. The landscape was fragile, the soil acidic and mineral-poor. It was subject to erosion, and, in the absence of regenerative care, a rapid loss of fertility. In the abandoned clearings that dotted the region, broom sedge and pine trees advertised that the land was exhausted. Production in Meshack's fields had probably declined substantially after some thirty years of continuous cultivation. In parts of the state with better soil, land prices were high. North Carolina had no big cities, but it was the nation's fourth most populous state in 1820. For the Lewellings as well as many other North Carolinians, emigration seemed a good path to more, better, and cheaper land.

Meshack managed to sell his land in Randolph County, but some of his fellow Carolinians were in such a hurry to leave that they abandoned their fields and even, occasionally, their slaves. Some *had* to leave, because of debts; according to one Guilford County farmer, the sheriff had three hundred foreclosures in hand on one day in 1820. Nearly half of North Carolina counties would lose population by 1840.

Struggles Against Slavery

But a shortage of good land wasn't the main reason for leaving. The Quakers' biggest frustration in North Carolina was slavery. Meshack and Jane owned no slaves, nor had Meshack's parents. Some of their neighbors—not Quakers, certainly—did keep slaves, though seldom more than one per household. Still, with cotton plantations expanding to the south, demand for slaves was increasing. From the perspective of farmers like the Lewellings, slaveholding provided an unfair economic advantage and led to increased land prices. Worse, slavery was cruel. Since importation of slaves from Africa had been banned in 1808, North Carolina slaves were ever in greater danger of being sold out of their communities and families, while free Black people faced the risk of being kidnapped back into slavery.

The Religious Society of Friends, founded in the mid-1600s, naturally took leadership in the anti-slavery movement. The Quaker creed was essentially democratic. Because everyone possessed the Inner Light of God, Friends believed, all human life was sacred. The Society had no paid ministers, because Friends recognized no distinction between clergy and laity. They dressed plainly so none would appear wealthier than others, and they used "plain speech"—*thee* and *thy*—because no one deserved to be elevated about others by the formal singular *you*. They believed that men and women were spiritually equal, that Indians should be paid for their lands, and that Blacks and Indians both should be treated kindly. George Fox himself, founder of the Society, had preached against slavery on his American tour in 1672, after witnessing the misery of captives in Barbados. He did not inspire slave-owning Quakers to immediately free their human chattel, but over the following century Quakers gradually came to ameliorate their slaves' living conditions, to treat them more like indentured servants or wage workers, and, finally, to free them. By the late eighteenth century, the Society of Friends had completely renounced slavery.

By the early nineteenth century, non-Quakers were joining the Friends in opposing slavery, but slaveholders dominated North Carolina politics. Free Black people, the slaveholders maintained, were too dangerous an influence on their slaves; the freemen might inspire slaves to rebel. So the laws got harsher. Slaves could be freed only with the permission of the county court. Illegally freed slaves were seized and sold, and informants got half the sale price. From 1801 on, anyone liberating a slave had to post a bond of $1,000—about $24,000 in 2023.

Some Quakers, especially in the eastern counties, had apparently delayed freeing their slaves for long after the Yearly Meeting required their doing so, and other Friends inherited slaves after legal emancipation became too difficult. Freeing these people without removing them from the state would likely result in their being sold back into slavery. So, in 1808, the North Carolina Yearly Meeting devised a way to circumvent the law: A committee of trustees would take "all suffering cases of people of color" from Friends who wanted to release them. The committee would formally hold the slaves in trust for their former masters, while members of each quarterly meeting provided direct care and protection. This meant that the Blacks, though still legally enslaved, could live as though they were free, while local Friends instructed the Black children in morality and trade skills. By 1814, more than 315 slaves had been transferred to the Yearly Meeting, which would in time become North Carolina's largest slaveholder.

Always led by the Piedmont Quakers, the North Carolina Friends fought slavery in other ways as well. They involved themselves in legal wrangling with the heirs of people who had granted their slaves freedom upon their own deaths. They sent frequent petitions—regarding colonization, kidnapping, slave traders, and related matters—to both the North Carolina General Assembly and the U.S. Congress. The work grew more difficult and frustrating over time.

The year Meshack Lewelling joined the Back Creek Meeting, 1816, was one of marked agitation against slavery in North Carolina. Charles Osborn, a Quaker minister from Tennessee, organized small manumission (emancipation) groups among Friends' meetings in Guilford County, his birthplace, and the groups together formed the North Carolina Manumission Society. Osborn recruited Presbyterians, Methodists, and others with anti-slavery leanings to join. In Virginia, the American Colonization Society began its Liberia Project, with the goal of resettling Black people in Africa. Despite reservations, the North Carolina Friends contributed heavily to the cause. The same year, Back Creek set up a school for Black children, the first in the area.

Meshack wholeheartedly devoted himself to helping the poor and enslaved. In 1818 he contracted with a slave-owning neighbor to provide three Black children with food, shelter, and apprenticeships, apparently at no charge; in fact, he had to pay a bond to ensure he would not remove the children from the county. In 1819 Meshack joined a committee of elders charged with caring for poor and needy Back Creek Meeting members. These actions, along with the community's continual discussions over the best path to ending slavery, must have strongly affected his children's moral development.

The "gradualists" who came to dominate the Manumission Society favored freeing the slaves only if they accepted colonization—resettlement in Haiti, Africa, or a far-western desert. To many of the Quaker District Friends, this was deportation, not liberation. When a large faction in the Manumission Society managed to change the name to the Manumission and Colonization Society, the group fizzled, until it was revived in more radical form in 1824. In the meantime, North Carolina Friends pursued alternatives. Vestal Coffin, of Guilford County's New Garden Meeting, initiated what came to be known as the Underground Railroad. At the same time, Quakers began leaving North Carolina and taking along with them willing slaves, to release in free territory. In 1823, the trustees of the North Carolina Yearly Meeting announced that they had found nothing in the laws of Ohio, Indiana, or Illinois to oppose this, and advised their agents to begin removing Black people from the state "as fast as they are willing to go." At this point, the Lewellings may have already participated in the removal.

Owen A. Garretson, son of one of Henderson's anti-slavery comrades in Iowa, would write that Meshack had brought slaves along with his family on the journey from North Carolina to Indiana, that he later traveled to Louisiana to take possession of two slave children whom a relative had inherited, and that Meshack freed all these slaves in Indiana. No one has found manumission certificates or other documents that verify these claims, but they are credible. When North Carolina Friends decided to move to Ohio or Indiana, they were often asked to take along a group of Quaker-held Blacks. As early as 1814, the Yearly Meeting heard reports on the numbers of Black people in its ownership and of those who had been taken to freedom in Haiti, Liberia, Pennsylvania, Ohio, and, especially, Indiana. If slaves accompanied the Lewellings to Indiana, someone besides Meshack may have signed the manumission papers, since the family probably made the journey as part of a larger group of Friends: "Rarely did a family travel alone," writes one Quaker historian. Meshack's purported trip to Louisiana would have entailed about two months of travel, assuming he took a steamship down the Ohio and Mississippi rivers instead of walking. But he wouldn't have been unusual among North Carolina Friends in his devotion to the cause; Levi Coffin boasted that he walked from North Carolina to Indiana three times in his efforts to free slaves.

If the Lewellings took Blacks along on their move to Indiana, they weren't among the first or the last of the Quaker District Quakers to do so. From 1815 to 1820, the population of Randolph County dropped by 158 white households and by 100 individual Blacks, nearly all of them in bondage. From 1823 to 1825, Friends took at least four groups of Black people to the Western states, despite encounters with slave rustlers. In 1830, North Carolina Friends counted a total of 652 Blacks in the trustees' care who had been transported to free lands.

Indian Territory

Friends were moving to the Midwest not only from North Carolina but also from Pennsylvania, Virginia, and Maryland. By 1821, at least twenty thousand Friends lived west of the Allegheny Mountains. About one-quarter of them had come from the Philadelphia Yearly Meeting, and most of this group had settled in Ohio. The rest had come mainly from the South and mostly settled in Indiana. Many more were to come. More than one hundred wagons a day were counted moving westward through Richmond, Indiana.

The great attractions of Indiana were its abundant, cheap land; its deep, dark soil; and, for the Quakers, its status as a free state. Farming families without slaves didn't have to compete with those that had them. For a time, Black people could move into the towns already established or create their own hamlets, and live unmolested. But the status of the people for whom the state was named was somewhat more complicated. The Northwest Territory—or the Territory North-West of the River Ohio—was organized by the Congressional Ordinance of 1787 to plan for the gradual incorporation of this vast area, stretching north to the Great Lakes and west to the Mississippi River, into the United States. The plan followed centuries of conflict in the region, involving Britain, the Netherlands, France, the Continental Army, American settlers, and various native groups, whose alliances shifted according to their interests. There had been the Beaver Wars, the French and Indian War, Pontiac's War, Lord Dunmore's War, and the Yellow Creek Massacre, in which white men murdered thirteen Iroquois women and children. Then came the Revolutionary War, which further damaged relations between the

Americans and native people, especially following the Gnadenhutten Massacre of ninety-six Delaware tribal members and the Crawford Expedition, an attempt to destroy the Indian towns along the Sandusky River, in today's north-central Ohio. The American forces were fighting not just for liberty from British rule but for control of Indian land. The natives who supported the British did so because Britain had promised, with the Proclamation of 1763, to keep the white squatters out.

Quakers were among those white squatters. Even before 1787, Friends from Virginia and Pennsylvania had crossed the Ohio River and established settlements in what would become eastern Ohio. Southern Friends had journeyed northward through Kentucky to build communities in southwestern Ohio. William Penn had taught the Friends that Indian land must be bought fairly before it could be colonized—although his own son violated this rule when he swindled the Delaware in the Walking Purchase of 1737. But some Friends were less scrupulous. Knowing they were on Indian land, these Friends relied on their identity as Quakers—clearly signaled by the men's broad-brimmed hats—to protect themselves from attack. The Friends knew the Indians knew that Friends were friendly—although the Friends, like other Americans, depleted game stocks, destroyed forests, and bred profusely.

The Treaty of Paris, signed in 1783, had awarded the northwestern lands to the United States, but it had not stopped the British from occupying forts in the region and aiding the natives' struggles. With British help, the Indians continued to fight the U.S. Army until 1794. That year, General "Mad Anthony" Wayne and his men won the Battle of Fallen Timbers, the last battle of the Northwest Indian War. Leaders of a dozen Indian nations signed the Treaty of Greenville in 1795. In doing so, they gave up claims to what would become Ohio and part of Indiana, although they managed to preserve their peoples' hunting rights.

Land-hungry Americans soon poured over the Appalachians into the Northwest Territory. Disregarding the fact that the Indians had been forced through war to sign the Treaty of Greenville, Southern Friends joined the migration. By 1800 there were six Quaker settlements in Ohio Territory, and in 1803 Friends established Ohio's first monthly meeting, in Miami County, just north of Dayton.

In 1800, the Northwest Territory was divided into Ohio Territory, which would soon become the state of Ohio, and Indiana Territory, which was all the rest. William Henry Harrison, the first governor of Indiana Territory, was tasked with acquiring more land from the people for whom the territory was named and who vastly outnumbered the white residents. By the end of 1805 the Indians had ceded about 46,000 square miles to the United States, and Congress had passed laws allowing sales of government land in sections (640 acres), half sections (320 acres), and quarter sections (160 acres).

That year three families from Maryland settled in what would become Wayne County, barely within the boundary of lands then open to Americans. In 1806, three Quaker families built cabins nearby, on the Whitewater River. Although they had traveled from Miami County, Ohio, their home before Ohio was North Carolina. They must have wasted no time in promoting their new home to Carolina friends and relatives, because the following year more than eighty Quakers in the Whitewater area requested permission to start a new meeting. Their log houses and meetinghouse were the beginning of the town of Richmond, which Addison Coffin would later describe as "the great center of Carolina emigration, and the Jerusalem of Quakerism for all the northwest." Richmond would become the hub of a county named for a famous Indian slayer, General Wayne.

Governor Harrison continued extinguishing Indian land titles; by the end of 1809 he had personally secured thirty million acres for the United States. Up until this point most of the Piedmont Friends had postponed their migrations, but the news of the Twelve-Mile Purchase—a twelve-mile-wide strip just west of Richmond obtained from indigenous people in 1810—produced excitement back in the North Carolina Quaker District. In 1811, the federal land office in Cincinnati was ready to sell off parcels. But by this point the Indians were fed up with their lands being invaded and their people murdered. In 1808 a Shawnee man called Tenskwatawa had proclaimed himself a prophet, condemned white ways, and provoked a witch hunt against his opponents. He and his followers formed a new community, Prophet's Town, near where the Tippecanoe River runs into the Wabash. His brother Tecumseh joined him and turned the movement political. Tecumseh formed a confederacy of native nations, denounced past treaties, and urged the nations not to sell any lands without the consent of all. He gave Governor Harrison a choice between returning lands or going to war. But Harrison would not let Indiana remain "the haunt of a few wretched savages." The result was the Battle of Tippecanoe, in which Harrison himself, in November 1811, led the destruction of Prophet's Town.

The War of 1812 soon followed. With their British allies, the Indians attacked American forts and massacred both soldiers and settlers, and for a time held the whole of the former Northwest Territory. But Harrison, now a major general, finally triumphed. At the close of 1814, the native peoples agreed to peace, and the United States agreed to restore all the rights and possessions they had had in 1811.

American migration to Indiana Territory rapidly increased. In 1816 Indiana met the requirement for statehood: About 65,000 whites lived in the territory. The new state was divided into eighteen counties. Three-quarters of the land, however, was still in Indian hands. So, in 1818, at St. Mary's, Ohio, the United States signed treaties with the Wyandot, Seneca, Shawnee, Ottawa, Potawatomi, Wea, Lenape (Delaware), and Miami peoples. Through these treaties the United States gained rights to a huge parcel of land in central Indiana, about one-third of the state. The Miami gained a reservation, though it would be taken from them, through more treaties, by 1840. The Lenape, who had already been driven from New Jersey and eastern Pennsylvania, first to Ohio and then to Indiana, were now required to remove themselves to west of the Mississippi by 1820.

Finally, the area that would become Henry County, just west of Wayne County, was open for American settlement. The newcomers couldn't get titles until 1820, after the land had been surveyed, but they squatted anyway, settling on claims. Dozens of families settled in Henry County in 1819. Some of them were Quakers. Although the Friends never used violence against Indians, they were happy to occupy lands from which the natives had been forcibly removed.

Emigration to Indiana increased so rapidly after the end of the War of 1812 and the signing of the St. Mary's treaties that the state's population grew to almost 150,000 by 1820. So many of the new residents were Friends that, in 1821, the year before the Lewellings arrived, the Indiana Yearly Meeting formed, dividing off from the Ohio Yearly Meeting.

If the Lewellings had brought enslaved people along from North Carolina, they probably parted from them at Richmond. Newly freed Blacks tended to settle near Friends' communities, where they could get help with such matters as employment and housing and, once established, could engage in business as equals with white people. But the first Black family in Henry County didn't arrive until 1827. Until then, the newly incorporated county may have seemed too wild for newly freed people. They may have preferred to live where they could find wage labor.

For Meshack, however, Wayne County may have seemed too civilized. He favored an area with ample unclaimed land. He probably left his wife and children with a cousin or friend while he explored the Twelve-Mile Purchase. Then the family headed together into the woods.

They walked thirty-five miles or so to their new home near the Blue River. Perhaps they were able to follow a rough road cut by prior settlers; if not, the trip must have been slow going. The forest was dense with big sugar maple, beech, and hickory trees. Although the land had been long settled by various native peoples, the clearings were sparse and small. Just a year earlier, another settler had spent two days cutting his way through seven miles of woods to take a wagon from New Castle to the Greensboro area, where the Lewellings would settle.

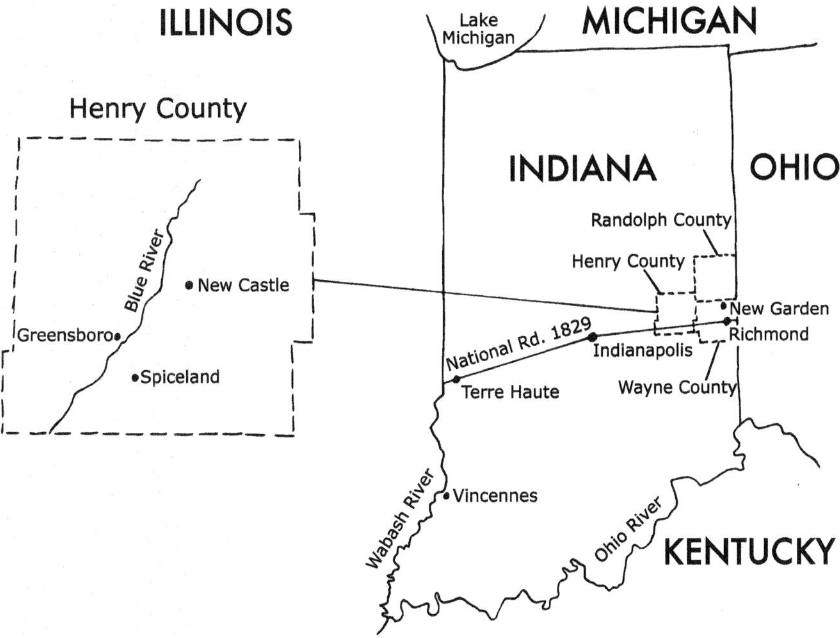

Indiana and Henry County. Map by Rebecca Waterhouse.

Meshack had chosen eighty acres on a headland, above Blue River's boggy bottom lands. The land was just a few miles north of what would become the village of Greensboro. The country was gently rolling, not broken and steep like the Piedmont. The deep, black soil, once cleared of trees, would sometimes be too wet in spring for planting grain, but the land would prove excellent for orchards. The Lewellings squatted on the site while awaiting the next government land sale. Then Meshack bought the land for the bargain price of $1.25 per acre.

The family immediately set about sawing, hacking, and burning trees to clear enough ground for a cabin and a cornfield. It was already May or June when they arrived; they would have had to plant their corn soon if they were to harvest a crop that year. If the Lewellings had brought along fruit trees, those would have needed planting, too. While the family was busy with the initial clearing and planting, they probably slept in a shelter assembled from poles and bark, or in their wagon. Before the onset of winter, however, they had undoubtably turned some of the trees on the site into a snug log cabin. Maybe they finished even before Jane gave birth to her seventh child, on August 29, 1822.

Chapter 2
Sweet Home Indiana

> Half the beauty and pleasure that brightens the life of youth and childhood . . . is found in the orchard of the old homestead—the sight of the trees in bloom, the waiting and watching for the first ripe fruit, the in-gathering of the fruit in the fall, and the storing of it away in bin and cellar for use in the winter around the ingleside.
>
> —J. R. Cardwell, "The First Fruits of the Land"

The Lewellings came to a gently rolling land with rich, deep loamy soil "that needed only to be tickled with a hoe to be made to laugh with a harvest." The soil was underlaid with limestone, which would eventually prove useful for building, and with gravel, which would be good for roads. A family would settle by a spring or a stream, both of which were abundant, and immediately commence the work of clearing trees before planting corn, vegetables, and an orchard.

The orchard was essential. Newly planted fruit trees, along with a cabin, were a clear sign to all that the land was no longer wilderness, that a farmer had claimed it. Land companies in New York, Vermont, and Ohio required settlers to plant orchards immediately. This was no great imposition, because other crops could be planted in the orchard while the trees were growing up. If the settler wasn't truly ready to settle down, the fruit trees, unlike grain, would grow untended; you could walk away and leave the trees to prove up your claim. For the family, planting an orchard was a promise that they would be eating well, and drinking plenty of cider, a decade in the future. In addition, after the native forest was cut down, the orchard would be the family's shady grove. An established, well-tended orchard, no matter how remote, was a sign of prosperity and civilization. It was an inheritance due one's children.

If the orchard had been planted entirely from seed, an occasional tree might produce fine dessert apples. But the most admired orchards comprised trees that were grafted, either before or after planting. Like fencing, manuring, and a big, sturdy barn, an orchard of grafted rather than seedling trees indicated higher class status. It symbolized ambition, wealth, and industry.

Henry County, Indiana, received ample rainfall, about forty inches annually. Some of the rain came in heavy storms, which would cause localized flooding every year. But Meshack had chosen his first eighty acres carefully, on well-drained land above the Blue River. Although some areas may have been boggy in spring, all the land would have been suitable for fruit trees. And fruit trees would provide two sources of income: the fruit, and the young trees propagated from older trees. The Lewellings' grafting skills would prove profitable when newcomers to the area sought fruit trees to plant on their own homesteads or grafts for their seedling trees.

When the Lewellings arrived in Henry County, their eldest child, by coincidence also named Henry, was fifteen. Henderson and John, who would become partners in a nursery business, first in Indiana and later in Iowa, were thirteen and eleven. William, who would join the nursery business in Iowa, was five, and Seth, who would take over Henderson's nursery in Oregon, was only two. The new baby was called Thomas. The only daughter in the family was Mary, age seven; Jane would be born three years later.

The Lewelling boys spent their youth much as their father had back in North Carolina. Clearing land took the most effort. After the trees were felled, most of the logs were rolled into huge piles and burned. The great trees were so abundant that they had little value, and, besides, the first sawmill wasn't built in the area until 1836.

With some of the reserved timber, the boys must have helped to build the family's cabin, probably of round logs, to save the trouble of hewing. The cabin likely started as a single room with a big stone or adobe fireplace, a puncheon floor, and perhaps a greased-paper window. Other rooms may have been added later, but starting small would have allowed more space for the first planting.

Families like the Lewellings kept their Southern foodways. The first year they probably ate mostly bacon and corn in various forms—dodgers, pones, hoe-cake, hominy, and samp. These they may have supplemented with store-bought wheat and coffee. The Lewellings probably let their pigs run loose in the woods, as was the custom in North Carolina. After a few years the family likely enjoyed an abundance of beechnut-fattened pork. In the meantime, they probably sampled the abundant game in the area: bear, bison, deer, squirrel, and turkey. To save on ammunition, the family probably did more trapping than shooting. They must have trapped plenty of raccoons, whose pelts were "the principal circulating medium" in Henry County when the Lewellings arrived. The children probably gathered wild foods, too: acorns, wild rice, and wild barley to pound together into cakes; hazelnuts, hickory nuts, walnuts, and beechnuts; and sassafras roots and spicebush (*Lindera benzoin*) twigs, leaves, and berries for infusing. The years of waiting for the orchard to produce wouldn't have been fruitless: The woods offered pawpaws, elderberries, black raspberries, plums, chokecherries, and grapes. Undoubtably, the family also tapped some of the ubiquitous sugar maple trees and boiled down their sap.

The early stores carried novel manufactured goods, such as calico and silk dresses and fancy shoes and boots, which could be had in trade for deer hams, deerskins, and furs as well as coonskins and ginseng (or "sang"). But the Society of Friends required plainness in dress as well as address. Although many Quakers accepted expulsion because they refused to conform to rules about clothing, the Lewellings presumably upheld the old standards. Meshack almost certainly wore the Quaker patriarch's broad-brimmed beaver hat and, at least in public, a "shadbelly" coat, short in front and sloping gradually to the tails. The women dressed in plain, prim dresses of homespun flax or wool. The boys may have worn deerskins and moccasins at first, but eventually they began dressing like their father.

The family had few neighbors in the early days. There were almost fifteen thousand nonindigenous people in Indiana by 1820, but the settlement of Henry County had begun only in 1819. Even in 1824, the county had no more than five hundred white residents.

The Lewellings were probably grateful for the neighbors they had. Most of the county's early white residents were Quakers, usually born in Virginia or North Carolina. Meshack's sister Mary and her husband bought an adjacent claim, thus providing the Lewelling children cousins to play with. At first families would have visited by following narrow paths through the woods, often depending on blazes to find their way.

As more people came to the neighborhood, some relationships apparently soured. Friends routinely disciplined their members for such offenses as fiddling, dancing, joining the militia, and failing to live up to standards of apparel. Both Meshack and his eldest son, Henry, were denounced for treating neighbors rudely. In 1830, Meshack got "in a passion" and "threatened to strike two of his fellow creatures." Two years later, Henry "manifested a malicious and unchristian disposition" and used "an expression shocking to Christian feelings." Jane must have had a more tranquil nature than her husband, because her three sons who would reach the West Coast would often be described as gentle and kind.

Indians among their neighbors presented little trouble for the Lewellings. Some Lenape tribal members lingered in the area, and they may have sometimes begged for things they needed, but they didn't steal or threaten violence. Friends not only treated individual Indians respectfully but also, through the yearly meeting, monitored the tribes' well-being and established reservation missions and schools.

By the end of 1826, the Lewellings' household and local clan had both expanded. An eighth child, Jane, named for her mother, was born in 1825. The next year, the elder Jane's sisters Sarah and Peggy arrived from North Carolina—Sarah with her husband, Tom Newby, and their children, and Peggy with her twelve-year-old son, Emsley, and her three-year-old daughter, Anna. Emsley and Anna had been abandoned by their father, who was married to another woman. The three moved in with the Lewellings and lived with them for years. Sarah and Tom established a homestead on an adjacent claim.

Although the country was lightly populated, Meshack may have found plenty of demand for his doctoring skills and medications. Indiana, like much of the Midwest, was ridden with one of the major plagues of westward expansion, malaria. The anopheles mosquitoes that transferred the disease were native to the region, but the plasmodia protozoa that caused it were not. The latter were carried inland, along rivers, in the blood of some of the emigrants themselves. The abundance of standing water in the spring, especially in the low areas closest to the rivers, allowed the mosquitoes to breed prolifically. Until much of the land was drained by ditches and tile, "fever and ague," or "the shakes," was a nearly universal affliction each year. Victims might treat themselves and their family members with roots, "yarbs," and whiskey, but Meshack probably used quinine, though it caused roaring in the ears and other side effects. Some people suffered so much from malaria that they moved away, leaving their pigs to go feral. The Lewellings were fortunate: Since their farm was on high ground, they probably suffered less than other families.

Meshack may have also treated victims of a cholera epidemic, in 1833, that struck the town of New Castle, seven miles from Greensboro. Fifteen of one hundred and fifty residents, including the town's physician, died in the epidemic. Asiatic cholera, a fast killer caused by the bacterium *Vibrio cholerae*, had traveled by ship to western Europe and crossed the Atlantic in 1832. Cholera became the country's first rapidly advancing pandemic, spreading mainly through contaminated water and surfaces and from victim to victim. The disease would revisit North America from 1849 to 1852, when it would kill many among the Shawnee and other native peoples and thousands on the Overland Trail. John and Seth Lewelling, who took the trail to California in 1850, would luckily escape infection.

As the Lewelling boys grew up, they found opportunities to earn money. They probably cut cordwood and split rails for neighbor's fences. They may have performed road work as well. In 1825, when Henry was only eighteen, he was appointed Henry County's official surveyor. When the country's first interstate highway, the National Road, reached Henry County in 1827, Henry laid out townships along the right of way.

The money the boys earned helped to pay for land. Federal lands sold slowly in their part of Indiana, and so the government sales continued until 1848. Henry was able to buy an eighty-acre parcel in 1830, Henderson and John each bought one in 1833, and their cousin Emsley Brookshire bought a forty-acre parcel the same year. Meshack and Jane almost certainly contributed funds for their sons' purchases, and Meshack bought more land in his own name as well. By the end of 1835, he owned six hundred acres in the neighborhood, all on fertile, rolling lands above the Blue River. When the federal land sales ended, the Lewellings had one of the largest holdings of any family in the township. In North Carolina, Meshack had been a middling farmer, less propertied than average. The move to Indiana made the family wealthy.

Henry, Henderson, and John had already married and started families when they bought their farms. In 1827 Henry married Rachel Presnall, a Friend and former neighbor from Randolph County, North Carolina, who had migrated to Indiana with her family in 1826. In 1830 Henderson married Rachel's sister Elizabeth. According to her granddaughter Jane Harriet Luelling, Elizabeth was "a very pretty woman, with fair complexion, blue eyes and wavy brown hair, almost auburn, very long and beautiful." John married another Friend, Elvina Elliott—Elvy, for short—in 1832. In the few years that Henderson and John would spend clearing their parcels and planting them with trees in Indiana, Elizabeth would bear three children, Elvy two. Henry and Rachel, who would stay in Indiana, would have ten children in total.

Meshack and Jane's fifth child, William Lewelling, never bought land in Indiana; he would make his first land claim in Iowa, where he would assist in his brothers' business. William married Cyrena Wilson, another Friend, in 1838—just months before they, along with John and Elvy, asked the monthly meeting for a certificate of transfer to Iowa.

Henderson's farm was a few miles north of Greensboro, between Blue River and Duck Creek. The land was nearly all level, and, like the families' other parcels, it was well drained. John's parcel, though not adjacent, was a short distance away. The two brothers probably began planting the same year they began clearing the land. They may even have started their nurseries on the parents' land so that they could set out grafted trees in their first year of ownership.

In their early years of farming their own land, building their own houses, and starting their own families, the Lewelling brothers lost their mother. Jane Brookshire Lewelling died in 1835, at forty-six; the cause was unrecorded. Meshack would remarry just two years later, to Margaret Williams, and have three children by her before his own death, in 1840, from pneumonia. His North Carolina–born children would all be grown and independent at this point, and Henderson, John, and William would have made their second migration westward, to Iowa.

The Fruit Business

Indiana's first city was Vincennes, a former French fur-trading post on the Wabash River. Fruit trees of Eurasian species were planted there as early as 1735, when the first white families settled in the area. By 1796 Vincennes had fifty houses with enclosed gardens, most of them with apple, pear, and peach trees. Few of the trees, if any, were grafted. Like the people of the Eastern Seaboard, the French Americans of the area made most of their apples into cider, for which they didn't need fancy fruit. When William Henry Harrison became the first governor of Indiana Territory, he built a fine house in Vincennes and surrounded it with grafted trees, but if he or an employee shared scions we have no record of it.

The grafted cultivars the Lewellings grew in Indiana had diverse origins, though few, if any, came from Vincennes. You can trace the paths of many of the cultivars from the East Coast over the Appalachian Mountains and on to the Midwest. A main path was from New Jersey to Ohio and thence on to Indiana, Illinois, and Michigan. Other cultivars came from the South into Ohio and Indiana. Friends brought some of these varieties, and Friends took the lead in spreading all of them through the Midwest.

At the annual meeting of the Ohio Pomological Society in 1859, members reminisced about the nurserymen who had proceeded them in Ohio and Indiana. Most often mentioned was Silas Wharton, who moved from Pennsylvania to Warren County, Ohio, in 1810, bringing grafted fruit trees of cultivars from the collection of William Coxe, of Burlington, New Jersey. Coxe's collection included various apples that the Lewellings would later sell. These included Jenneting (or Junating), which Coxe called "the earliest table apple of our country" (its original name may have referred to St. John's Day); Drap d'Or, a very old French dessert apple; Summer Pearmain, an American variety, early and favored for fresh eating; Bellflower, a yellow apple from New Jersey, preferred for baking; Black, a deep red apple from New Jersey; Seek-No-Further, from Massachusetts; Gloria Mundi, whose fruits could weigh two pounds each; Lady, probably the same as Api, from Brittany; Newtown Pippin, a tart winter apple from New York; Swaar, from the Hudson River Valley; Vandevere, probably from Delaware; and Rambour d'Eté (or Rambour Franc or Summer Rambour), one of several Rambour apples said to have originated in the northern French village of Rambures; and, finally, Rambo, not to be confused with Rambour but a seedling of a Swedish apple brought to America by a Swede named Rambo. The Lewellings would also grow at least two of Coxe's pear cultivars, the sweet little Seckel and the enormous Pound Pear.

When Silas Wharton started his nursery, grafted fruit "was looked upon by many, in that new country, as a curiosity, and rather an innovation upon the works of nature," wrote David Evans for the Ohio Pomological Society. But Wharton found plenty of demand for both his fruit, which he sold from a wagon, and for his trees, at least sixty cultivars. He probably also sold scions to frugal or hurried homesteaders who had planted fruit trees from seed (or who had bought seedlings from less formal nurserymen like John Chapman—"Johnny Appleseed"—at a small fraction of the price of grafted trees) and to traveling grafters. Wharton eventually partnered with seven nurserymen, five in Ohio and two in Indiana, to whom he would furnish grafted trees in return for a share of the profits when the trees were sold. Before Wharton's business was long under way, grafted fruit trees had become a homesteader's essential.

One of Silas Wharton's associates in Indiana was Andrew Hampton, who lived in Randolph County, just north of the Wayne County line. Hampton moved there in 1816 from Warren County, Ohio, where Wharton had his nursery. Perhaps Hampton learned the nursery trade from Wharton; at least Wharton must have inspired Hampton to go into the business himself. In any case, Hampton—a Quaker who wore the signature broad-brimmed hat and "drab"—brought young grafted trees with him to Indiana. He then bought seeds from local homesteaders to grow into more trees, to which he would graft scions or buds from his initial stock. By 1819, three years before the Lewellings' arrival in Indiana, he probably had trees ready to sell. By the 1840s he was grafting, planting, and selling 65,000 fruit trees a year. People came from as far away as fifty miles to buy trees at his nursery, and he and his nephews took fruit trees by boat on the Ohio, Mississippi, and Missouri rivers to sell in riverside settlements. Hampton's 1843 catalog included many of the Coxe-Wharton apple varieties, including "Jenneting of Cox," but also varieties from other sources, such as Carolina June, which the Lewelling brothers would grow in Iowa. Like the Lewellings, too, Hampton also sold pears, peaches, quinces, cherries, plums, grapes, currants, and gooseberries.

The Lewellings could have acquired fruit trees or scions from Andrew Hampton as early as 1822. The distance from Greensboro to Hampton's nursery was about forty miles. For a lover of fine fruit, this wasn't too far to travel.

As budding horticulturists, Henderson and John Lewelling may have found a strong role model in Andrew Hampton. Not only was Hampton a Quaker, but like Meshack Lewelling he was known for his opposition to slavery. He refused to buy products of slave labor, including rice, sugar, and cotton, and he was known to harbor fugitives from slavery. At the same time, he was carrying on a thriving nursery business.

Becoming a nurseryman, like opposing slavery, was a very Quakerish thing to do. "Nearly all the earliest nurserymen were members of the Society of Friends," according to a local historian. By 1840, there were eighteen nurseries in Indiana, most of them run by Friends. In that year the nurserymen joined with Henry Ward Beecher to form the Indiana Horticultural Society. Henderson Lewelling would probably have attended this gathering if he hadn't already left the state. Perhaps John was among the group.

Other Quaker farmers contributed to the fruit industry even if they didn't own commercial nurseries. One such Friend was Solomon Horney, who emigrated from Guilford County, North Carolina, to Wayne County, Indiana. Horney was credited with introducing the Never Fail apple—also known as Rall's Genet, Rawle's Janette, and other variations on that name—which must have reached North Carolina from Virginia, where Caleb Ralls grew it (it may have originated in Normandy; Thomas Jefferson, Ralls's neighbor, may have got a scion from the French envoy Edmond Genet). The Horse apple, perhaps a true Guilford County cultivar, was said to have been introduced to Indiana by John Morrow, another Quaker and one of the earliest white settlers in Wayne County; he came in 1808. The Lewellings would sell both the Never Fail and the Horse in Iowa, along with Carolina, Carolina Sweet, and Carolina June.

When Henderson and John began considering leaving Indiana, Iowa's greatest attraction may have been that it was a new market for fruit and fruit trees—a market that would expand very quickly, without competition from a lot of other Quaker nurserymen.

Among Friends

The Indiana Yearly Meeting split off from the Ohio Yearly Meeting in 1821, a year before the Lewellings arrived. The new meeting was destined to become the center of Midwestern Quakerism, encompassing thirty-five quarterly meetings in six states. In fact, it would eventually have more members than any monthly meeting in the world.

In their early years in Indiana the Lewellings belonged to the Milford Monthly Meeting, which met in the village of Milton, over the Wayne

County line. As a Milford member, Meshack wasted no time in displaying his radicalism. In 1824 he refused either to join the militia or to pay the tax required in lieu of service. This behavior was expected among the Friends, who objected to supporting war in any way. But whereas most Friends gave in to the authorities at some point, Meshack kept on fighting. After two years the unpaid tax had doubled, and the sheriff sought the permission of the court to enforce the levy. The sheriff and two other men came to the Lewelling farm and seized a horse, which was then sold at public auction. When he was offered the difference between the sale price and the levy, Meshack refused to accept it. Again, this was standard Quaker practice, but Meshack went further: He sued the men for trespassing. The case eventually went all the way to the Indiana Supreme Court, which ruled that Meshack must pay all legal costs and fees. Meshack was ornery, but his righteousness made a strong impression—especially, I imagine, on his children.

Greensboro, the town nearest the Lewelling farm, was a Quaker settlement long before it was platted in 1830. The Lewellings and other local Friends broke off from the Milford Monthly Meeting to found the Duck Creek Monthly Meeting in Greensboro in 1826. They built their new meetinghouse of logs.

The Lewellings were active members of the meeting. In 1826 Meshack and Jane were appointed to the committee for the care of the poor. Meshack also became "supervisor of the road" that led to the meetinghouse, with the authority "to call on all hands" for help in maintaining the roadway.

In 1828 Duck Creek members who came to be called Hicksites split off and built their own meetinghouse in Greensboro. The Hicksite separation wasn't just a local phenomenon; it divided the Friends throughout the United States and Canada. Elias Hicks, a Quaker minister and abolitionist from New York, emphasized the individual's Inner Light over the Scriptures as a source of spiritual truth—at a time when many Friends, inspired by the fiery preaching of evangelical Methodists and Baptists, leaned toward Bible reading over introspection. Hicks's implied refutation of concepts such as the Trinity, original sin, and even the divinity of Christ troubled the opposing faction, who came to be called Orthodox. When William Bond, of Duck Creek, proclaimed that "Elias Hicks is as good a man as Jesus Christ and a certain approved minister aught to be killed off," he was disowned, and the Hicksites created their own parallel system of meetings.

The Lewellings stuck with the Orthodox Friends. Although they shared Elias Hicks' views on slavery, they must have objected to William Bond's behavior. Besides, at least some of the family had a taste for fiery preaching.

In 1831 a prominent Friend from Guilford County, North Carolina, settled in Greensboro and joined the Duck Creek Monthly Meeting. He was Seth Hinshaw, a man Meshack's age who, like Meshack, had a passel of children and a passion for the abolitionist cause. Hinshaw opened a store in which he would sell "free produce"—goods produced without the use of slave labor, such as wool and maple syrup instead of cotton and sugar. In the 1840s Hinshaw's house would become "the meeting place of all grades of reformers, or setters forth of new doctrines—Mesmerism, Grahamism, Spiritualism, Socialism, Fourierism, etc., besides being headquarters for all abolition meetings," according to Addison Coffin. Hinshaw would lead anti-slavery meetings in Greensboro's Liberty Hall, and he and his wife would entertain Frederick Douglass in their home. Even in the 1830s, the Hinshaws may have occasionally harbored fugitives from slavery—as perhaps the Lewellings did, too. In any case, Meshack Lewelling and his sons undoubtably spent much time in Seth Hinshaw's company, and slavery was probably a frequent topic of conversation. Henderson, John, and Seth Lewelling would explore the other "new doctrines" later, possibly with Hinshaw's ongoing influence (Seth Lewelling received a letter from him in Oregon in 1859, he noted in his diary).

Seth Hinshaw must have been a compelling speaker, because at some point he began mentoring young William Lewelling, a budding minister. William was fourteen years old when the Hinshaws arrived in Henry County, and at that point he may have already shown interest in preaching. William almost certainly adopted his middle name, Lorenzo, in honor of Lorenzo Dow, a long-haired Methodist circuit rider who preached so powerfully that many in the crowds who turned out to hear him "were made to cry for mercy" and others "took the jerks." Lorenzo Dow provided William's inspiration, but Hinshaw must have taught the boy to refine his performances and to speak cogently on the topic of slavery.

The Duck Creek Monthly Meeting proved itself unusually fractious when, in 1837, the congregation divided again, ostensibly over a spiritual question, and a third time in 1840. This third time the division was over what to do about slavery, and it extended far beyond Duck Creek. Henderson and William would take their stand on the issue not in Greensboro but in Salem, Iowa.

Black Neighbors

After the state constitution of 1816 banned slavery and involuntary servitude, Indiana became, for a time, a refuge for Black people. In 1820 the state had 1,230 Black residents. mostly from North Carolina, Virginia, or Kentucky. By 1840 there were more than seven thousand.

Black migrants tended to concentrate, for security, near Quaker settlements. Richmond had the biggest Black population, and in New Garden, a short distance north, Black shopkeepers ran businesses as equals with their white counterparts. Henry County had only four Black families in 1830, but soon thereafter William and Sarah Trail founded Trail's Grove, a Black farm settlement near Greensboro that was large enough to support a school.

Indiana Friends assumed the responsibility of protecting their free Black neighbors. From its beginning in 1821, the Indiana Yearly Meeting maintained a Committee on the Concerns of People of Color. Friends lent Black people land, found them places to live, gave them apprenticeships, and helped them pay doctors' bills and funeral expenses.

Not all Indiana Friends were wholly sympathetic to Black settlers, however. In 1826, a Quaker in Richmond wrote others in North Carolina that "the prejudice against a colored population was as great in Indiana, as in North Carolina, and that there was as much of it in the minds of members of our Society there as in other people." When Governor James B. Ray suggested that slave states were burdening Indiana with their old and disabled Blacks, some Quakers may have quietly agreed. In some ways the Friends were friendlier to their Black neighbors in the Midwest than they had been in North Carolina; the Indiana Friends did not officially segregate their schools, meetinghouses, or graveyards. Yet very few Black people joined Quaker meetings. Friends seem to have encouraged Blacks to join the Methodist Church, as a more appropriate spiritual home, and the Friends more often helped set up and maintain schools for Black children than they invited Black children into Friends' schools. Quakers had always felt a need to guard their communities by maintaining social separation, and perhaps few of their Black neighbors envied the Friends' emotional suppression and enforced conformity.

Yet the Friends remained committed to the struggle against slavery. The Ohio River, which formed Indiana's ragged southern border, marked the boundary between slavery and freedom. The riverfront was scrutinized by slave patrollers and slave hunters, and, whenever a slave escaped, free Black people in the area fell under suspicion. White people who favored slavery or were indifferent to it were growing in number in Indiana, and Quaker leaders understood that no Black person could be safe as long as slavery remained legal anywhere in the republic. Quakers sometimes rescued free Black people who had been kidnapped to be sold into slavery; Friends from Hamilton County, just north of Indianapolis, pursued a kidnapper and his Black victim all the way to Louisiana. In New Garden, Levi and Catherine Coffin, Friends from Guilford County, North Carolina, famously took in fugitive slaves fleeing for Canada, despite that anyone caught rescuing a slave could be sued for twice the value of the "property." Their neighbors, meanwhile—Wesleyan Methodists as well as Quakers—organized a sewing society to provided clothing for the runaways.

Friends also continued their political campaign against slavery and the "Black codes"—laws intended to keep Black people subordinate or away from white people altogether. The Indiana Yearly Meeting sent a memorandum to the Indiana legislature, in 1831, protesting a proposed law to require people of African descent to post a bond upon entering the state. This was the year of Nat Turner's Rebellion, when revolting slaves and free Black men killed at least fifty-one whites in Virginia, provoking alarm and retaliatory measures throughout the country. This was also the year that William Lloyd Garrison began publishing *The Liberator*, a weekly paper that demanded immediate emancipation of every slave. The issue of slavery was splitting the country, and many Indiana Friends took a radical stance. They decried the popular Indiana Colonization Society, which aimed to end slavery by deporting Black people to Africa, Haiti, or a western desert—purportedly so they wouldn't have to compete with a superior race. Black migrants sent to Haiti in 1826, the Friends remembered, were miserable two years later, when they reported that they would rather be slaves in North Carolina than sharecroppers in Haiti. In 1836, the Indiana Yearly Meeting called the Colonization Society's efforts the "unrighteous work of expatriation." In 1837 the Yearly Meeting protested to Congress the proposed annexation of Texas, which would extend and perpetuate slavery. With other anti-slavery advocates, Friends formed the State Anti-Slavery Society of Indiana in 1836 and local anti-slavery societies in Henry County and elsewhere. Some of the Lewellings probably joined the local society.

For many Friends, however, joining anti-slavery societies and harboring runaway slaves went too far. Although all Quakers opposed slavery, some advocated gradual emancipation. They believed that Friends should work at turning public sentiment against slavery instead of fraternizing with strangers in abolitionist societies. Besides, abolitionists' methods were odious to many. Helping slaves escape to freedom was tantamount to stealing property, and stealing property was, to most Friends, unquestionably immoral as well as illegal.

Conservative Friends began speaking out against abolitionism, first in the East—in New York, New England, Virginia, and Pennsylvania. Then the Indiana Yearly Meeting advised in 1836 that Friends should stop joining outside associations. Everyone knew which associations were meant.

Leaving Indiana

In 1837 the Duck Creek Monthly Meeting was in complete discord. Some members interpreted the Bible so literally that they insisted that, come Judgment Day, actual bodies would rise from their graves. To the more traditional Friends, this was ridiculous. Resurrection was spiritual, not physical.

In reaction to the controversy over resurrection, the quarterly meeting closed Duck Creek, for a time, and sent its members to the monthly meeting in Spiceland, four miles south of Greensboro. Duck Creek Friends were forced out of their meeting house, but they couldn't escape one another. The monthly meetings must have been tense.

Amid all the wrangling over slavery and theology, and all the hard work of establishing the orchard and nursery, Henderson Lewelling's thoughts drifted westward. Now twenty-eight, he had lived in Indiana for fifteen years. He may have believed that he and John would face growing competition and lessening demand for their trees as Indiana grew into a settled country. Maybe he sought an escape from his fractious community; perhaps, he just longed for adventure.

Immediately west of Indiana was Illinois, but Henderson wouldn't move there. Perhaps he couldn't countenance the state's Black codes, and the fact that Illinois permitted slave holding under certain circumstances. Perhaps he felt that that Illinois was already too well occupied by white people. It was hardly more a frontier than Indiana.

Across the Mississippi River from Illinois were Missouri, a slave state and therefore intolerable, and, to the north, Iowa, then part of Wisconsin Territory. Iowa was free, and newly open to American settlement. And Indiana Friends were all talking about Iowa.

The opening of Iowa was much like that of Indiana. Events followed the familiar pattern: Indians suffering from a loss of land and game would harass the newcomers, the U.S. military would defeat the natives, the government would force them to relinquish more land, and then white settlers would move into the uninhabited country. In the territory that would become Iowa, the U.S. military attacked a group of Sauk, Meskwaki (Fox), and Kickapoo Indians, led by a Sauk named Black Hawk, who had crossed the Mississippi River in violation of a disputed treaty. So began the Black Hawk War, which the United States won in August 1832. With Black Hawk in captivity, other native leaders were forced to sign a treaty relinquishing six million acres and their rights to plant, hunt, or fish on the land. That land, a forty- to fifty-mile strip extending along the west side of the Mississippi River from the Missouri line north to the Upper Iowa River, became known as the Black Hawk Purchase. The treaty went into effect on June 1, 1833. Other such purchases would follow.

As in Indiana, Friends were among the earliest white settlers in Iowa. Several Quaker families met in southwestern Iowa in 1835 after separately crossing the Mississippi. They didn't know one another, but Friends couldn't remain strangers, so they banded together. Using a long grapevine as a measuring stick, the men laid out a town on the bank of Little Cedar Creek. Aaron Street, from Salem, Indiana, named the town for that Salem and two others that he or his father had founded on their westward migrations.

Reports soon spread through Indiana's Quaker network: Iowa was fertile and healthful—free of malaria, that is. It had ample grassland for pasture, hay, and crops; settlers didn't have to clear forests. Several Friends from Randolph County, Indiana, made the trek on horseback in 1836 to inspect the land for themselves, and they returned home with promising accounts. The first train of wagons arrived the following June, bearing Friends from Aaron Street's old meeting in Wayne County, Indiana. More Friends followed that summer. Salem would become a magnet for Quaker emigrants and other homesteaders as well.

Henderson and Elizabeth waited until after the fall apple harvest. Then they loaded a wagon with food, supplies, and whatever other possessions they couldn't live without, just as Meshack and Jane had done in North Carolina. They took their four children—Alfred, Mary, Asenath, and Rachel, the eldest only six and the youngest just a baby, born in March of that year. Like Meshack and Jane, the family probably drove livestock along with them on their journey. John and William may have joined the family on horseback, to serve as drovers and, perhaps, to see the new country before committing to moving there. The group had four hundred miles to cross between their old home in Henry County, Indiana, and their new one in what would soon be called Henry County, Iowa.

Chapter 3
Radical Quakers on the Prairie

> A good tree takes no more room than a poor one. Have the good one."
> –Luther Burbank

The journey from Indiana to Iowa was easier than the one from North Carolina to Indiana. This time there were no mountains to climb, no forests to scramble through. Henderson and his family drove a team of young mares instead of oxen, and they and the horses traveled part of the way down the Ohio River on a flatboat. After leaving the river they mostly traveled across flat prairie land, with only occasional groves of trees. The trip took about a month and climaxed with a Mississippi River crossing on a flatboat ferry.

From the river, Salem was only about forty miles farther on. The Lewellings found themselves in a throng. An observer at Burlington, John B. Newhall, described roads "lined with the long blue wagons of the emigrant slowly wending their way over the broad prairies—the cattle and hogs, men and dogs, and frequently women and children, forming the rear of the van—often ten, twenty, and thirty wagons in company."

Hawkeye Farmers

Henderson and his family arrived in a "moderately undulating" land with an "admirable distribution of prairie and woodland to the wants and convenience of the husbandman," in Newhall's words. They chose a place about three miles northwest of Salem, in a neighborhood that came to be called Cedar Creek or Cedar Grove. Their land bordered Big Cedar Creek, whose forested edge included oak, elm, walnut, hickory, ash, and maple trees as well as Eastern red cedar. There were also thickets of hazelnut and abundant native fruits—plums (*Prunus americana*), blackberries, rosehips, and strawberries. The native grasses, which grew to eight feet and taller, made good hay and pasture, though you might have had to stand on top of your horse to find your cattle. Rainfall would prove sufficient for crops, about thirty-five inches per year.

Because trees were scarcer in Iowa than Indiana, they were more valued; the settlers needed them for buildings, fences, furniture, and firewood. Still, the Lewellings and their neighbors were happy not to have to cut and burn acres of forest before planting. The prairie sod was hard to break, but with four yoke of oxen and a steel plow—then a novelty, invented precisely for the Midwestern prairie—you could turn over two acres in a day.

Because the family arrived in late autumn, they probably didn't do any plowing right away. More likely, they concentrated on building a cabin, as both shelter from the cold winter to come and a sign that they had claimed the land. Just as Meshack, Jane, and their children had done in Indiana, these younger Lewellings would squat while waiting for the government to survey the land and put it up for sale in parcels. (This custom of taking a "preemptive claim" would be legalized through the Preemption Act of 1841.) After the winter snows melted, they would plow the prairie and plant corn—and many, many apple seeds.

For the Cedar Creek site, Henderson envisioned not just a nursery and orchard but also a botanic garden. Traditionally, botanic gardens had been public institutions that maintained collections of plants for study. These gardens began in Europe as "physic" gardens, specifically for medical research, but in time their directors came to collect plants from around the globe with known or conjectured culinary and aesthetic as well as medicinal value. New World plant enthusiasts established some of their own botanic gardens; George Fox, at his death in 1675, willed a parcel of land in Philadelphia for a physic garden, and John Bartram, a Quaker farmer and plant explorer, established such an impressive collection of native plants in Pennsylvania that in 1765 he was appointed the king's botanist in America.

Henderson, however, planned a commercial operation. His main interest wasn't medical or native plants but those with culinary and landscaping uses, and he intended not to send them to England, as Bartram had done, but to supply them to frontier homesteaders. Henderson's closest model was almost certainly William Prince's Linnaean Botanic Garden in Flushing, New York.

Episcopalian rather than Quaker, the Prince family had established, in the 1730s, one of the country's first commercial nurseries. George

Washington, Thomas Jefferson, and James Madison were all customers, and in the early nineteenth century, throngs of New Yorkers visited by regularly scheduled stage and sailboat trips to "delight in a rural retreat during the verdant season."

Although the Prince nursery's annual catalog included vegetables, herbs, and ornamentals, it emphasized fruits. Always listed first and second in the catalog were apples and pears, which the Princes had begun grafting in the 1790s. The 1837 catalog included 331 cultivars of apple, 481 of pear. The apples were classified as good for the table, for cider, for cooking or preserving, or just for ornament, and the pears as "melting" (juicy), "breaking" (crisp), "buttery," or "baking." Earlier catalogs also included "perry pears," for fermenting.

Although Henderson must have pored over the Prince catalogs, he probably never visited the Prince nursery. But he certainly ordered Prince trees or scions—pencil-size twigs for grafting. Shipping arrangements were complicated, but the Linnaean Botanic Garden advertised that "the proprietors are in the constant habit of sending trees, and even the most delicate plants, to the remotest part of the Union with success."

Henderson patterned the brothers' business after Prince's. He would always advertise apples first—in 1841, the Lewellings offered forty-five varieties—and pears second. From the start, the Cedar Grove Botanic Nursery and Garden also sold cherries, plums, peaches, red currants, raspberries, roses, and herbs. And Henderson and his brothers would create permanent plantings of their chosen cultivars in a display garden, the first in the region—although to see the plantings visitors had to come by horse and wagon, usually over long distances, instead of in quick trips by stage and sailboat. Sales were both retail and wholesale. In his newspaper ads, Henderson would specifically invite "those who feel an interest in the nursery business" to visit.

While establishing the Cedar Grove business, the ever-industrious Henderson found another way to make money: He opened a general store in Salem. Soon he was Salem's most prosperous merchant. The store supported the family while Henderson established his Iowa orchards and got the fruit and fruit-tree business underway.

In June 1838 Henderson was back in Spiceland, requesting a certificate of transfer for himself, Elizabeth, and the children to Vermilion Monthly Meeting, the nearest monthly meeting to their new home.

Although the transfer was a doctrinal requisite, the main purpose of this trip was probably to fetch a batch of fruit trees, tended by John over the preceding winter and spring. The return journey to Iowa may have been the first dry run for Henderson's later trip to Oregon.

If John, William, and their wives hadn't already agreed to join Henderson in Iowa, on this first trip back to Indiana he must have convinced them to go. On September 19, three months after Henderson and Elizabeth received transfers from Spiceland to Vermilion, John, Elvy, William, and Cyrena got theirs.

John and William must have left Indiana soon thereafter, because they were in Iowa in time for the first government land sale, on November 2 and 3, 1838. Cyrena was probably with them, with a wagonload of household goods and a belly swollen with her first pregnancy. Elvy and her two children—Sarah, five, and Eli, two—probably stayed home, awaiting John's return. According to Owen Garretson, John continued running the Indiana nursery and orchards until 1841, when he sold the business there and joined Henderson and William in Iowa. Seth Lewelling, still a teenager, also stayed home in Indiana.

At the land sale, parcels weren't free, as they would be later in Oregon, but their cost was only $1.25 per acre, and any man over twenty-one could file a claim for as much as 160 acres (women were ineligible). The town of Burlington, on the Mississippi River, was filled with the tumult of prospective buyers and moneylenders, arriving by steamboat and ferry as well as by horse and wagon. So many Salem Friends attended the sale that their monthly meeting had to be canceled. Like other settlers, the local Friends knew exactly what parcels they wanted; most had staked them off even before the land was surveyed. Henderson bought the two adjacent eighty-acre tracts that would become the core of the Cedar Creek Botanic Garden and Nursery. John bought eighty adjacent acres just east of Henderson's tracts, and William bought eighty acres nearby.

David Diamond, in his dissertation on Henderson Lewelling, imagines the brothers and their assistants at work in winter, grafting tens of thousands of little trees. (They probably hired and trained other local farmers, though no record of the employees has survived.) Diamond pictures the group in a shed, gathered around a stove and working by lantern light, surrounded by bundles of seedling trees and scions. A can of a wax mixture for sealing the grafts would have been placed at the edge of the stove to warm. The men—and perhaps women, too—would have donned leather aprons and rolled up their sleeves. With well-sharpened knives, they would make matching cuts in each scion and stem, tie and wax the graft, and label the tree with a number indicating the cultivar.

To produce many trees quickly, the Lewellings used a technique popular at the time but nearly forgotten today. It was developed by a teenager, Joseph Curtis, who in 1818 moved with his family from Ohio to Illinois. There he established what may have been Illinois's first nursery. Joseph had the idea of grafting scions onto root pieces cut up by a plow. He tried cutting a main root of a two-year-old apple seedling into pieces several inches long, to each of which he grafted a scion of about the same size. The technique worked, and it became popular on the frontier. A nursery might make five hundred such grafts per day in the winter, and then store the baby trees in dark cellars, where root segment and stem segment would knit. The tiny trees would be set out in rows in spring, to grow for at least a year before they were sold. In Oregon, Seth Lewelling would multiply trees through root grafting until at least the late 1870s and probably until his death.

In 1840, the Cedar Grove nursery was established to the extent that the Lewellings could advertise "about thirty-six thousand Apple trees, a considerable number of which will be ready for transplanting the ensuing fall or spring. The trees will be large and fine, in point of size and vigor not often equalled."

It was already clear to the Lewellings, by this time, that Iowa was a difficult place for fruit growing. Winters were colder than in Indiana, with strong winds and frequent violent storms. But the Lewellings considered the climate an advantage. The ad continued:

> One great advantage the trees of our nursery will have over those coming from the eastern States, is, their being grown upon the prairie, where they are exposed to the winds, which will tend admirably to acclimatize them to more northern countries, and trees thus hardened by nature, will be found to succeed best in our southern States.

The ad proved prescient: The winter of 1842–43 would be so harsh that the trunks of some fruit trees split completely in two. The Lewellings must have lost many young trees, and after that winter they probably removed some Southern cultivars from their catalog.

I can't say how well Henderson succeeded in creating a botanic garden; no testimonies have survived. But as nurserymen the brothers were clearly successful. Their ad promised free delivery of orders of a thousand trees or more within twenty-five miles of the nursery, including to the Mississippi River towns of Burlington and Fort Madison, from where they could be shipped further by boat. Through this service the Lewellings intended to serve other nurseries as well as commercial orchards. Soon, according to Owen Garretson, "almost every homestead in the southern part of Henry County and the northern part of Lee County was bountifully supplied with fruit trees from the Lewelling nurseries."

Fruit, of course, was another Lewelling product. "As soon as the summer apples began to ripen," wrote Garretson, "the roads would be lined with covered wagons hauling the fruit to Ottumwa, Oskaloosa, Newton, Marshalltown, Cedar Rapids, and intermediate points."

What exact form the Lewelling partnership took isn't clear. William considered himself primarily a minister. Though his religious activities afforded him no salary, he spent much of his time traveling and preaching. Yet, when he died, in 1847, he left his own nursery land, nearly two thousand pear trees, more than five thousand apple trees, and sixty-five hundred apple seedlings as well as eighteen acres of timber. John, who described himself simply as a farmer, ran the Indiana side of the business until 1841. After that, he probably did more actual farm work than his partners, because both Henderson and William traveled so much. John also kept the accounts and handled legal matters for the shared business, and he would continue to do this work after Henderson left for Oregon. Henderson, who called himself by the new term *horticulturist*, took charge of marketing, sales, and shipping. Henderson's son Alfred later reported that his father made a total of fourteen trips east over his ten years in Iowa, gathering trees, shrubs, and vines from the Blue River nursery and orchard; he sold trees on these journeys as well. At least some of the trips were made partly by water, down the Mississippi and up the Ohio, allowing for sales in Missouri as well as Indiana.

After Meshack died of pneumonia, in 1841, Henderson was back in Indiana for the sale of his father's property. He returned to Iowa with some of Meshack's medicines and medical books, bags, and implements.

He may have used some of the medicines to treat malaria, which the whites had brought with them into Iowa. (Unaware that the disease was mosquito-borne, they blamed the disease on "the effluvia from the decaying sod" after plowing).

In the summer of 1841, the Lewelling brothers' younger sister, Jane, joined them in Salem. At sixteen, she had probably been living unhappily in her stepmother's house, helping to care for three little half brothers, the last one born after their father's death. So, Jane followed Henderson, John, and William to try her chances on the Iowa frontier.

Life in Quaker Salem

Within a few years, all three of the Lewelling brothers, with their families, had moved off their farms to live in the town of Salem. There they were among not only Friends but friends: All of the early settlers had roots in North Carolina, most had lived in Indiana for a time, and many were committed abolitionists. Town living offered an advantage the brothers must had missed as children: proximity to local gathering places.

Life still centered around Friends' meetings. The earliest settlers had met for worship in one of their cabins. In October 1838, soon after John and William and their families arrived, the Salem Monthly Meeting won full authorization. Henderson became the meeting's first overseer. Because the congregation was growing fast, through both migration and births, the Salem Friends soon rented a building for their meetings, and the following spring the Friends bought land for a new log meetinghouse, a school, and a cemetery. The new meetinghouse, completed in the spring of 1840, was huge for its day, with two rooms of twenty-two square feet each.

Education was a special concern, because the juvenile population was growing fast. The Lewellings were typically fecund: By late 1846, William and Cyrena had five or six children, John and Elvy had added four to their initial two, and Henderson and Elizabeth had also added four to their brood. In 1841, the Lewelling children who were old enough for school could walk there. One hundred eighty-five children in the monthly meeting attended Friends' schools in town or in the surrounding countryside. Beginning in 1845, Salem even had a small college, the Salem Seminary.

Of the three Lewelling families, Henderson's was the wealthiest. In 1844, his assessed property valuation was twice that of John's and three

Henderson and Elizabeth's stone house in Salem, Iowa. Photo courtesy of Jean Leeper and the Lewelling Quaker Museum.

times that of William's. So, while John and William and their wives built wood frame houses, Henderson and Elizabeth outdid all their neighbors with their two-story Greek Revival house made of locally quarried sandstone blocks. It was "the largest and most commodious of all the surrounding country." (Today the house accommodates the Lewelling Quaker Museum, and it is listed on the National Register of Historic Places.) Begun in 1842 and completed by 1845, the house had five fireplaces and, like many a Quaker meetinghouse, two front doors, on either side of the porch stairs. An ell, centered on the main part of the house, held the dining room and kitchen, and below these rooms was a shallow, dirt-floored basement, inaccessible from the main, brick-floored basement. A trap door in the kitchen floor, easily covered by a throw rug, opened onto a small dugout space below. This was apparently meant as a place to store plant materials, so that the family could graft while sitting around the kitchen table.

All three of the brothers had sufficient funds to invest in real estate beyond their homes and homesteads. Henderson bought about thirty-two acres just south of Salem in 1842, and John bought an adjacent parcel. William bought two lots in town. Henderson and Elizabeth felt wealthy enough to give away a small parcel to a widow, in "consideration of the natural love & affection which they . . . bear unto the whole human family & unto the said Ann Bennet, widow in particular."

Fighting for "the People of Color"

The more radical of the Salem Friends enthusiastically provided fugitives from Missouri with food, shelter, and transport to the next stop on their way to freedom. In what would come to be called the Underground Railroad, Salem became a hub, a crucial junction on the way to Canada or Chicago. No records were kept of this network, and children were taught neither to ask questions nor to share information about anxious Black visitors. Not only did the fugitives' well-being depend on secrecy, but federal law imposed a penalty of five hundred dollars on anyone who helped harbor or hide a runaway. Still, many stories of slave rescues in the Salem area have been handed down—stories of Blacks hidden in cellars, attics, blind closets, and weed patches; of slaves hidden in a wagon under sacks of bran (which looked just like sacks of wheat but were much lighter); of fugitives concealed in a hollow within a pile of hay or straw; and of Black men riding in carriages wearing Quaker bonnets, dresses, and veils. None of these stories name any of the Lewelling brothers, but Henderson, in particular, had ample opportunity to transport runaways in his commercial wagons. The cellar space under his kitchen trap door is believed to have been a frequent and infallible hiding place for fugitives, and he owned another building, known as the Beehive, with a wooden wheel in the attic to which a strong rope was attached. By turning the wheel, a person could raise a section of the first floor and thereby expose a staircase to a cellar. William and Cyrena, too, are said to have harbored escapees—in the Beehive, which they acquired when Henderson left Salem, and also perhaps in their own house. John, too, apparently assisted fugitives: After William died, John acquired the hidden Beehive cellar while Cyrena and her family retained ownership of the rest of the building.

Collectively, the Salem Friends posed such a threat to Missouri slaveholders that the Missourians regularly patrolled the Des Moines River and the roads of southeastern Iowa, and they were said to enter Friends' stables in the morning to check whether the horses seemed sweaty or tired from laboring during the night.

Free Black people as well as fugitive slaves found no true sanctuary in Iowa. In 1839, Iowa's first legislature had enacted Black codes. As in other

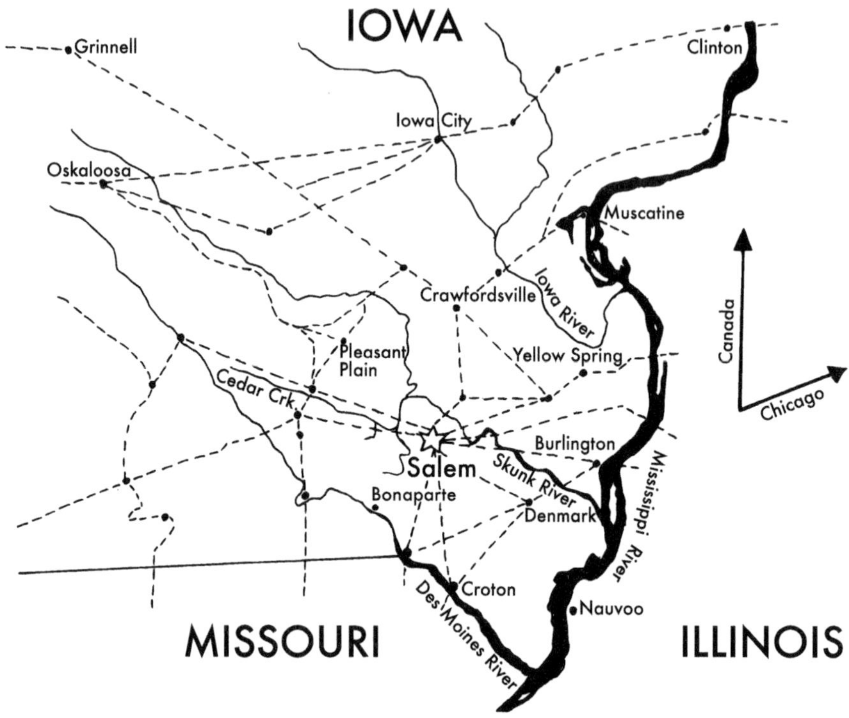

Underground Railroad routes in southeastern Iowa. Map by Rebecca Waterhouse.

"free" states, these were intended to keep Blacks out. Public education was limited to whites. Only white male citizens could vote or join the militia, and any "negro, mulatto, or Indian" was forbidden from testifying in court against a white person. Marriage between Black and white Iowans may have at first been beyond the legislators' imagination, but the next year they banned that, too.

Although the Black codes were unevenly enforced, they signified an officially lower status for Black residents. The codes helped legitimize events such as a mob's beating to death, in Dubuque in 1840, a Black cook and waiter who was accused of stealing a suitcase. The Friends couldn't abide such laws. In January 1841, sixty-five Salem men—including every man of any prominence in the town—petitioned the Iowa legislature to repeal the Black codes, reminding them that "all men are created equal." Their request was rejected.

In reaction, Salem Friends organized the Salem Anti-Slavery Society. Henderson and William were among the founders, and John was on the initial executive committee. The following year John would serve as treasurer of the organization, William would serve as the corresponding secretary, and Henderson and Cyrena would also hold seats on the executive committee. The group reported their activities in the *Free Labor Advocate and Anti-Slavery Chronicle,* a journal published by separatist Friends in New Garden, Indiana. The Salem group formed a library to circulate abolitionist literature, and in 1844 they seriously considered founding a newspaper, to promote education, morals, and temperance and to "advocate for the rights of the oppressed" as well as to cover agriculture, mechanical arts, and manufacturing. It must have been William who wrote in the group's 1842 report to the *Free Labor Advocate,* "When the people of the nominally free states and Territories, imbibe the idea that they have nothing to do with slavery, they imbibe an opinion directly at variance with the sad reality; for we have to do with it, both morally and politically."

In February 1841, the newly appointed governor of Iowa Territory and his territorial secretary both arrived with retinues of slaves. Other white people had been bringing slaves into Iowa and denying them their liberty; of the 188 Black residents counted in the territorial census, close to 10 percent of them were recorded as enslaved, and many of the others were probably also in bondage. But for the governor and his secretary to flout the territorial ban on slavery was an outrage too great to ignore. Soon reports came that the slaves not only hadn't been told that they were now officially free, but they were being whipped and otherwise mistreated. The radicals pushed the Salem Monthly Meeting to send a delegation to protest. The group presented the governor with copies of an anti-slavery pamphlet and "an address on civil government."

Friends had long supported Whig politicians in government, but through their fight against the Black codes the Salem Friends found that, in Iowa, Whigs were generally no more opposed to slavery than Democrats were. In the summer of 1841, the Salem Anti-Slavery Society resolved that it would oppose any candidate for the coming legislative session "who was not favorable to abolition and temperance." The group appointed a committee to attend the county Whig and Democratic party conventions and let the parties know their decision. Democratic candidates proved more receptive, but they lost the election. That winter 286 Friends from Salem and adjacent Jefferson County petitioned the legislature to appeal the Black codes. Again the petition was rejected.

As the Salem radicals found themselves more and more embroiled in state politics, they turned to local allies. Just twenty miles away was the Congregationalist town of Denmark, Iowa. The forebears of Denmark's citizens may have tortured Quakers in New England, but these dairy farmers were now fighting for social equity, thanks largely to the influence of their minister, Asa Turner Jr. Turner had led his parishioners in forming the territory's first abolitionist organization, the Denmark Anti-Slavery Society, in 1840. Situated on the way to the Mississippi River, Denmark was for many fugitives the next stop after Salem on the Underground Railroad. Other communities that became Salem's allies in the abolition struggle were also religious, Presbyterian or Associate Presbyterian. Political unity overwhelmed the denominational differences among these Iowa communities.

But Salem society itself began to fracture. Although the Salem Monthly Meeting was unified in opposing the Black codes, many members disapproved of the secret work they knew was going on around them: the feeding, hiding, and transport of runaway slaves, and the collaboration in this work and in politics with people who were not Friends.

At the same time, feelings both for and against abolition were reaching a peak back in Indiana. Levi Coffin's Newport was the district's anti-slavery hub, while the Lewellings' old meeting of Duck Creek, re-established in 1840, was the most radical, thanks largely to William's old mentor, Seth Hinshaw. Charles Osborn, the man whose anti-slavery preaching had inspired Meshack Lewelling back in North Carolina, worked with Levi Coffin in organizing abolitionist conventions. Quaker women led the formation of ecumenical anti-slavery societies, including one in Henry County (among the members were a Brookshire and four Presnalls, relations of the Lewelling brothers' mother and Henderson's wife). And in 1841 Friends organized the Wayne County Free Produce Association, with the goal of boycotting slave-made goods and inducing merchants to sell free-labor goods. We don't know how far Henderson went in incorporating free-produce principles into his store in Salem, but he must have brought back news of all these activities after his trips to Indiana.

For the Friends of the Indiana Yearly Meeting—which included Salem, Iowa—a breaking point came in 1842. When Henry Clay came to speak at the yearly meeting, in Richmond, Indiana, he was presented with a petition signed by about two thousand abolitionist Friends requesting that he free his slaves. Embarrassed Quaker leaders hastened to assure Clay that the Friends in general had nothing to do with abolitionists. The meeting's leaders then denounced eight prominent abolitionist members—including Thomas Frazier, a prominent minister from Salem, and Charles Osborn—and appointed a committee to direct Friends in every community to stay out of anti-slavery societies and to keep abolitionists from using their meetinghouses.

And so the Quaker world experienced yet another schism. In 1843, about two thousand Friends left their old meetings to join the Indiana Yearly Meeting of Anti-Slavery Friends. In Salem, the three Lewelling brothers and their wives joined a group of about fifty, including many of Salem's earliest and most prominent residents, in creating the Salem Monthly Meeting of Anti-Slavery Friends. Although historians have identified Henderson as one of the lead organizers, neither he nor William took an official role. John and Elvy, however, became two of the four overseers. John took the job of treasurer as well, and Cyrena became a clerk. The Anti-Slavery Friends built a new meetinghouse a block from Henderson's home and bought a five-acre parcel for a graveyard. Salem would host a quarterly (that is, regional) as well as a monthly meeting of the Anti-Slavery Friends.

As reports about the "separatists" flowed into the original, "body" Salem Monthly Meeting, the meeting censured the anti-slavery radicals, one by one, and eventually disowned them. Reuben Joy was denounced first, for "keeping company with others who encouraged a prisoner to escape"; presumably the prisoner was Black. Second was Aaron Street Jr., who had joined his father in Salem in 1838, after he and his wife had become Quakers in Ohio. Street was chastised for "being out of unity with Friends and writing slanderously about them"—probably because he had told a newspaper editor about plans for a territory-wide abolitionist convention. Henderson was the fifth among the radicals to be censured, for "being concerned with others in setting up a meeting contrary to discipline." Elizabeth, Cyrena, William, and John were all denounced a month after Henderson, and Elvy got her turn the following month. Condemnation of the separatists continued until May 1846, when little sister Jane was attacked for marrying Reuben Johnson in the separatist meeting. In total, about fifty separatist Friends were disowned by the regular monthly meeting. I've found no record of how the separation affected either the Lewellings' businesses or their friendships, but relations in the town must have been severely strained.

Gradually, the Salem abolitionists turned more and more to politics. They looked to the Liberty Party, which had been established in 1839 in New York with the goal of divorcing the federal government from slavery. In 1843, in a two-day, territory-wide meeting that included Congregationalists and Presbyterians as well as Friends, they formed the Iowa Anti-Slavery Society. William, Elvy, and Jane Lewelling were all in attendance. Aaron Street was chosen president, William was chosen recording secretary, and Henderson, although he was absent, was elected one of the directors. After wrangling over William Lloyd Garrison's idea that abolitionists should abandon both the political system and the churches, the assembly instead abandoned the Whig and Democratic parties but directed their focus to third-party politics. They adopted not Garrison's *Liberator* but the Chicago *Western Citizen*, a Liberty Party newspaper, as their official organ.

Back in Salem, all three Lewelling brothers joined the Liberty Party, and they and their fellow abolitionists organized a Liberty Party ticket for the upcoming legislative election. One of the two candidates was Henderson's friend Joel Garretson, who had been raised by Quakers, though he never joined the sect.

The election results were discouraging. Neither of the local Liberty candidates won many votes. Nor did James Birney, the Liberty Party's presidential candidate. In fact, votes for Birney may have thrown the victory from Henry Clay to James Polk, a pro-slavery Democrat.

The Iowa abolitionists had another concern: During the 1844 presidential race, Iowa, still a territory, held a convention to write a state constitution. The assembly talked much of excluding Blacks from the state altogether, for fear of both miscegenation and violent interracial struggle. When the abolitionists repeatedly petitioned the assembly for equal treatment for Black people, the governor suggested outlawing any such petitions. The state constitution, finally approved in 1846, allowed only white men to vote, to join the general assembly, or to serve in the state militia and only white residents to be counted in the state censuses. And the 1839 Black codes were to remain in effect. (Little did the Lewellings know that Iowa's constitution would become the model for Oregon's provisional government.)

1845 and 1846 were sad years for the Friends—body, separatist, and Hicksite alike. The United States annexed Texas, which became a new slave state, seized California and New Mexico, and conducted "Polk's War" to wrest away more than half of Mexico's territory. Friends could do little but petition the U.S. Congress. From 1846 to 1848, Congress was besieged with at least 254 anti-war petitions.

Meanwhile, the break between the "body Friends" and the Anti-Slavery Friends showed no sign of mending. So, in 1845, the London Yearly Meeting sent a delegation to bring about a reconciliation. The visitors, however, didn't try to investigate the break or mediate between the groups; instead, they simply advised the Anti-Slavery Friends to stop gathering separately and to rejoin their old meeting. The Londoners were politely turned away.

Oregon Beckons

In this atmosphere of social and political gloom, Henderson Lewelling once more set his sights on the West. As a boy he had read the journals of Lewis and Clark and had dreamed of seeing the Oregon country and the Pacific Ocean. Lately he had read newspaper accounts by Overland Trail emigrants of 1843 and 1844, and he had also perused John Frémont's report of his expeditions to the Columbia River. He may have also heard about plans for a western exodus by his Mormon neighbors, who lived not only across the Mississippi River in Nauvoo, Illinois, but in scattered settlements in southeastern Iowa. Henderson knew about the mild climate and fertile soil of the Willamette Valley, where land was free for the taking. No one had yet paid the native peoples for it, but Henderson must have known that two Missouri senators, Lewis Linn and Thomas Hart Benton, had long been proposing that the United States offer Americans land in Oregon without charge so they would pour into the region and push out the British. Linn died in 1843, but few doubted that Congress would eventually approve his plan, by which a married couple would be able to claim 640 acres of Oregon land. That was far more than a family could farm, but the excess could be sold in pieces to later settlers. For ambitious men like Henderson, this was a very attractive proposal.

That same fall, according to his son Alfred, Henderson decided to move to Oregon. We don't know how his family reacted; presumably, Elizabeth consented to go, and William and John agreed, however reluctantly, to run the nursery and fruit business on their own. Henderson's friend Joel Garretson objected: How could a man who had prospered so in a place leave everything behind? Joel's son later quoted Henderson's response: "It makes no difference how much a man has around him[,] if he is not satisfied he will go off and leave it."

The following winter and spring Henderson bought oxen and put land up for sale in preparation for the trip. But when it came time to begin the journey in the spring of 1846, he hadn't completed his land sales. He decided to wait until the following year to leave for Oregon. In the meantime, he used the oxen to break new prairie and planted plenty of corn for the trip. And he prepared to take a good supply of grafted trees with him; surely the new Oregonians would be just as hungry for good apples, pears, cherries, and plums as the Indiana and Iowa pioneers had been.

Henderson and Elizabeth ended up selling at least six parcels, including twenty-five acres of their original claim. They profited well: Iowa land values had multiplied about ten times by 1840 and had continued rising since. Henderson and Elizabeth pocketed almost $1,400. They kept the stone house in town, but they rented out the front rooms for the office of the justice of the peace.

In the summer of 1846 Henderson was pleased to learn that, without waging another war, the United States had managed to negotiate with Britain for all the Northwest lands to the forty-ninth parallel, including the Puget Sound. He probably also heard that Oregon's provisional government had banned slavery. These developments must have seemed good omens—good enough, perhaps, to outweigh any misgivings he might have felt about Oregon's moral prospects. If he knew that, in 1844, the provisional legislature had banned the settlement of free Black people he may have felt relief that this law was removed the following year. And perhaps Henderson overlooked a truth about Oregon that should have made even a moderate Quaker quake—that some of the native people were far from ready to surrender their rights to the land.

Chapter 4
The Traveling Nursery

> That load of trees contained health, wealth and comfort, for the Old Pioneers of Oregon. It was the mother of all our early nurseries and orchards, and gave Oregon a name and fame that she never would have had without it. That load of living trees and shrubs brought more wealth to Oregon than any ship that every entered the Columbia River.
>
> —Ralph C. Geer, address to the Oregon Pioneer Association, 1879

Years after railroads had supplanted the Overland Trail, Henderson's eldest child, Alfred Luelling, described his father's preparations for the traveling nursery. Henderson and a Quaker neighbor, John Fisher, "had procured a stout wagon and made two boxes 12 inches deep and of sufficient length and breadth that set in the wagon box side by side they filled it full. These boxes were filled with a compost consisting principally of charcoal and earth, into which about 700 small trees and shrubs, embracing most, if not all of the best varieties in cultivation in that section of the country, were planted." Most Henderson had propagated himself, but "to complete his assortment he bought a few" from Robert Avery, who had a fruit-tree nursery—established even before Henderson's—near the neighboring Iowa town of Denmark.

Emigrants' wagons were generally only about ten feet long and four feet wide. No record remains of the dimensions of the nursery wagon, but it was substantially bigger. Filled with damp soil and trees, it was also extremely heavy. At times more than six oxen would be required to pull it. "Three good yoke of cattle were hitched to that wagon," reported Alfred. "All other arrangements being completed we started from Salem, Iowa, on the 17th day of April 1847."

The trees, from twenty inches to four feet high, were protected from the horses and cattle by a fence of thin hickory strips. Soon a carpet of clover would sprout in the boxes, helping to hold in moisture and providing some nitrogen.

The Lewellings brought no livestock besides their draft oxen and a saddle horse. Perhaps cattle or sheep would have been too much trouble to handle in addition to the traveling nursery, especially since the animals would try to eat the leaves of the young trees. Besides, the Lewellings were probably vegetarians by this time, followers of Sylvester Graham. (Henderson was still hunting in 1852, but he may have given the meat to relatives or hired hands. In 1848 he was a "vegitearian or Grahamite," an acquaintance noted.)

There were now eight Lewelling children, four born in Indiana, four in Iowa. Alfred, the eldest, was fifteen; Mary, Asenath, and Rachel were fourteen, twelve, and ten. While Alfred drove one of the wagons, the older girls looked after four Iowa-born siblings, Jane, eight; Hannah, six; Levi, four; and Albert, two. The younger children rode amid sacks of provisions, dry goods from the Salem store to sell and trade, seeds, tools, and plenty of schoolbooks.

The family wasn't yet complete. Like many other Overland Trail emigrants, Elizabeth was pregnant. If the Lewellings made good time, the child would be born in Oregon.

The Lewellings had, besides the traveling nursery, three wagons for the family and their goods. Joining the party were two other Salem families and a few single men. Nathan and Rebecca Hockett and their four children—the oldest sixteen, the youngest just a baby—were emigrating in hopes of improving Rebecca's epilepsy (Rebecca had accidentally killed one of her babies during a seizure). The Hocketts brought two wagons and fifty head of cattle. John and Rachel Fisher, who had buried three children in Iowa, occupied another wagon with their only living child, two-year-old Angeline. They also brought along a milk cow. The other members of the party were the young schoolteacher Enos Mendenhall, who brought twenty-five head of cattle; Nathan Hockett's younger brother Thomas; Spicer Teas, who drove one of the Lewellings' wagons; and another teamster, Munson Robinson. The little train included, altogether, seven wagons, each with three yoke of oxen, seventy-five head of loose cattle, and several horses.

Munson Robinson may never have been a Friend, but all the other Salem emigrants were from Quaker families with roots in North Carolina.

All the adult Friends had been charter members of the Salem meeting—though Thomas Hockett had been disowned in 1843 for drinking and "making an uproar." The Fishers were especially close to the Lewellings; like Rachel's father, Reuben Joy, the Fishers had been Anti-Slavery Friends in Salem. I wonder if this group knew, as they headed out for the Pacific coast, that they were leaving Quakerdom behind for good.

Before leaving Salem, according to Alfred, Henderson had an odometer—or "roadometer"—attached to one of the wagons; it was probably the first ever used on the Overland Trail. On the rainy, muddy first leg of their journey, through southern Iowa and northwestern Missouri, they covered about fifteen miles a day, according to the roadometer.

The little train reached the Missouri River, ten miles above St. Joseph, on May 17, Alfred recalled. Upon learning that they would have to wait a week to cross at St. Joseph, they bought provisions—flour, cured pork, coffee—in the village of Savannah. Then they took a one-hundred-thirty-mile detour to Independence to cross the river with no wait before joining the crowd of emigrants opposite St. Joseph. Or else, according to William Hockett—nine years old at the time—they traveled for about four days along the east side of the river before crossing at what would become Brownville, Nebraska. William Hockett was amazed at the sight of hundreds of wagons swarming on the riverbanks, many of them belonging to a Mormon train bound for Salt Lake. "As far as I could see it was just covered wagons, cattle, and horses," he remembered.

Obviously, the group would have plenty of company on their journey. By early June, a St. Joseph newspaper editor estimated, fifty-two hundred people had started west from Missouri—along with thirteen thousand cattle, twelve hundred horses, seven hundred sheep, and ninety mules. The overland migration of 1847 would be two and a half times the size of the 1846 migration.

The Salem emigrants set about meeting their fellows. "A few days after crossing the Missouri River we took part in the organization of what was known as the Lot Whitcomb Company," Alfred remembered. Whitcomb was slightly older than Henderson and, like him, a serial emigrant. Born in Vermont, he had moved to Michigan and then Illinois, where he served a term in the legislature. For his family of seven, including one-year-old Queen Victoria, he had seven wagons, and this show of wealth alone may have been enough to get him elected captain of the company. The group organized themselves with military flair, appointing other men as lieutenants and sergeants. Thirteen Illinois families, the Iowa families, and the many others that joined them made up a train of about 114 wagons.

Most of the men and many of the women had prepared to practice their trades in the new country. Ralph Geer, who made the overland journey the same summer, noted preachers, doctors, lawyers, schoolteachers, millers, millwrights, wheelwrights, carpenters, blacksmiths, gunsmiths, silversmiths, tailors, shoemakers, dressmakers, milliners, and "a lumberman with his heavy log wagon" among the emigrants in his wagon train. All of them carried the tools of their trades. Stockmen drove fine cattle, horses, and sheep for breeding. Geer also mentioned "nurserymen with their trees and seeds." He hadn't yet met Henderson, but Geer himself was a nurseryman. He had packed a bushel of apple seeds and a half-bushel of pear seeds to plant in Oregon. In addition, the captain of Geer's train, Joel Palmer, had arrived in St. Joseph with a box of grafted fruit trees from his son's nursery in Indiana. Lacking room to take them himself, he turned the trees over to Geer.

Among the many other emigrants encumbered by the things they needed to practice their crafts, Henderson was one of the most encumbered—and most dogged. His pertinacity may have been matched only by that of Henry Davis, a miller who brought along two granite millstones. Joel Palmer's trees would not survive the trip, and the log wagon would be abandoned along the way at Fort Laramie, in what is now Wyoming. The millstones and the Lewelling traveling nursery, however, would be borne all the way to the Willamette Valley.

From St. Joseph, Oregon was more than two thousand miles away. Getting there would take at least four and a half months. With the nursery wagon, the Lewellings must have known, their trip would probably last longer. The entire journey, from Salem, Iowa, to the Willamette Valley, would in fact take seven months.

Americans had first traversed the Overland Trail with wagons in 1842, moving boulders and filling holes along the way. Thanks to the efforts of these early emigrants and those who followed over the next four years, the route was no longer just a trail. It was, in large part, a well-worn road. But it was still a hard road indeed. Because it followed rivers, it included many crossings, with no bridges and few ferries. Along the Platte River to the crest of the Rockies at South Pass the emigrants would cross nine hundred miles of sandy prairie almost entirely devoid of trees. Then they would follow the Snake River through dusty desert for nearly four hundred miles, to the Blue Mountains of Oregon, and finally they would follow—and ride—the Columbia River to the Willamette. Just a few fur-trading posts would serve as supply stations along the way. The travelers might take a detour to the Whitman Mission, near today's Walla Walla, Washington, if they badly needed a rest or if Marcus Whitman could entice them to come. From the mission only a stretch of ten days or so remained to the Dalles, where emigrants would build or hire boats to carry them down the Columbia River.

Just a few days after starting out, the Whitcomb Company understood that their wagon train was too big. The cattle needed to spread far from the trail to find enough grass to graze, and gathering and sorting them every morning proved too time-consuming. So the Salem group parted ways with Lot Whitcomb, on good terms. In Oregon, Lot and Henderson would become neighbors and business partners.

The Salem emigrants joined with a smaller group led by John Bonser, who had built and operated flatboats on the Ohio River, developing skills that would prove invaluable on the Columbia. John and his wife, Rebecca, may have been the first among several emigrants to turn over their collection of fruit seeds to Henderson. In return, Henderson would later supply the Bonsers with grafted trees for their orchard, on Wapato (now Sauvie) Island, just downstream from Portland.

For at least one of the emigrants of 1847, Hugh Cosgrove, the overland journey "was a long picnic." The emigrants got to see immense herds of buffalo, Indians of various nations, and awesome geological formations. The journey was, "although daring in the extreme, a summer jaunt." But Cosgrove was bluffing. The Salem contingent could not be so blithe, at least not for long. Four of them would perish on the journey, and a fifth, Spicer Teas, would die soon after arriving in Oregon (no one seems to have recorded when and where exactly he died).

Sickness and Death on the Platte

John Fisher was the first to fall sick, as the train headed northwest and approached the Platte River. Like most of the other people who perished on the Overland Trail, Fisher was almost certainly infected by a water- and food-borne pathogen, probably campylobacter or salmonella. These bacteria proliferated in crowded camps. Most emigrants were wise enough not to take drinking water straight from rivers; instead, they would dig a shallow well at some remove. But this didn't help if the previous night's campers had had a latrine nearby, and if rain had spread contaminants over the surface of the soil, as happened frequently during that particularly wet spring. The emigrants may have thought they were journeying into pristine wilderness, but as they moved up the shallow, mile-wide Platte River they brought their contagious diseases with them. Only the cold of the Rocky Mountains would put a stop to the epidemic.

John Fisher was buried on June 6, nine miles from where the group first reached the Platte River. Eighty to one hundred people attended the burial, according to Nathan Hockett. Then the caravan pushed on, although others among the Salem party were ill. Unwilling to turn back alone, Rachel Fisher continued on with little Angeline, sleeping and cooking with the Hocketts for company. Thomas Hockett or one of the other men drove her wagon.

With John Fisher gone, Henderson drove the nursery wagon and tended to his plants. As summer approached and the emigrants traversed ever drier country, the trees needed watering every day. They leafed out and bloomed, and some of the berry canes bore fruit. Later the family would jest that Henderson took better care of the trees than he did of his family.

At times the heavy nursery wagon slowed progress for the entire train. Other emigrants complained. "But to every discouraging criticism," wrote Alfred, "Father invariably answered that as long as he could take that load without endangering the safety of his family he would stick to it." The Lewellings, with Enos Mendenhall and Spicer Teas, began to lag behind the Hocketts, the Fishers, and the rest of the Bonser train.

Their on-and-off separation from their friends may have contributed to the Lewellings' good health during the trip. Perhaps they chose less trampled campsites. They may also have drawn drinking water farther from the river or boiled the water—simple sanitation measures Henderson may have learned from Meshack, his medical books, or the writings of Sylvester Graham, who advised preventing dysentery or cholera by boiling water with toast or grain and then straining and cooling the water before drinking it. However they managed, none of the Lewelling family got sick on the Overland Trail.

Encounters with Natives

While crossing the buffalo range the emigrants saw "many band of Indians, as many as 500 or 600 in a company, but they did not give us much trouble yet," reported William Hockett. Although the Pawnee and Sioux were preoccupied with fighting each other, no one could have been more alarmed by the size of the overland emigration of 1847 than the native peoples in its path. By shooting buffalo, deer, and antelope and destroying grazing lands, the emigrants drastically shrank the natives' food supply. Many Indians expected compensation for the damages, and when payment wasn't freely given they sometimes seized it.

Just a few days after John Fisher's death occurred what for many 1847 emigrants was their most exciting encounter with Indians on the Overland Trail. The Lewellings may have missed the event—perhaps they were camped down the trail—but several other emigrants told the story in their letters and diaries. The Bonser trains had laid over—"on the account of high water," wrote Rachel Fisher—along with another train, led by Asa White, a Methodist missionary from Illinois. That morning some of the Bonser men had already gone off hunting when along came

> a party of about forty mounted Pawnees, clothed only in buffalo robes . . . asking for sugar and tobacco, as usual. But as they rode off, they disclosed their purpose—making a sudden swoop, to stampede the cattle and the horses of the train. The young men of the train, however, instantly ran for the trail ropes of their horses, and began discharging their pieces at the Indians, who, perhaps, were more in sport than in earnest, or, at least, simply "saucing" the immigrants; and wheeled off to the hills, letting the stock go.

But the Indians were serious, William Hockett recounted. As the emigrants rounded up the cattle, they found thirteen draft oxen dead. And at the end of the day two of their men were missing.

Thomas Hockett and Munson Robinson had been out hunting when the Pawnees raided. The men reappeared only around sundown, naked, looking like "two white birds coming over the distant hill," according to Martha Bonser Armstrong, who was ten years old at time.

The Pawnees, explained Hockett and Robinson, had surrounded the two men and demanded their guns. Thomas Hockett resisted; "in fact he tried to kill the Chief," according to his young nephew. After wrestling the gun away, the Pawnees made Hockett and Robinson strip off their clothes, and the chief beat Hockett across the back with his bow, cutting through the skin with each stroke. The Indians then commanded the two men to run for camp, and threw the men's boots after them.

Back in camp, the naked men got little sympathy. After all, Hugh Cosgrove observed, "They were notorious boasters, and from the first had been declaring that they would shoot, first or last, one Indian a piece before they reached Oregon."

The emigrants, for the most part, made light of the Indians' depredations and avoided provoking more. The Bonsers bragged that their two mastiff dogs "were death on Indians" and "could smell an Indian for a mile." Yet Indians managed to steal four of John Bonser's five brood mares before the company reached Oregon, and once the Bonsers had to ransom their prize racehorse with a folding knife.

At Fort Laramie the Bonser company met Sioux Indians, enemies of the Pawnees. Rachel Fisher described the Sioux with the mix of sympathy and annoyance that many emigrants must have felt toward Indians in general.

> They complain that the Buffaloes has all left from near the road they have to go 30 miles for their subsistence there fore they Expect a Smal contribution from each co of the emegrants but they are verry thakfull of the smallest gift but yet they are Friendly and Beggarly and thieveish they have stelen several horses in our knowledge.

By July 2, the Lewellings, with Enos Mendenhall and Spicer Teas, had fallen far enough behind the Bonser train that they seldom caught up by nightfall. But the family didn't mind camping near other emigrant groups or even on their own. The wolves that howled all night long were no great threat, since they were getting their fill of expired oxen. The greatest fright Enos later recalled was petting an ox one night only to discover it was actually a bear. Apparently the Lewellings didn't fear Indians, either. "Instead of standing guard at night," wrote Alfred, "we put bells on our cattle and watched them evenings until they had fed and would lie down, and Father would invariably hear the first tinkle of the bells in the morning."

Jane Harriet Luelling, Alfred's daughter, later recalled the story of the night the family camped near a large band of Indians. Five chiefs came to visit the camp, and Elizabeth fed them cornmeal mush. Henderson gave them beads and trinkets but refused them powder or bullets.

Later a Christian Indian told Henderson that the trees had probably saved the Lewellings' lives. Indians, the man said, believed that the Great Spirit lived in trees, and that anyone crossing the country with a wagon-load of them must be under the Great Spirit's care, and so must not be harmed. The family's hospitality, and their lack of horses and loose cattle, may have helped ensure their safety. But during the whole of the 1840s, Indians killed only a handful of emigrants on the Overland Trail. The natives, in fact, more often helped than harmed the newcomers.

The Mormon Ferry

The emigrants crossed the South Platte where the river forks in western Nebraska, continued up the south side of the north fork, forded the Laramie River where it joins the North Platte at Fort Laramie, and crossed the North Platte 150 miles further on, where the river bends to the south, near present Casper, Wyoming. There, in June, Mormons bound for Salt Lake had first experimented with rafts and with boats made of wagon boxes before building a sturdy ferry from cottonwood dugouts with a deck of pine poles. When they finished, they saw more than one hundred non-Mormon wagons, stretching in a line of more than four miles, waiting to cross the river. Nine Mormon men immediately went into business. They stayed to run the ferry through the season, charging non-Mormons three dollars cash or $1.50 worth of flour or other provisions for each wagon and family. They also built a blacksmith's shop for repairing wagons.

To avoid paying additional fees for transporting cattle, most emigrants drove their livestock across the water. Both animals and their drovers would have to swim part way. Many oxen drowned.

The Bonser company reached the North Platte crossing by July 9, when the White company caught up with the group. The Lewellings soon caught up, too, and camped with the rest of the Bonser company, taking time to grease the wagon axles and sell the Mormons a hundred dollars' worth of dry goods from the Salem store. The oxen must have welcomed the lightening of the load, and the family the extra space in the wagons.

The river level had dropped substantially since the Mormons built the ferry, so many emigrants forded the river without it. Henderson wouldn't take that chance with his nursery: He sent the big wagon, with all its waving green trees, across the river on the ferry.

More Sufferings

Although the Lewellings' fellow travelers looked more and more dubiously at the nursery wagon, they gave up trying to talk sense into Henderson. "The last time that I recollect anyone trying to discourage him," Alfred wrote, "was on the North Platte." There Captain Asa White pointed out that the Lewellings' oxen were "weary and footsore." The increasing weight of the growing trees would kill them, White was sure. "Father's answer was such an emphatic NO," Alfred remembered, "that he was allowed to follow his own course after that without much remonstrance."

The Bonser train never left the Lewellings far behind, however, because the company was often slowed by sickness and death. Soon after the incident with the Pawnees, Thomas Hockett had fallen sick, probably with Rocky Mountain spotted fever. Before the invention of antibiotics, this tick-borne disease was very often deadly. For two weeks Thomas was too sick to drive a team. Fourteen-year-old Solomon took charge of a wagon while nine-year-old William rode a horse all day to keep the cattle from straying.

From the North Platte River the emigrants followed the Sweetwater, its tributary. The Sweetwater's semi-arid, nearly treeless valley provided an almost direct path to the continental divide at South Pass, but its alkali deposits were notorious. The Lewellings lost two oxen in this 238-mile stretch, Alfred reported, one from drinking alkali water and the other from walking in it. But the family hitched up a spare team, and the other oxen began to improve as the two wagons of provisions lightened.

Some of the emigrants crossed the river to visit Independence Rock, a big granite outcropping on which travelers had been carving names and messages since trappers started the custom in 1824. As Henderson would almost certainly later learn, this was the approximate point at which William Barlow, in 1845, had "dumped on the ground . . . at least $50,000.00" in the form of "the best grafted fruit trees that Illinois could produce." Men returning east from Oregon had told Barlow that he couldn't get them through and that anyhow Fort Vancouver and French Prairie already had productive orchards. They failed to tell him, though, that none of the trees in those orchards were grafted. (Barlow did save a small sack of apple seeds, which he would plant in about 1849 on Upper Molalla Prairie. Impatient for their maturity, he would also plant some of Henderson's grafted saplings.)

Just six miles beyond Independence Rock was Devil's Gate Canyon. Near this landmark the Bonser train stopped out of concern for Tom Hockett, who was still in a stupor. The Bonsers and Rachel Fisher soon continued on, however, with Munson Robinson driving Rachel's wagon. The Lewellings didn't stop for long, either, after they arrived from the ferry. Henderson no doubt worried that the falling nighttime temperature would damage his fruit trees. Left behind, the Hocketts rested for several days. Then they traveled on, falling in with another company, despite Tom's continuing fever.

As the emigrants began ascending the Rocky Mountains, disease was again growing rife. Flies spread bacteria from animal carcasses—carcasses of oxen who died from strain and starvation or from drinking infected water, and from buffalo who had been shot, skinned, and left to rot. Some people got sick from eating their own infected livestock.

For Henderson Lewelling, cold was a greater concern than disease. Near South Pass, where the emigrants crossed the Continental Divide, some of them noted nighttime frosts and patches of snow along the trail in late July, though the days were hot. Henderson must have noticed damage among his trees, especially those at the outer edges of the boxes. He probably improvised a nighttime canopy for the nursery, perhaps from the cover of a wagon abandoned by other emigrants. The nights continued to be very cold all the way to Fort Bridger. Even after the descent to the lower Bear River, which the emigrants would follow northwest toward the Snake, the trees weren't safe; in early August, along the river, a snowstorm struck, and the Lewellings probably awakened to a frozen world most days. Some of the damaged trees must have gradually died.

The Lewellings were probably a few days behind the Bonser company when tragedy struck for Rachel Fisher. On August 11, as the Bonser wagons followed the Snake River past Fort Hall, Rachel's two-year-old daughter, Angeline, suddenly grew feverish and mysteriously lame. The next day she was dead. Rachel, now without any family, was more devastated still when Munson Robinson drowned about a week later, in attempting to swim across the Snake River. He had wanted to explore Thousand Springs, the source of waterfalls on the opposite canyon wall, but a whirlpool sucked him under.

The Hocketts' sufferings, meanwhile, had only multiplied. Although they never caught up with the Lewellings, they had shortened their trip by about eighty-five miles by taking what would become known as the Sublette Cutoff, bypassing Fort Bridger. This meant crossing almost forty-five miles of desert without water—a great hardship for the livestock and the emigrants, too. According to William Hockett, "About this time it seemed the entire company was doomed. . . . There was scarcely a night but there was someone buried."

Nathan and Solomon Hockett were both too sick with fever to drive, so Thomas Hockett and seventeen-year-old Rachel drove the two teams. As the train approached the Snake River, the Hocketts stopped, too weak to continue. Nathan and Solomon were still very sick, and now William and Rachel "took the fever," too. Of the four Hockett children, only two-year-old Jesse remained healthy. Most of the rest of the company had recovered, and so they moved on without the Hocketts. The family let their oxen loose and lay exhausted in their wagons.

They were rescued on August 3 by a five-wagon company led by James Raynor, a Methodist preacher originally from England. Unfortunately, the Raynor company brought measles, which Solomon and Rachel both caught. With Nathan Hockett still very ill, the Hocketts left one of their wagons behind and moved on with the Raynor train. On August 19, in a nearly treeless landscape of black volcanic rock, sage, and abandoned wagons, Nathan Hockett died.

Rebecca Hockett had seemed well, but she died in her sleep about eleven days later, as the Raynor train prepared to cross the Snake at Three Island Crossing, a particularly difficult ford. A sudden, quiet death of this sort happens sometimes among epileptics, though decades later her son William would maintain that his mother died of a broken heart.

Soon thereafter William came down with "black measles," probably not measles at all but Rocky Mountain spotted fever, which produces a rash over much of the body. He suffered even more than his Uncle Tom had. The boy was in a stupor for six weeks, after which time his "hip and backbone had worn through the skin." The disease can also cause partial paralysis. Until the following June, William would need crutches to walk.

Unaware of the Hocketts' misery, the Lewellings reached Fort Boise, the Hudson's Bay Company trading post near the last ford of the Snake River, by early September. They traveled west through stony desert and began the rugged trek into the Blue Mountains—probably the most difficult climb of the journey with the nursery wagon. After about ten days they entered the Grande Ronde Valley, a beautiful, fertile round valley surrounded by timbered mountains. Here the Nez Perce and Cayuse pastured their horses and cattle, and Indians of various nations gathered camas bulbs.

It was likely in the Grande Ronde Valley that the Lewellings met the physician Marcus Whitman. With his wife, Narcissa, Whitman had founded the Presbyterian mission at Waiilatpu, thirty-one miles north of the primary route of the Overland Trail. The eleven-year-old mission was in trouble. Because the Whitmans had had little success in converting the local Cayuse to Christianity, the church had stopped supporting the missionaries' work. Marcus's real mission at this point was helping to fill up Oregon with white, Protestant emigrants from the United States and enticing some to join his own small colony. The measles epidemic that the emigrants had brought was ravaging Waiilatpu and the nearby Cayuse village, yet Whitman took the time to greet many of the wagon trains passing through.

Shortly before approaching the Lewellings, Whitman had tried, unsuccessfully, to convince Henry Davis to set up his flour mill at Waiilatpu or to at least sell Whitman his millstones. Now the physician-turned-missionary-turned-colonizer talked with the Lewellings for hours and ended up staying the night with them. Henderson and Whitman discovered "a great bond of sympathy," Alfred remembered. Whitman "expressed high appreciation of the effort Father was making to introduce grafted fruit into the country," and the Lewellings were much impressed by the stories of a white family's life alone in Indian country.

But they weren't tempted to go to Waiilatpu. Instead, the Lewellings moved the boxes of fruit trees to one of the smaller, lighter wagons, doubled up the teams, and abandoned the heavy nursery wagon. Then Whitman led the Lewellings over a new route he had developed to the Dalles, out of the mountains and across the windy desert of northeastern

Oregon to the John Day River. The route avoided difficult hills and troublesome Indians along the Columbia and allowed for an easier, upstream crossing of the John Day. Whitman must have spent several days with the Lewellings before turning back to continue his recruitment efforts among the emigrants: he would try, unsuccessfully, to convince James Raynor, the Hocketts' savior, to take a teaching job at Waiilatpu. Little did the Lewellings know that only about two months later their new friend, his wife, and a dozen others at Waiilatpu would be massacred by a group of Cayuse, who blamed the missionaries for the disease that was killing half their tribe while sparing the lives of most of its white victims.

Alfred didn't describe the family's last river crossing, at the mouth of the Deschutes, but it was difficult for all the emigrants. Until a dam turned the area into a lake, in 1957, the Deschutes hurtled into the Columbia over large rocks between basalt cliffs. Some emigrants rode across in

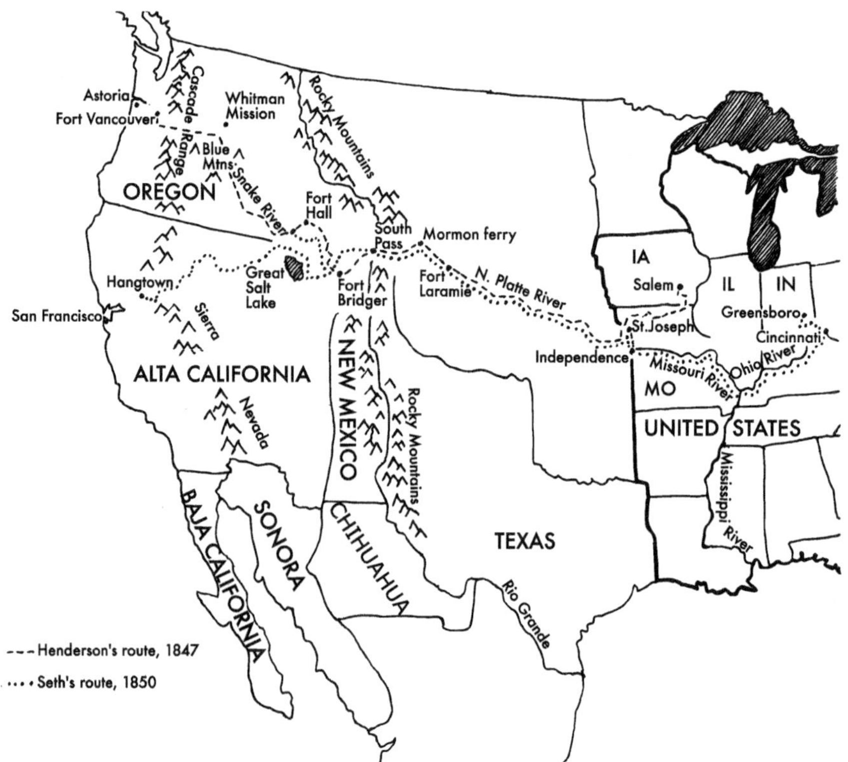

Henderson and family's route to the Pacific Coast in 1847 and Seth's in 1850. Map by Rebecca Waterhouse.

Indians' canoes, paying for the service in calico shirts. Some floated their wagons, which often turned over in the rapids; this is how Ralph Geer lost Joel Palmer's fruit trees. Other emigrants found they could drive their teams across over a sandbar. The Lewellings may have succeeded with the last method.

The Final Ordeal

About thirteen miles downstream from the Deschutes was the Dalles, the end of the Overland Trail. Here the Columbia River contracted from nine hundred feet wide to sixty as it entered a long, narrow channel between vertical basalt walls. From time immemorial, Indians of many Northwestern tribes had met in the area to fish and trade. Now the Dalles was the site of a small Presbyterian mission—"It looks like starvation," noted one traveler—and the last big emigrant encampment of the Overland Trail. Taking wagons farther along the river was impossible. An alternative was a rough toll road around the south side of Mount Hood, developed the preceding year by Sam Barlow, whose son William had dumped his fruit trees at Independence Rock. But in 1847 the Barlow Road was impassable once the snows started, and nearly impassable before then. So most emigrants chose to float the river for eighty-eight miles to Fort Vancouver, the Hudson's Bay Company's western headquarters, and then a few miles more to the mouth of the Willamette. Speculators were ready to help, for stiff prices. The emigrants might secure places in one of the swift, strong, thirty-foot-long native canoes. They might buy passage in one of the Hudson's Bay Company's flatboats, large enough for forty dismantled wagons with their passengers and baggage, and also piloted mainly by Indians. Or the emigrants might build their own raft or boat from the abundant timber in the area. Here on the eastern flank of the great volcanic mountain range that separated wet western Oregon from the dry interior, many emigrants camped for weeks, eating potatoes, onions, and peas bought from Indian farmers while constructing their simple vessels.

The Lewellings arrived at the Dalles in early October. Henderson immediately joined John Bonser in boat building. Martha Bonser Armstrong described the construction of one great boat for the whole Bonser party, but Alfred mentioned two boats, so perhaps Henderson took charge of building the second one. The two boats were probably built in the same way, as Martha described:

> The trees were cut and whipsawed into boards, beams, and gunwales, and all were put together with wooden pegs, for they had no nails. The gunwales of the boat were heavy timbers hewn from huge trees, measuring 6 feet deep and a foot thick. To make the big boat water-tight, pine gum was gathered by the children and boiled in a big iron kettle which John had brought along on the long journey. The hot pitch was applied to the caulked seams so water could [not] seep through.

The work took a month. Elizabeth, with her baby due just two months after their arrival at the Dalles, may have welcomed the opportunity to rest. But as the weather grew colder and wetter she must have longed for her big stone house in Iowa, with its fireplaces—or for any kind of house at all.

Before the Lewellings could settle in for the winter they would have to endure the hardest, most perilous part of the emigrants' journey. The boats were completed about the first of November, according to Alfred. Martha Bonser Armstrong described the launch:

> Since the heavy boat had been built bottom side up, a monstrous task confronted its builders when it was finished. How to get it right side up and launch it! But as always, John had a plan. With long Chains he hitched several yoke of oxen to the side of the boat furthermost from the river and pulled it up and over onto skid rollers onto which the cumbersome craft was slid down into the water.

Henderson and his family readied the now dormant fruit trees. They "were taken out of the boxes, "wrote Alfred, "and duly wrapped in cloths to protect them in the various handlings and from the frosty nights."

Martha continued,

> Everything was then put aboard the big boat. The wagon beds were placed close together, running-gear piled high, people crowded close, the Argonauts set forth on the breast of the great river. Not relying on the current of the river for progress, John had equipped the craft with long "Sweeps," oars on the sides and another long oar at the back to guide the boat with its precious load.

Neither Alfred Luelling nor Martha Bonser Armstrong mentioned the weather. Elizabeth Smith, who also traveled from the Dalles to Fort Vancouver in November1847, described the nearly constant rain and snow, "icicles hanging from our wagon beds," and winds that whipped the river into waves as high as four feet and forced the travelers, over and over, to land and wait for calmer weather, sometimes for several days.

Alfred remained on land. He and Enos Mendenhall were among the men who drove the livestock along narrow and steep Indian trails against the rock walls of the Columbia River Gorge. For the cattle, wrote one drover, a misstep could mean a fall of "one or two hundred feet and nothing could be found of them but a grease spot."

About halfway between the Dalles and Portland were the Cascades, a two-mile stretch of rapids through which the river dropped about forty feet. In the late 1930s these rapids were submerged by the Bonneville Dam, but for travelers on the Overland Trail they were such a notorious obstacle that they gave their name to the mountain range surrounding them. At the head of the Columbia River Gorge, the emigrants would have to unload their boats on the north bank. They would make a five-mile portage around the rapids on what Elizabeth Smith called "the worst road a team could possibly travel," with "snow, mud, and water almost to my knees."

Alfred described how the boats

> went down as far as Wind River [at today's Carson, Washington], where they were unloaded and used to ferry our cattle and horses over to the north side of the Columbia, and then reloaded and taken to the Upper Cascades, again unloaded, the wagons set up and hauled to the Lower Cascades, the boats having been turned adrift at the Upper Cascades went bumping and tossing down the seething current and were captured below.

According to one account, Bonser cleverly stabilized the boats: "He cut a tree, took the bushy portion of the top, and lashed the boats to this and set them adrift."

The boats were caught, Martha Bonser Armstrong explained, "by the help of Klickitat Indians in their canoes. Again, the wagons, the people and their belongings were loaded on the boat, and the journey down the river was continued." The drovers and livestock, now traveling down the river's north shore, would meet the others at Fort Vancouver.

The Lewelling and Bonser boats finally reached Fort Vancouver, on the north side of the river, on November 17. The emigrants must have been awed by the sight. The palisade alone was 220 yards long and 15 feet high. Nearby was a workers' village, made up of log huts in neat rows. Stretching far into the distance were at least twelve hundred acres of cultivated fields, plus pastures for sheep and cattle.

The families pulled their boats out of the water and joined an encampment of tattered tents and wagons outside the fort. Three days later, Alfred and Enos arrived with Enos's cattle. The Lewellings must have taken care to ensure that the roots of the fruit trees stayed damp—though this was little trouble in the cool, wet weather of late autumn in western Oregon.

Settling In

As every family or single settler began a search for better winter shelter, the Salem emigrants and their friends dispersed. Enos Mendenhall went to teach school at the home of his distant cousin Isaac Mills, a former Quaker from North Carolina. Isaac and his wife, Charity, and their children had emigrated to Oregon in 1843 and had settled on the Tualatin Plains, west of Portland. Rachel Fisher spent a month in Portland, then just a string of about a dozen riverbank houses, half made of logs, half framed, with one store and with pieces of emigrant wagons scattered around. Lacking good forage for her cattle, Rachel joined Enos at the Mills homestead, where she became his arithmetic student, although she was already twenty-five years old. The following spring, the Mills family would enjoy a double wedding: Rachel Fisher to Isaac and Charity's twenty-one-year-old son William, and Enos to their sixteen-year-old daughter, Rachel Emily (who went by Emily).

The Lewellings may never have seen the Hocketts again. The orphans and their uncle had reached the Willamette River via a Hudson's Bay Company bateau from Fort Walla Walla, twenty-five miles west of the Whitman Mission, on the Columbia, taking nothing but one cow, William's horse, and food and bedding. Like Rachel Fisher, the family moved into a Portland shack, though they may have already left town by the time Rachel arrived. After fifteen-year-old Rachel Hockett, armed with a fireplace poker, fought off a drunken sailor who had broken into the house, she begged her uncle to move them out of town, and Tom found the family a home on the Tualatin Plains.

The Bonsers, who had left their cattle in the care of Indians at the mouth of the Sandy River, found an empty cabin at Linnton, a short distance up the Willamette River. Eight weeks later they moved into a bigger, better cabin, across the river at present-day St. Johns. Martha Bonser Armstrong, who later described these events, remembered nothing of the first cabin, because she was unconscious with fever all the time the family was there.

Henderson was away exploring the country when Elizabeth went into labor, on December 3. Probably hoping to give birth in a comfortable room at Fort Vancouver, she started off in a hired Indian canoe with her two eldest children, Alfred and Mary. But the contractions came on so fast that the boatman had to turn the canoe around and paddle fast for the southern shore. In the rain, on the riverbank across from the fort, Elizabeth delivered her ninth child. The birth of a healthy baby must have seemed a great triumph following the Lewellings' exhausting seven-month journey. They called the boy Oregon Columbia.

Three days later came news to dampen the family's joy. Thirteen people had been murdered at the Whitman Mission. Besides Marcus and his wife, Narcissa, the victims included several new emigrants, whom the Lewellings might have met along the trail. In addition, fifty-four people from the mission were now captives of the Cayuse. Suddenly Oregon seemed a less safe place, and the peace-loving Lewellings must have despaired at the talk of war against the Cayuse. When a makeshift militia rallied, neither Henderson nor Alfred joined in.

Henderson eventually found an empty log cabin on the bank of the Willamette River, across the river from Portland. With one-week-old Oregon Columbia wrapped against the cold, the family moved in about December 10. Finally they had a roof over their heads, a place to huddle through the winter when they weren't out searching for a home site. They may have heeled in the fruit trees beside the cabin, or placed them, still wrapped in their cloths, in a trench or pit, well covered in forest duff. Like the Lewellings, the trees would soon grow roots in Oregon soil.

Chapter 5
Webfeet

> It is related of some of the earliest settlers in the Willamette Valley that nothing more thoroughly and painfully accentuated their isolated condition than the absence of fruit trees on their newly-made farms.
>
> —J. R. Cardwell, "The First Fruits of the Land"

For nearly three chilly, rainy months, Henderson continued his search for a home and nursery site. He ended up buying the squatting rights to a parcel on the east bank of the Willamette River, halfway between Oregon City and Portland and adjacent to Lot Whitcomb's claim and what would be the town site of Milwaukie.

Although the indigenous people of western Oregon had kept much of the landscape open through controlled burning, for better hunting and gathering, Henderson had chosen a forested site. Perhaps he banished from his mind the years of his youth that he had spent clearing forest in Indiana. He must have weighed the value of frontage on the Willamette River—an aqueous highway through a roadless land—and access to the stream that would be called Johnson Creek, for irrigation and, perhaps, powering a mill. Henderson would not have forgotten the association of fever and ague—malaria—with damp lowlands, but he probably figured that the disease would be no concern in this healthful land. In fact, malaria had been a tribulation here and would be yet, even for the Lewellings.

I like to imagine Henderson, upon paddling to the mouth of Johnson Creek, encountering his friend Lot Whitcomb, who with his family had spent the winter in Oregon City. During January and February, Lot sought a site where he could build a sawmill. He preferred a forested site, so he would have his own trees to cut. He had found such a site with an abandoned shack by the river and with two creeks—Johnson and another, to be called Kellogg—running into the Willamette. In just a month or

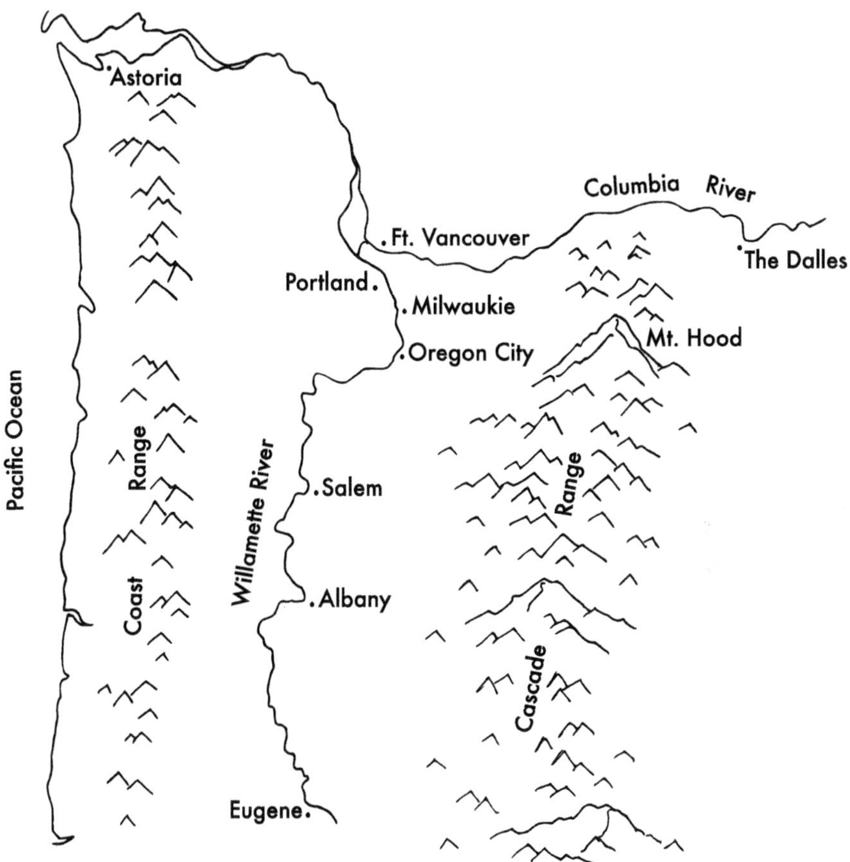

The lower Columbia and Willamette rivers. Map by Rebecca Waterhouse.

two, he would begin building his mill. Lot probably already planned to plat a town; he would do so before the end of the following year. He may have shared his dreams with Henderson and encouraged his friend to acquire the cabin and claim just downstream.

That claim belonged to Albert E. Wilson, the first judge in Oregon's provisional government (formed in 1843, this government had no authority recognized by the United States or Britain, and no way of enforcing laws). Wilson was at this point running a store in Astoria, near the mouth of the Columbia River. At the site of what is today the Waverley Country Club, he had built a log cabin and felled about five acres of trees. Henderson tracked down Wilson and paid him off with Iowa store goods, mostly woolen cloth, boots, and shoes.

Unlike the woodlands of Indiana, the western Oregon forest was largely coniferous, with Douglas firs as big as two hundred fifty feet tall and six feet in diameter and western red cedars with trunks as wide as nineteen feet. The trees Wilson had cut "lay in great heaps over the ground," Alfred remembered. The family moved into the cabin on February 5, 1848, and immediately began clearing timber. All the oxen that had survived the Overland Trail may have been needed to move a single felled tree trunk. Some of the trees were too large even for the oxen and had to be burned in place. The family must have lived for months in a cloud of smoke, but they persevered. Alfred recalled, "with ax and fire plied almost day and night, for we kept the fires well tended until ten o'clock at night and were up and at it again by four in the morning, we soon had land cleared on which to plant our orchard."

About three hundred of the plants from the traveling nursery had survived the trip. Among the trees were twenty-two varieties of apple (including one crabapple), eight of pear, five of cherry, three of peach, four of plum—three gage types and the large, oval, purple Smith's Orleans—and the Orange quince. Along with the trees were three American grapes (Delaware, Concord, and one start of Isabella), a single gooseberry, and a few currant bushes.

Somehow the Napoleon cherries ended up relabeled as Royal Ann—which doesn't sound like a name a Quaker would choose unless you consider that the two names share a central *l* and a final *n* and that, on a damaged tag, an *N* might look like an *R* and a *p* like a *y*. In any case, forever after in America the red-blushed yellow cherry would remain the Royal Ann, a prized Oregon product still today—although it is now best known in the form of the dyed, alcohol-free, industrial faux-maraschino cherry (true maraschino cherries are marasca cherries in marasca cherry liqueur).

The Lewellings planted all the living trees, shrubs, and grapevines in the newly cleared ground. In doing so Henderson must have felt enormous relief and satisfaction, despite having lost more than half his young plants to freezes. The survivors wouldn't begin bearing for a few more years, but they represented great promise.

Henderson filed a preemptive claim with Oregon's provisional government, and so did Alfred, on a neighboring parcel.

On Clackamas Land

The Lewellings were now in the territory of the Clackamas people, who had long occupied the area from the Willamette on the west to the Cascades on the east, and from the Columbia on the north to some distance south of Oregon City. The Clackamas had lived in permanent villages, with houses as long as one hundred feet and an economy centered on fishing. But when the Lewellings arrived only one small Clackamas village remained, three to four miles upstream of the Lewelling claim.

Foreign diseases had reached the Clackamas, by ship, long before the opening of the Overland Trail. First came smallpox, in the late eighteenth century; it probably killed at least 30 percent of the region's indigenous peoples. Then came malaria, transmitted from sick sailors in 1829 to native mosquitoes and from them to both Indians and whites. Returning each year through at least 1833, the malaria epidemic killed an estimated 90 percent of the Clackamas people.

The Clackamas people weren't the only natives affected. These diseases were the main reason western Oregon saw little conflict between Indians and white settlers. This is not to say there was no conflict at all. According to one source, Albert Wilson sold Henderson his claim because the local Indians were annoying. While the Lewellings settled in, and while a militia hunted for the perpetrators of the Whitman massacre, Cayuse emissaries visited neighboring peoples in hopes of forming a coalition to combat the whites. In the foothills of the Cascades, Cayuse, Klamath, and Molalla men harassed wives of militia volunteers, broke into cabins, and stole horses. In early March, a "home guard" of white settlers responded by killing thirteen Klamath men near Abiqua Creek. Indians were accused of minor depredations elsewhere in the Willamette Valley– cattle thefts, the killing of an old white man, and the rape of a white girl.

But the Lewellings were unbothered by Indians. The Clackamas were in no condition to battle white people in the winter of 1847–48; they were instead battling the measles, which the emigrants had brought to the valley from the infected tribes of the Columbia Plateau. In 1855 the Clackamas—that is, the twenty-five to thirty surviving tribal members—would sign a treaty ceding all their land to the United States in return for an annuity of $2,500 a year for ten years. In the meantime, the newcomers would divide the land among themselves with impunity.

First Grafts

The little Lewelling orchard was a novelty in the region. Unlike any other, it was made up entirely of luscious-fruited exotic clones.

The Willamette Valley had abundant wild fruits—crabapples, elderberries, blackberries, thimbleberries, salmonberries, blackcaps, strawberries, currants, gooseberries, salal berries, serviceberries, chokecherries, Oregon grapes (*Mahonia*), and black haws. The blackberries—*Rubus ursinus*—and the blackcaps were beloved by natives and newcomers alike, but most of the other fruits were less appealing; they were too small, too tart, or bitter, bland, or tannic. Returning gold seekers would soon add to this collection the wild plums and grapes of southern Oregon and northern California (*Prunus subcordata* and *Vitis californica*), whose fruits were small but sweet.

Oregon also had fruits that had originated in Asia or Europe. In 1821, Governor George Simpson determined that food imports were cutting too far into Hudson's Bay Company profits and that through farming the company could reduce its dependence on both Indians and Yankee ships and eventually even supplant the Yankees as suppliers to Russian fur traders in Alaska. Wheat became the company's main crop, but fruit culture soon followed. According to an oft-told story, women at a Hudson's Bay Company dinner in London, in 1824, put seeds of apples, pears, peaches, and grapes into the vest pockets of all the men bound for the Pacific Coast. By the close of 1827 at least one apple tree had been planted from seed at Fort Vancouver; an orchard and vineyard were planted about two years later. By 1832 the orchard apple trees, though still small, were bearing so heavily that their branches had to be propped. Other fruits came from California; in 1844, John Minto noted a 'Mission' grapevine covering one end of a building at the fort. The next year Minto bought Mission Bottom, the original site of Jason Lee's Methodist mission, and there he found peach trees, currants, gooseberries, and a rhubarb bed. The original seeds and or plants had probably come from Fort Vancouver.

John McLoughlin, chief factor at the fort, shared seeds with his employees who retired to French Prairie, twenty miles or so up the Willamette from Oregon City, and with American emigrants. The Fort Vancouver nursery also sold some two-year-old trees, but they were expensive—$5 each (about $190 in 2024 dollars)—and most of the emigrants had little or no cash. One French Canadian settler, Joseph Gervais, had planted an orchard at Chemawa by 1830, and in 1849 his apples sold for $3 a bushel (about $120 in 2024). Whether any of Gervais's apples were particularly good for fresh eating we can't know; no testimony survives. But none of his trees was grafted. The fruit was probably most suitable for cider.

Americans, however, were no longer great cider drinkers. They had grown accustomed to eating large quantities of dessert fruits. Now Oregon's new settlers, having left developed orchards behind, pined for grafted fruit trees. Some were planting nurseries from seeds they had gathered at cider mills before leaving on their westward journeys, and hoping somehow to obtain good scions to graft to their trees later. The Lewellings' trees would provide those scions, along with tens of thousands of already grafted trees, to fill the emigrants' orchards and gardens. But these would-be orchardists would have to wait a few years.

News from Home

Since mail from the States took five to six months to reach Oregon, the Lewellings probably received their first letters from Iowa and Indiana in the spring of 1848. Whenever news from home came, it was by turns inspiring and devastating. The Anti-Slavery Friends had continued their shift into civic activism. The Iowa Anti-Slavery Society's fifth and last annual meeting, in fact, had morphed into the first convention of the Iowa Liberty Party. Salem's William Lewelling, Aaron Street, and Elwood Ozbun had all become Iowa Liberty Party officers. But then William went on a speaking tour in Indiana. He died there, suddenly, on October 17, 1847, while Henderson and his family were still on their way to the Willamette Valley. Cyrena was left with six young children to raise on her own, and John Lewelling was left to run the Iowa nursery alone. Many years later, Henderson would add the name William to his own, probably in honor of his brother the preacher.

A New Partner

Another William may have helped to distract Henderson from his grief. William Horry Meek arrived at the Lewellings' cabin in March. Henderson knew William Meek from Iowa; he had probably been one of Henderson's customers. Although Meek (as I'll call him, because of the surfeit of Williams in this story) wasn't raised Quaker and was eight years younger than Henderson, the two men had much in common. Meek had also had an orchard in Iowa. Like Henderson, too, Meek was the son of a serial emigrant and a serial emigrant himself. His father, also named William, had been born in Pennsylvania and had lived in West Virginia, Ohio, and Michigan before settling in Iowa in 1837, on the Des Moines River, about fifteen miles from Salem. William Meek the younger had been born in Ohio and had moved along with his family.

Together the Meek family had dammed the Des Moines River and, in 1844, built a grist mill. The elder William and two other sons would go on to build a sawmill, a brickyard, and a woolen mill, all in the little town of Bonaparte, Iowa. But the younger William Meek, like Henderson, was restless. He had lost two young children and divorced his first wife for "insanity" (perhaps schizophrenia or postpartum psychosis) before marrying Sarah Stone, in late 1845. The following summer Sarah delivered a premature baby and, a week later, died. According to family lore, Sarah Charlotte was so small at birth "that her father wrapped her in a handkerchief, put her in his pocket and rode several miles on horseback" to his wife's parents' place, where her thirteen- and eight-year-old sisters took charge of the tiny baby. Somehow, they kept little Sarah alive.

But Meek had had enough of Iowa. When Henderson told him about his plans to go to Oregon and to take along the traveling nursery, Meek decided to go, too. Leaving his daughter behind and taking along one of his deceased wife's brothers, Lysander Stone, Meek departed for Missouri, where he planned to meet Henderson for the westward trek.

The Lewellings arrived late, however. They didn't find William Meek. He had already left for Oregon.

Meek had decided to carry along some young fruit trees himself. He took about twenty, according to Alfred, in a box attached to the back of his wagon. Because he crossed the Rockies earlier in the summer than the Lewellings did, he avoided freezing temperatures. He didn't risk his trees on the Columbia River but instead carried them through on the Barlow Road. His trees were still alive, heeled in on a friend's preemptive claim in the Forks of the Santiam, about seventy miles southeast of the Lewelling claim. Since he had arrived in the valley in September, William Meek, not Henderson, was in fact the first to bring grafted fruit trees to Oregon.

But now Meek saw that Henderson was the first to have planted a grafted orchard. The quince trees must have been already leafing out, and buds were probably opening on some of the pear trees. Meek wanted to join the enterprise.

Meek spent several days with the Lewellings as he and Henderson made plans. Meek would fetch his trees, and he and Henderson would add them to the Lewellings' orchard. According to one source, Meek had also brought seeds; these, with any seeds Henderson had brought himself and those John Bonser had given him, would be the start of the nursery. Henderson and Meek would run the orchard and nursery business together. Together, they would hold about thirteen hundred acres.

While acknowledging Henderson's greater horticultural expertise, the two men may have considered applying Meek's special skills in a second enterprise. Rather than burn all the timber they would be cutting on their lands, they would set up and run a sawmill.

Meek filed for a provisional claim adjacent to Henderson's on the north side. Then he and Henderson "threw their claims together and divided the whole by a line running north and south, Meek taking the eastern portion and Lewelling the western."

Now Meek needed a wife, not only as a helpmeet but as justification for a bigger land claim. The land-claims act passed by Oregon's provisional government in 1843 provided 320 acres to any white man and 640 acres to a married couple. The emigrants expected the U.S. Congress to pass a similar law soon, validating their provisional claims. Single men, therefore, were especially eager to marry. The demand for wives would intensify in 1850, after passage of the federal Donation Land Claim Act, at which point, according to an 1893 newspaper account, "no young girl over the age of twelve was safe from the stampede of young farmers wanting to add another half section to their land." But Meek didn't wait. He turned his attention to Henderson and Elizabeth's eldest daughter, Mary—a pretty girl, according to her niece Jane Harriet Luelling, "with black eyes like her father's and dark hair and fair complexion and a sweet expression." Mary celebrated her fifteenth birthday about the time of Meek's visit. In July she married him, a man twice her age, a few days after he filed his provisional land claim. She may have eagerly anticipated owning her own big piece of Oregon land.

The family chose their neighbor George Wills to perform the wedding service, even though he was a "hard shell" or "primitive" Baptist preacher. A brand-new arrival from Kentucky, Wills and his son would soon build and operate their own sawmill on Johnson Creek, one of four along the creek by late 1849.

Among the Forty-Eighters

The newlyweds barely had a chance to get settled before Meek made plans to leave for California. News of the discovery of gold there came in July, after the captain of the schooner *Honolulu* brought his ship to Portland empty and hurriedly loaded it with flour, picks, and shovels. The news flew from cabin to cabin, town to town. Gold fever spread like an epidemic. Soon as many as two-thirds the adult males of Oregon would be among the "forty-eighters," who beat the forty-niners to the California goldfields, leaving their wives and children to fend for themselves in little log shacks on lands still formally held by native people.

Whether his family or his business exerted the stronger pull, Henderson decided he couldn't leave Oregon for California anytime soon. Instead he sent William Meek and Alfred Luelling.

Alfred told the story of the trip years later in a letter to Ralph Geer. He and Meek joined a company who would accomplish something never before attempted: taking wagons through the rugged mountains of southern Oregon and northern California into the Sacramento Valley. The company comprised 150 "stout, robust, energetic, sober men" with fifty wagons and ox-teams. The train traveled down the western edge of the Willamette Valley to Dallas and then southeast along the Applegate Trail, cut two years before to provide an alternative route around the Cascades into western Oregon. At Klamath Lake, Meek joined the leaders of the expedition in blazing a new trail south into California. Eventually they came upon a newly cut wagon road, which, they thought, might lead to Peter Lassen's ranch on the Feather River. After following the rough road for weeks, they came upon Lassen himself, wandering in the woods with the small band of half-starved emigrants he had urged to come to California by a direct route to his ranch—a route that he had not, unfortunately, yet explored. The Oregonians scouted out a new trail to Lassen's ranch and cleared it for the wagons. The Oregon company, along with Lassen's party, arrived at the ranch on November 28, and Lassen celebrated by killing "a fat beef."

After a few days' rest, Alfred and Meek tried their hands at mining, first on the Yuba River and then on the North Fork of the American River. Having little luck, they left their wagon and five yoke of oxen at Sutter's

Fort, bought ponies from another miner, and headed for the Bear and Yuba rivers. But snow drove them back to Sutter's Fort. There Alfred waited while Meek visited San Francisco.

We don't know how Meek spent his time in the City by the Bay, but any trip there had to be an adventure. The two-thousand-some residents, nearly all men, were mostly, at this point, from Mexico, South America, Hawaii, Oregon, and other parts of California. They slept amid sand hills and mud puddles in canvas tents, rough-board shacks, and packed hotels and boarding houses. The harbor was crowded with ships, many of them abandoned by sailors who had left for the mines, and hundreds of gambling saloons provided the chief entertainment. But Meek was a serious man. I imagine he spent most of his time checking out business prospects.

On Meek's return to Sutter's Fort, in February, he and Alfred explored the diggings near the Stanislaus and Tuolumne rivers and finally bought a claim at Angel's Camp, east of Sacramento. Sifting gravel in their rocker for a few weeks' time, they made $16 to $160 dollars a day.

Perhaps Alfred would have stayed longer, but "not being suited with the prospect of mining life Wm. Meek decided that we would better return to the Fort, sell our ponies, oxen and wagon and return home." In San Francisco—whose population had doubled since Meek's solo visit—they caught a ship for Portland at the end of June 1849.

Alfred didn't say how much money they gained in total, but Oregon men who were luckier or more dogged made small fortunes in the California mines. In total, Oregonians mined about $5 million of California gold. Perhaps unwilling to leave all the gold for other families, Henderson encouraged his brothers John and Seth to come west and have a go in the goldfields. Yet Henderson may have also heeded the advice of the Oregon City newspaper editor, who asked, "Is not a market for your wheat, beef, pork, potatoes, peas, beans, garden vegetables, fish, and lumber, a desirable matter?" Although the editor neglected to mention apples, his argument was compelling:

> And will not such mines draw to them a sufficient population to provide you a market for all these articles? . . . [T]he mines have already brought the desired market, the mines will bring facilities for carrying provisions to the mines; and the mines will materially contribute to make Oregon known, and develop her great resources.

Wise Oregonians would go back to farming, but in a more capitalistic mode.

California gold would provide a much-needed medium of exchange, and Oregon would even use it to issue its own "Beaver money" in 1849. Before that year, ships rarely visited the lower Willamette River, but in 1849 fifty or more docked there, the captains eager to fill their holds with grain and timber. California would be the chief market for Oregon products. The "webfeet" would mine the miners.

Gaining Ground

Much had happened in Oregon while Meek and Alfred were away. In reaction to the massacre at Whitman's colony, Congress had passed a bill to create the Oregon Territory, which encompassed Idaho, Washington, and parts of western Montana and Wyoming along with present-day Oregon. The bill had been delayed two years by the debate over whether slavery would be permitted in the new territory. To Henderson's and Elizabeth's relief, no doubt, slavery was ultimately forbidden—although the appointed territorial governor, Joseph Lane, favored slavery's spread (and the following year Black people would be banned from entering the territory). A new legislature took office—though when it first assembled, on December 5, 1848, it immediately adjourned for two months, because half the members had left to hunt gold in California.

While the absentee legislators prospected for gold—or idly waited out the rain and snow—Henderson must have seen plenty of riches in his own orchard. The trees would have produced almost no fruit in the fall of 1848, although according to an apocryphal story "the first big red apple produced by Oregon soil was borne that year. So great was the fame of it, and such the curiosity of the people, that men, women, and children came from miles around to see it, and made a hard beaten track through the nursery to this joyous reminder of the old homestead so far away." Henderson no doubt saw more wealth in the form of young branches suitable for use as scion wood and buds. To his frustration, though, he was short on rootstock on which to graft. He acquired seedling trees—probably hundreds—from Ralph Geer, who had settled in the Waldo Hills, east of Salem, and who must have planted his seeds soon after arriving in Oregon. In return, Henderson gave Ralph buds for his orchard—an exchange for which Ralph was ever grateful. But these little trees were too few for Henderson, and, besides, they were only apples and pears. Henderson must have spent much time in the woods, perhaps with his children's help, hunting for seedling trees of native crabapple (*Malus fusca*), hawthorn (*Crataegus douglasii* or *C. suksdorfii*), and bitter cherry (*Prunus emarginata*), because he tried grafting onto all of these—apple, pear, and quince onto the crabapple and hawthorn, and sweet cherry onto bitter cherry. But he had little success.

Henderson may have looked with some envy at his neighbor Lot Whitcomb, who had also concluded he could better ensure a path to fortune by staying in Oregon than by running off to California. He and William Torrance, his business partner and new son-in-law, connected a grist mill to their sawmill. In early 1849, the two commissioned Joseph Kellogg, another 1847 emigrant, to build a schooner to carry flour, bacon, and lumber to San Francisco. The partners made so much money on sales of the cargo, and of the schooner itself, that they were able to buy a larger ship, the brig *Forrest*. The saw-and-grist mill ran around the clock, turning out six thousand feet of lumber a day. Soon Lot and his son-in-law bought a second ship. They repeatedly loaded both vessels with lumber that would sell in San Francisco for two hundred dollars per thousand feet. Unable to keep up with demand, Lot sought both lumber and flour from other millers, for whom he would serve as agent—though he would struggle against Portland competitors to prove the navigability of the upstream Willamette. Soon after Meek returned from California, he and Henderson began building their own mill on Johnson Creek. They would rely on Lot to market their products.

The Lewelling family continued to grow. On September 9, 1849, Elizabeth gave birth to her tenth child, Eliza Ann.

The next day the village acquired a new resident, Hector P. Campbell, a schoolteacher from Massachusetts. "In reply to a taunt concerning the poverty of the New England soil," Campbell replied, "They build schoolhouses and raise men." His zeal for education so impressed the locals that they quickly erected a schoolhouse, on land and with lumber donated by Lot Whitcomb. Hector Campbell was hired as schoolmaster; later he would become a judge and a legislator. In April 1851, Alfred Lewelling would marry Hector's daughter, Mary.

The 1849 fruit harvest must have been only slightly larger than that of 1848. There was not enough crop to sell. But about this time the partners made sudden headway in the nursery business: They were able to buy large quantities of fruit seeds from a "Mr. Pugh." From these seeds Henderson and Meek would have, in the fall of 1850, eighteen thousand "splendid stocks from two to four feet high," to which they would graft scions or buds over the following winter.

Also in the fall of 1849, Lot Whitcomb platted a town on his claim and named it Milwaukie, after Milwaukee, Wisconsin, whose name derived from a Pottawatomie word meaning "meeting place of waters." (The spellings of both towns' names varied for a time before permanently diverging.)

In the winter that followed, a flood destroyed at least two mills on Johnson Creek. Henderson and Meek's orchard, on the riverbank, may have been submerged, but the trees survived. So did the Lewelling and Meek cabins, close by but on slightly higher ground, along with the nursery and Lot Whitcomb's saw-and-grist mill. It's unclear whether Henderson and Meek's mill was damaged, but perhaps at this point the partners had built only a dam. Henderson remained invested in Lot's struggle against competition from Portland, so much so that he went out onto the swollen river in a boat to take soundings.

The year 1850 must have been a mostly happy one for the Lewellings. Congress passed the Donation Land Claim Act, the most generous federal land act yet, which legitimized the claims of 320 acres for every white man already residing in Oregon and 320 acres for his wife. Henderson, Alfred, and Meek all filed claims under the new law.

We don't know whether Henderson and Elizabeth fretted over the exclusion of Blacks and Hawaiians from the Donation Land Law or over the expropriation of Indian territory that the law entailed. Perhaps the Lewellings were relieved to learn that authorities would negotiate treaties with the Indians—though the goal was, of course, to remove the natives from their land.

Nor do we know whether the Lewellings lamented the outcome of the Cayuse War, when five Cayuse tribal members were tried in an Oregon City tavern for the Waiilatpu massacre. Although the five probably hadn't been involved in the murders, and although Cayuse law authorized the killing of a medicine man who has given bad medicine, and although the United States had no jurisdiction in the case, because Oregon wasn't yet a U.S. territory at the time of the murders, the five men were hanged, in June 1850. The violence against the Cayuse, sadly, wasn't over; it would continue for five more years.I like to imagine that Henderson and Elizabeth sympathized with the accused, despite the family's affection for Marcus Whitman.

Milwaukie's second schoolmaster, Oliver Nixon (who, like Henderson and Elizabeth, was raised Quaker in North Carolina), described the Luelling family in 1850. Oliver had just been dropped ashore by Indians paddlers when Henderson was "at my side and offering me his hand." Although some his family members were sick, Henderson insisted on bringing Oliver home. "The young people, Alfred, Rachel and Jane, just growing into young manhood and womanhood, and the good wife and mother, made me feel that my lot had been cast among friends."

Still weak from the cholera he had succumbed to while mining in California, Oliver soon got a dose of Henderson's unconventional medicine. "Throw away your cholagogue and other drugs and I will soon cure you and make your cheeks rosy," Henderson assured him. Henderson introduced Oliver to the (cold) "shower bath," much touted by Sylvester Graham and his followers. "I thought it was the coldest water that ever flowed from Greenland's icy mountains," Oliver recalled.

And Henderson found Oliver a job. "In less than two weeks after my arrival I was a teacher."

In the autumn of 1850 Henderson and Meek, with help from Lot Whitcomb, completed their sawmill. In the federal census Meek identified himself as a miller, while Henderson, modestly, called himself a gardener. Henderson and Meek would turn the milling operations entirely over to others in 1852, but in the meantime the mill would provide the nurserymen with cash while the fruit business got underway.

It was probably soon after the partners began producing their own lumber that Henderson replaced his cabin with a frame house. This house could not compare with the family's grand stone house back in Iowa; in fact, Joseph Lambert, who would take over the Milwaukie site in 1859, would build a new house on the old foundation. But in his journal Seth consistently called Henderson's home a house, whereas he called Meek's home a cabin. (Both were on Henderson's claim, just 150 feet apart.) Meek would replace his cabin with a frame house later.

Milwaukie, with its muddy, stump-ridden streets and unpainted shacks, was losing the competition with Portland to become Oregon's

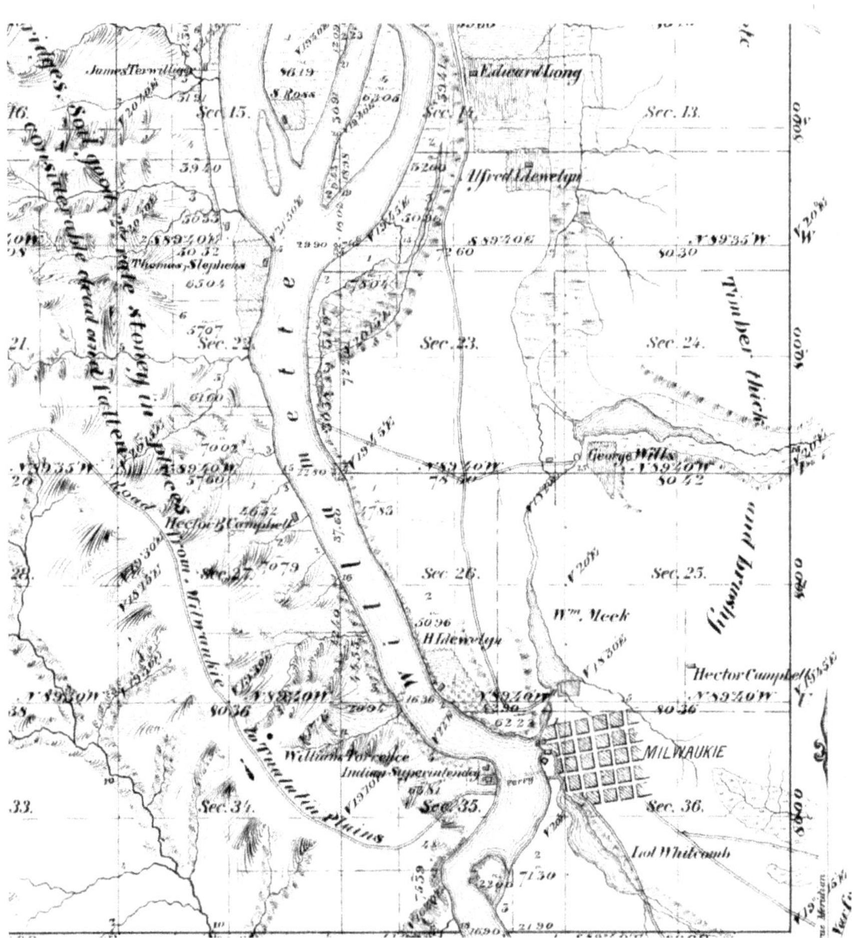

The Milwaukie area, from the 1851 U.S. survey by Butler Ives. Identified are the land claims of Henderson and Alfred "Lewellyn," William Meek, Lot Whitcomb, and Hector Campbell.

leading city. Yet the little settlement was developing into a real town, with two hotels, three taverns, and an assortment of shops as well as a school. Wagon roads reached from Milwaukie to Molalla, Portland, and the Tualatin Plains, and a free ferry crossed the Willamette. In February Lot Whitcomb opened a post office, and in November he founded a newspaper, the *Western Star*, which he would lose the following year, for failure to pay his printer-partners. Lot also began constructing a steamboat, to provide freight and passenger service on the Willamette and Columbia rivers from Oregon City to Pacific City—and thereby to ensure high profits for Milwaukie's lumber and flouring mills. He hoped to stop at all the small towns but bypass Portland altogether.

In the summer or fall of 1850 the orchard finally produced enough fruit for Henderson to take into Portland to sell. People bought up his apples for a dollar a piece, which is equivalent to about forty dollars in 2024. From a single box of apples—Newtown Pippin, according to one account—Henderson made seventy-five dollars.

Happily, the Lewelling family continued to grow. In May, Henderson and Elizabeth's second daughter, fifteen-year-old Asenath, married John S. Bozarth, a son of a large family of emigrants from Missouri. And in June Asenath's sister Mary bore a child, Andrew Jackson Davis Meek.

Seeing the Light

Andrew Jackson Davis Meek was quite a handle for the grandson of a man who had no middle name at all. But Henderson had become entranced with the original Andrew Jackson Davis, and Mary may have shared his fascination.

Not long after arriving in Oregon, Henderson must have acquired a copy of Davis's newly published *Principles of Nature, Her Divine Revelations, and a Voice to Mankind*. The book gave him much to ponder.

Andrew Jackson Davis—or the "Poughkeepsie Seer," as he called himself—dictated this tome of more than eight hundred pages while hypnotized, or "magnetized," in the language of the day, during public appearances in New York in 1846. Only twenty-one years old when the book was published, Davis claimed that he had had very little schooling and that he didn't read books. Yet *Principles of Nature* seems to have been written by someone of great learning, in theology, history, geography, linguistics, and science. Davis said that spirits dictated the book through him. Perhaps the truth was that he secretly read books by philosophers like Emanuel Swedenborg and regurgitated the authors' ideas. If so, Davis must have possessed a phenomenal memory. Those who doubted his clairvoyance couldn't deny his genius.

A middle section of the book concerns Davis's own theological system, with God replaced by "the Divine Mind" and mysterious proclamations such as "Motion became an organized soul." Another, more practical section advocates a homegrown style of socialism, in which groups of six or more families are advised to set up farming cooperatives, to increase profits, reduce labor, and promote happiness. But most of the book consists in a thorough and critical analysis of the books of the Bible, one by one. Jesus, to Davis, was a reformer, a medium, and a natural man, not a man-god and not a messiah. Altogether, *Principles of Nature* is a mostly measured but occasionally forceful polemic against Christianity, faith, the clergy, and the authority of the Bible.

Besides targeting mainstream Christianity, Davis allied himself with the anti-slavery and feminist movements and other "isms" of the day. He shrewdly associated himself with a new movement, Spiritualism. This quasi-religion got its start in 1848, when two girls in Hydesville, New York—fourteen-year-old Maggie Fox and her eleven-year-old sister, Kate—found they could scare their mother by dropping apples on the floor, cracking their toe joints, and talking to the imaginary ghost they blamed for making these noises. Neighbors succumbed to the prank as well, and the family soon deserted their seemingly haunted house. The girls were sent to live with older siblings in Rochester. There their older sister, Leah, saw opportunity in the hoax, and declared herself a "medium" between the spirit and natural worlds. A radical Quaker couple, Amy and Isaac Post, invited the girls into their home, listened to the "rappings," and grew convinced that the girls were truly communicating with the dead. The Posts spread the news among their radical Quaker friends, whose mystical religion rendered them—and ex-Quakers, as well—particularly susceptible. "Spiritualism is Quakerism enlarged and revised," said the Quaker preacher Priscilla Cadwallader. Spiritualism thus became associated with radical Quaker causes—temperance, abolition of slavery, and women's rights. In late 1849 the girls gave a public demonstration at Corinthian Hall in Rochester, and no one detected the fraud. The girls went on tour, and Spiritualism became a phenomenon, with mediums, séances, and Spiritualist journals and assemblies popping up all over the country. Conveying messages from the spirit world served at once to soothe the bereaved, entertain the curious, and promote unpopular political views.

As the movement got underway, Andrew Jackson Davis saw its potential value in boosting his own career. He invited the Fox girls into his home and admired their demonstration. Afterward, he reminded the world that in *The Principles of Nature* he had predicted the rise of Spiritualism: "It is a truth that spirits commune with one another while one is in the body and the other in the higher Spheres," he had written. "The world will hail with delight the ushering in of that era when the interiors of men will be opened, and the spiritual communion will be established such as is now being enjoyed by the inhabitants of Mars, Jupiter, and Saturn."

In fact, the Fox girls had no interest in denizens of other planets. Still, for Davis, the girls had ushered in the new era of spiritual communion. The day the Fox girls had demonstrated their prank to a neighbor, Davis claimed, "a warm breathing passed over my face and I heard a voice, tender and strong, saying, 'Brother, the good work has begun—behold, a living demonstration is born.'" Davis had lost some supporters when his writings proved his disdain for the Bible. But now, by associating himself with the Foxes, the Poughkeepsie Seer became a leader of a mass movement. His "Harmonial Philosophy" provided a theory to support the Fox phenomenon. Sales of his books surged.

As so often happens with long journeys, the trek from Iowa to Oregon promoted reflection and, for Henderson, personal transformation. Soon after the family's arrival in Oregon, Henderson changed the spelling of his name. By the time he and Elizabeth filed for a donation land claim, in 1850, he was spelling the name, at least sometimes, *Luelling*. Perhaps he admired Noah Webster's ideas about spelling reform, as many social radicals did. Maybe he meant this outward change to reflect an inner metamorphosis. In any case, his children also adopted the new spelling, as would his younger brother Seth, from shortly after Seth moved to Oregon until after Henderson's death.

Henderson and his family also left their Quaker ways behind. We don't know when Henderson gave up wearing his Quaker hat and coat, but apparently no one noted them in Oregon. In Iowa, Henderson was probably clean-shaven, as male Friends were expected to be, but sometime after leaving Iowa he let a beard grow in. In his only existing photograph he wears a thick ruff of hair, reaching across the underside of the jaw and up to the backs of the ears, while his face remains bare. Henderson and Elizabeth broke another Quaker taboo by allowing their daughter Rachel to have an accordion.

None of the Luellings joined a Friends' meeting in Oregon. In fact, although many Quaker families took the Overland Trail to Oregon, the state had no Friends' meeting until 1878. And none of the Luellings joined even then.

Principles of Nature may have helped Henderson say farewell not just to Quakerism but to Christianity altogether. On November 28, 1850, soon after helping to organize the Young Men's Lyceum in Milwaukie (though at forty-one years he wasn't exactly young), Henderson debated another member on the question, "Has theology conduced to the happiness of mankind?" Henderson took the negative position. From then on, the Luellings would spend much time in in social, civic, and agricultural gatherings, but the clan would never again be noted for regular churchgoing. Perhaps they would be satisfied with what one of Alfred's children called "the principles instilled by his Quaker (Friends) upbringing, to be active in all good works and to do unto others as he would have others do unto him."

Joy and Sorrow

Shortly before the theological debate, Henderson experienced what was for him, perhaps, the year's greatest joy: the arrival of his brothers John and Seth, from Iowa and Indiana, respectively, via the gold fields of California. But about two weeks after John and Seth's arrival, the family suffered its greatest tragedy of the year. On December 9, Mary Lewelling Meek died, presumably of typhoid, a disease that had come with the emigrants and was now endemic in Oregon. Perhaps heavy rains contaminated the groundwater with effluent from the Willamette River, which was already polluted by the upstream settlements of Eugene, Albany, and Salem. Henderson and Elizabeth were unusual among American parents in that all of their ten children had, or would, survive childhood. But now the couple had lost their eldest daughter. And William Meek, thrice widowed, was left to raise six-month-old Andrew Jackson Davis alone.

Chapter 6
Family Reunion

> If you wish to avail yourselves of the blessings of Providence, which are within your reach, you must plant an orchard.
>
> "Apples," in *The Cultivator*, 1844

On March 23, 1850, Seth Lewelling, a thirty-year-old shoemaker, departed his home in Greensboro, Indiana, for California and its gold. He left behind his wife, Clarissa, and three little daughters—six-year-old Elva, four-year-old Addie, and Alice, just a year old—in the care of Clarissa's father, a widower who still had seven of Clarissa's siblings in his charge. Seth kept a diary, and after he met up with his brother John the two took turns making entries. True to Quaker ethos, the entries are matter-of-fact, but a brief introduction, added later, encapsulates Seth's feelings about his Gold Rush adventures and his first years in Oregon: "This was a trying time with me the most so I have ever experienced in my remembrance."

Bound for the Gold Country

Unlike his brother Henderson, Seth took no wagon and no animals. He walked to Knightstown, seven miles southwest of Greensboro. At Knightstown he got on a stagecoach for Cambridge, nineteen miles due east. He spent the night in Cambridge, and at seven in the morning he got on a stage for Cincinnati. The ninety-mile trip that day must have been wearying; he didn't arrive in Cincinnati until nine at night. The next day he bought some clothes for the journey and booked passage aboard the steamboat *Gladiator*, bound for St. Joseph. He paid $18 for his ticket, the equivalent of about $716 in 2024. The following day, March 26, Seth boarded the boat, and soon it was underway.

Seth found himself among other gold seekers. While all were hoping to get rich, many brought substantial riches along with them, to pay their expenses and perhaps to allow them to settle permanently on the West Coast. Their presence attracted opportunists of another sort. The first night on the boat, six California-bound "boys" were robbed—of $2,800 in total, or, in 2024 dollars, an alarming $18,660 apiece, on average. From then on Seth must have tried to sleep with one eye open.

On April 9, the boat arrived in St. Joseph. Seth found the city beautiful, though tents were pitched everywhere and all the vacant lots were fenced for emigrants' livestock. He immediately began searching for his would-be fellow travelers, a group from Iowa that presumably included his brother John, although Seth didn't mention John by name in his journal until the two began working together in California. Seth couldn't find the Iowa party, and a stranger told him that the group had started from St. Joseph four or five days before. So, Seth bought himself a pony and hurried off to overtake the group.

The pony must have been intended for carrying Seth's belongings, not for riding. Seth walked, as fast and as long as he could. His feet grew sore and so swollen that on April 13 he couldn't take off his boots. Three days later he began traveling with a mule train.

On April 21 Seth finally caught up with the Iowa party and their cattle. If he and John threw themselves into each other's arms, Seth didn't mention it. Also among the group were two of the "Johnson Boys" from Salem, "R. J."—almost certainly Seth and John's brother-in-law Reuben Johnson, their sister Jane's husband and an anti-slavery Friend—and "E. B.," Reuben's brother Elijah.

The Overland Trail was more developed than it had been during Henderson's trip three years prior; there were more and better-stocked trading posts, for example, with cabins to rent and robes to sell. But the journey was still hard, especially for men in a hurry. The party took the Sublette Cutoff and traveled all night through the desert, as the Hocketts had done. In crossing the Green River, just west of South Pass, they saw two men drowned, one of them from their party. They took Hudspeth's Cutoff as a shortcut to the main California Trail, and upon reaching the Humboldt River they saw another man drowned. As they trekked southwest across the Nevada desert, they encountered returning miners with provisions to sell—at shockingly high prices. "Men do not starve here," Seth wrote, "but many do not get half rashens."

On August 3 they reached the road to Hangtown (later Placerville), the leading miners' rendezvous spot, aptly named for its vigilante justice. The next day they moved on to Johnson's Ranch, six miles east, where John Calhoun Johnson ran a sawmill, store, and campground. There Seth and John sold their horse and some cattle and settled up with some of their fellow travelers.

Afterward, they set out on their own. They tried mining for the first time, probably with a pan, on August 7. Three days later they bought a cradle, a basic device but a technological improvement over panning. Over the next two and a half weeks, Seth and John shared their takings as partners. Their best daily haul was $73.33. On August 30, perhaps because they were tired or because their luck was running low, they headed north, toward the home of Enos Mendenhall, Henderson's wagoner on his overland journey.

Iowa Quakers in Illinoistown

Enos and Emily Mendenhall had settled in a little hollow a half-mile or so southeast of today's Colfax, California. Although they were the first white settlers in the area, and although they had arrived only a year before, they had plenty of company. Their little community attracted miners on their way to and from the diggings. It was a place to rest, gather supplies, and arrange for delivery of more supplies to the camps.

Henderson must have recommended that John and Seth visit Enos, whom John knew from Salem. But Enos's invitation had probably also reached Salem directly, for Enos was an inveterate letter writer. Some of the letters he wrote to relatives in Salem still survive, and no doubt there were many more. Enos missed Iowa and his family there, and, besides, he was a savvy businessman. With only a little encouragement, his gold-hungry friends in Iowa would become his best customers in California. In a letter to his brother in 1850, Enos named some of their mutual acquaintances in the area—Iowans all, most of them bearing common Quaker names.

Enos hadn't been in any hurry to join the rush for gold. He had kept his gig as an Oregon schoolteacher through early 1849. After the birth of their first child, though, he and Emily were both ready for adventure. In the spring of 1849 Enos, Emily, and six-week-old Elvira Ellen boarded a sailing ship for California. Off the coast of Eureka, a severe storm hit. According to family lore, the sailors lashed Emily and Elvira to the mast to keep them from washing overboard. Yet the ship arrived safely in San Francisco. Emily and Elvira took up residence in the tent city called Happy Valley.

Extending along today's Mission Street from First Street to Third, Happy Valley was so named for its sunshine, shelter from prevailing winds, oak trees, spring water, and optimistic spirit (which lasted until fall, when the community was racked by cholera). Only about one arrival in a hundred was a woman, and babies were even scarcer, but apparently Emily managed well enough. Enos left her and Elvira there and went off to explore the Sierra foothills.

Whether Enos did any prospecting on this first trip into the gold country is unclear, but he picked out a new home for his family. Alder Grove was a bowl-shaped area full of alders, which were well-watered by a spring and its stream. Situated at an elevation low enough to escape heavy snows and high enough to avoid major floods, Alder Grove would be a good spot for planting fruit trees in this piney country with its long dry season. More important, perhaps, Alder Grove was the highest point that wagons could reach on the dividing ridge between Bear River and the North Fork of the American River. The place could therefore become the distribution point of supplies for all the mining camps to the north, south, and east. As Alder Grove's first white settler, Enos would take his gold not just out of the ground but out of the pockets of miners.

When Enos returned to San Francisco, he may have struggled to find his wife and daughter, because the city's population had grown by at least half in his absence. After the family was reunited, they boarded the little schooner *Sea Witch* to sail across the bay and up the Sacramento River, a trip of a week or more. On July 29, they landed in front of what would become the city of Sacramento. There they found an Oregon man with a team who agreed to take them to Alder Grove. They arrived on August 3. Immediately they put up their tent and built a small shelter of poles and brush, according to a local historian, "and forthwith the first hotel of the place was established, where, for one dollar and a half, the wayfarer would be served with bacon and beans, bread, and pie made of dried fruit—all of the delicacies then obtainable—from the hand of the pioneer white woman of that whole region, Mrs. Mendenhall."

Enos left Emily to provide this service on her own while he panned for gold some miles away. Although he never counted himself lucky, he sometimes collected as much as three ounces of gold in three hours' time.

When the rains began, in October, Enos returned to Alder Grove to build a sturdier shelter. He constructed a double log cabin, a sort of duplex with a breezeway between the two sections. One section would be a house and hotel, and the other a store, to be run by two men who were presumably the Mendenhalls' employees.

By the end of the year, three other families had opened hotel-stores near the Mendenhalls'. At one of these establishments, a gathering of card-playing miners from Illinois renamed the community Illinois Town, or Illinoistown. Enos and Emily apparently accepted the new name with equanimity, but they called their hotel-store Iowa House.

The Mendenhalls suffered little discord with the local Indians, Maidu or Miwok or both, who proved such eager workers that two Illinoistown storekeepers hired fifty a day to pan for gold. But other local families lost stored food and cattle to hungry and resentful natives. In reaction, in 1850, some of the Mendenhalls' neighbors formed a militia, the California Blades, to kill Indians and burn their villages. Eventually, "at nearly all of the wayside houses on the road from Illinoistown were scalps on exhibit." This violence ended the resistance from local Indians in time for the summer arrival of the gold-digging hordes, including the Lewelling brothers. I don't know what the Mendenhalls thought about the slaughter. They must have known that no treaties had been made with the Indians, but their Quaker precepts about such matters were falling away.

The miners were making the Mendenhalls rich, though Enos and Emily worked hard for their money. Soon after John and Seth's arrival in Illinoistown, Enos described his business in a letter to his brother: "I have taken in from my customers about $300. To day. I have averaged more than that on this day of the week for five months. . . . I am running a small team and driving myself. I leave home Monday morning and drive to the city [Sacramento, fifty miles away] in two days, stay there one day to get a load, start home Thursday and reach home Saturday so as to be at home during Sundays."

Hired workers took responsibility for another part of the business: delivering the goods, by mule train, to miners in the steep and crumpled mountains. Often the muleteers would take the trail that became known as Iowa Hill Road, today the route to the little town of Iowa Hill. Iowa Hill is still so hard to reach, by a narrow road that winds nine cliff-side miles from Colfax, that the town got landline phone service only in 2010, and it is still off the electrical grid. In the early 1850s it was just one of numerous mining camps in the area.

And many of those camps were occupied by Iowans from Salem and the surrounding area. Among the Salem men, in the fall of 1850, were Elihu, Thomas C., and Isaac Frazier—all of whom had been found guilty, in June of the same year, of aiding escaped slaves—and Franklin Street and Joseph Cook, both also from radical Quaker families.

With the Johnsons and Miles Dobbins (the Dobbins family, too, were Salem Friends), Seth and John camped and mined near Cold Spring, where Enos had dug for gold before them. In the back of the diary, Seth or John recorded the lyrics of sentimental popular songs—songs about love, loss, and loneliness. It is touching to imagine young Quaker men, far from their homes and families, sharing these forbidden lyrics after a long day in the diggings.

According to a letter Enos wrote to his brother on October 13, the men were making about twelve dollars a day per person and figured they could do even better when the rains set in. The men planned to winter in their cabin, Enos wrote, while relying on him to have all their provisions packed in.

The Lewellings and their friends, however, were apparently considering more pleasant ways to spend the winter. The same day that Enos wrote his brother the letter, Seth, Dobbins, and the Johnsons trekked to Nevada City to choose a building site. They "did not succeed," Seth wrote in his journal, without explanation.

Back at their diggings, the men had little luck. Six of them together dug out $7.50 worth of gold on October 17, $18.50 worth the next day, and $33 the day after that.

Perhaps the others decided to overwinter in place, but the Lewelling brothers left for Oregon on October 20. They stopped at Iowa House on the way. Then John rode with Enos to Sacramento while Seth took their "plunder" to Hangtown. Together in San Francisco on October 26, the brothers bought passage to Oregon, for $135 apiece. They would spend the winter working for Henderson in Oregon.

The ship set sail on October 29. After days of "hard winds," a storm, and a sailors' strike that necessitated the passengers' assisting the captain (apparently in crossing the perilous Columbia bar), Seth and John transferred to the steamer *Columbia* for the journey up the Columbia River. They arrived at Henderson's, finally, on November 18, "amid a heavy rain."

Winter on the Willamette

"Quite rainy." "Still raining." "Rained very hard." Rained." So Seth described his first days in the Willamette Valley, with its typical late-autumn weather.

On November 25, Seth and John began working for Henderson. They labored in the nursery and stable. They dug up nursery trees, four hundred at a time, and set them out in the orchard. They harvested cabbage and hunted deer.

John was writing the diary entries when Mary Meek died. On December 9, he noted Mary's "cramping Spasms" and death. John, Seth, and Henderson picked the place for a graveyard—on Meek's claim, on high land east of the orchard. (You can glimpse the graveyard today, as you whiz down Southeast Seventeenth Avenue in Milwaukie, though the sign was hidden behind shrubbery when I visited.) The three brothers dug the grave. The family held a funeral the next day.

The farm work continued: more tree digging and planting, mostly, though John also built a table while Seth built stalls for the stable.

Seth failed to note, in his diary, the arrival of Christmas. To a Quaker, no day was holier than another. But on December 25, he—and probably his brothers and Henderson's family, too—went into Milwaukie for the launch of Lot Whitcomb's new steamboat, the *Lot Whitcomb*, the first steamboat to ply the Willamette. The event was celebrated with speeches and a performance by the Vancouver Brass Band. Although Seth didn't mention it, the captain of another ship, Frederick Morse, died when he tried to fire his cannon in salute and the fuse burst, hurling a fragment into his neck. Despite the tragedy, a ball and supper with more band music followed. Morse's death could not dim the locals' glee at Milwaukie's score in the race for supremacy over the neighboring port cities of Portland and Oregon City. The captain was buried in the Lewelling-Meek graveyard, which thus became a community cemetery.

The sidewheeler *Lot Whitcomb*. Salem Public Library Historical Photographs Collection. Photo by Ben Maxwell.

Work continued on the farm. On the last day of the year, the men began pruning trees. Seth spent three days planting apple seeds, perhaps ones he provided himself. He had carried "quite a lot" of fruit seeds from Iowa and had protected them through his stay in the Gold Country. John later remembered that he also brought seeds—a peck, or two gallons—and that they were planted the following spring. Seth trimmed canes in the "Raspberry Orchard." Whenever the weather was rainy or snowy, the men worked in the grafting room.

On January 14, 1851, John and Henderson returned from a three-day trip to visit another pioneer nurseryman. They brought back with them ten to twelve thousand one-year-old seedling apple trees, for which they had paid $300 (about $12,000 in 2024). Now the men spent most of their time grafting. Seth cleaned out the potato house and prepared it for storing grafts, and he built boxes to hold the trees.

Still the brothers took time for hunting and other projects. Seth made himself cobbler tools and a bench, and one day he "worked over about 105 lbs of Butter."

On January 25, John noted, Elizabeth miscarried, with cramping pains that she felt in her chest.

Over the next week the men grafted plums and peaches, and Seth mended Rachel's accordion.

Elizabeth was "very bad." Apparently the abortion had been incomplete. On January 31, Seth went to Portland to fetch a doctor. Evidently the doctor couldn't help; perhaps infection had set in.

The weather turned frosty, and the work went on. The men dug and grafted apple and cherry trees. On February 4 they sold $110 worth of trees. Seth killed two "pheasants" (he must have meant grouse) for his ailing sister-in-law, who may have suspended her vegetarianism for the sake of her health. He made shoes for ten-year-old Hannah and mended shoes and boots for others in the family. He and John began planning to return to California.

At noon on March 7, Elizabeth died without a struggle. The next day, clear and frosty, the family buried Elizabeth beside Mary.

Henderson was left with seven children too young for marriage, from fourteen-year-old Rachel to one-and-a-half-year-old Eliza Ann. The household had lost its center. Perhaps the same woman who nursed Elizabeth in her sickness took care of the children. In his diary, Seth didn't mention the woman's name.

The nursery work continued. In one day, Henderson, Meek, and Seth together dug 3,100 wild cherry seedlings for grafting (these were probably bitter cherry, *Prunus emarginata*, whose fruit is inedible). Apparently Henderson had figured out how to make these grafts take. The men grafted day after day. John and Seth grafted their own set of trees to take to California, and, on March 24, they boxed up trees for Henderson.

On March 27 John and Seth left for California. Henderson, three weeks widowed, went with them. So did loads of young fruit trees.

In the brothers' absence, the *Western Star* would note on April 3 that the peach trees were in full bloom and that the nursery had on hand about ten thousand trees and more than one hundred thousand scions.

Back to California

After a nauseating sea voyage, happily broken by clam digging and shell collecting on Humboldt Bay, the three brothers reached Benicia at midnight on April 5, 1851. On the north bank of the Carquinez Strait, which connects San Pablo Bay and Suisun Bay, the little city had become a bustling stopover on the way to the Sierra Nevada. While Henderson

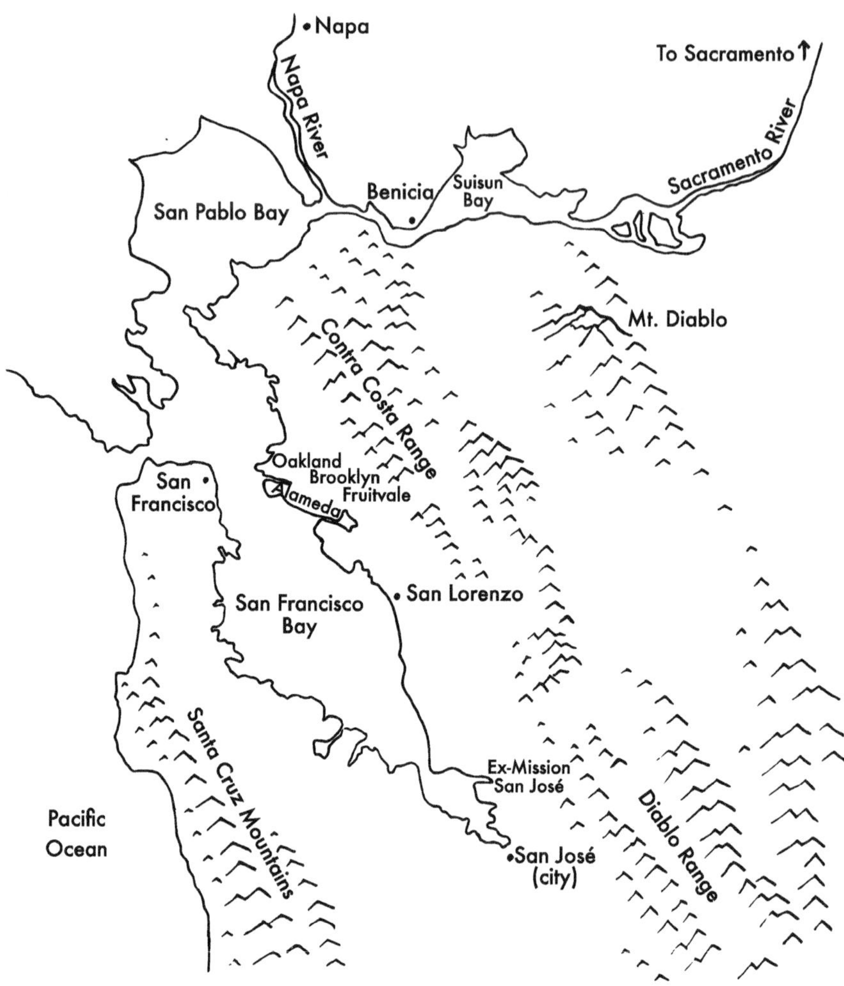

The San Francisco Bay Area in the 1850s. Map by Rebecca Waterhouse.

presumably did business in town, John and Seth headed off on a side trip up the Napa Valley. Perhaps they had trees to deliver there, but they couldn't have carried many, since they were on foot. Maybe they were only curious about the secluded, pretty little valley. The distance may have been greater than they expected; the town of Napa is about twenty-four miles from Benicia. After eight miles they stopped at a tavern for dinner, and Seth waited while John hired a horse and went on to town. John must have liked what he saw, because he would later return to live in the Napa Valley.

The next day the three brothers took passage from Benicia to Sacramento. After picking up mail, they bought mules, saddles, and other supplies, sharing the costs equally. Then they left for Illinoistown. They would camp out along the way.

On April 13, they set out their trees on Enos and Emily's land. Henderson planted 398 large fruit trees in an orchard. He may have sold the trees, and his labor, to Enos and Emily outright. More likely, he arranged to collect a share of fruit sales. John and Seth set out in nursery beds 560 grafts, "to be disposed of by JL and Seth Lewelling as way may Open & the proceeds of the latter to be equally Divided."

Some historians have written that Seth sold fruit trees in Sacramento in 1851, but his diary doesn't mention such a thing. I've found no record, in fact, that either Seth or John ever collected the trees that they planted at Illinoistown. It was probably Enos who sold some of the trees in Sacramento, taking a cut of the nursery sales. He probably sold some to his neighbors in Illinoistown, too. After all, in 1850 Americans and Europeans weren't only mining in the Sierra foothills; they were developing homesteads there, too. On September 18, 1852, the *Placer Herald* predicted "that Placer county will soon be third if not the second county in the state, in point of population." Although that dream was never realized, every new homestead still needed an orchard.

Enos now had the region's first grafted orchard. But it was not, as others have maintained, the first grafted orchard in California. Mission San José had hundreds of grafted pear trees, with fruit that was said to be of excellent quality (the trees were all re-grafted to the Bartlett variety in 1854). Cal Griffith, a later associate of John's, said his father, James A. Griffith, went to Oregon in 1849 to buy some of Lewelling and Meek's grafted fruit trees, which he planted near Sonoma. Also in 1849, two Napa County men, W. H. Nash and R. L. Kilburn, ordered thirty-six fruit trees from a nursery in western New York. Packed in moss, the trees survived the trip around Cape Horn and were planted in the valley in the spring of 1850. The Russians at Fort Ross, on the Sonoma County coast, planted apple, peach, cherry, and pear trees much earlier still, in 1820. Long after the Russians left, experts identified some of the fruits as named varieties, including Gravenstein and Bellflower apples. The scions were said to have come from Monterey, and perhaps they did. Other grafted-fruit orchards were planted the same year as Enos's: A Mr. Shelton of San Francisco brought fifty pear varieties from Valparaiso, Chile, in 1851, and George H. Briggs, of Marysville, brought fruit trees from the East the same year.

The Lewellings' first major gift to California wasn't the Mendenhall orchard, though it inspired other emigrants to plant their own. More important were the 560 little grafted trees that were sold from the nursery and planted in the Sierra foothills and around Sacramento. The number was trifling compared with the total stock of Henderson's nursery in Oregon, yet with scions from these trees—and probably from Enos's orchard as well—many more orchards were established. By the 1940s, Colfax would become "the fruit shipping capital of America," with fruit-packing sheds lining the railway. The transcontinental railroad provided access to distant markets, mountain snow provided refrigeration, and the ditches dug by gold miners provided irrigation for the orchards. The Colfax fruit boom is long over, and I could find no sign of fruit trees in the former Illinoistown. But the mountains around Colfax are still sprinkled with relics of old orchards, evidence of the local fruit industry that Enos and the Lewellings together launched.

When they finished their planting at Illinoistown, the Lewellings returned to the cabin at Cold Spring. But they found other miners inhabiting the building. So the brothers camped in the rain, prospecting a little, before returning, on April 19, to the Mendenhalls' place, where they met the Johnson boys. Seth sent gold pieces home with one of them.

Then Seth, John, and Henderson set off again, toward and beyond Grass Valley, looking at claims, buying and selling some, and working them. Finding little gold, they headed south, stopping again at the Mendenhalls', where they "found our trees growing fine."

They continued south, to Sutter Creek and Jackson, and across the North Fork of the Mokelumne River to San Andreas (or St. Andrew, as Seth called it). With a company that had probably organized at the Mendenhalls'—it included Ike Frazier, who must have spent the winter in California—they took claims on the North Fork of the Calaveras River.

On May 25, just as the men began building a long tom—an advance in mining technology comprising a shallow trough, with a sieve and cleats, through which a constant stream of water would flow—Henderson left for home. Seth didn't note why.

The remaining seven miners built a race and a dam for their long tom, and on June 2 they began serious mining. By June 27 they had made, in total, \$445.25—scant earnings for seven men. That same day Seth and John, at least, departed for Sacramento. They had had enough of gold mining.

They didn't stop at Iowa House this time, because Illinoistown was not on their way. Enos probably continued to correspond with the Lewellings, but no evidence suggests that any Lewelling returned to Illinoistown.

Seth and John spent three nights in Sacramento and several more in San Francisco, where "the Town was in quite an uproar the people ware Shooting & Celebrating the glorious fourth." Then they bought their tickets for Oregon, via a Pacific Mail steamship, for what must have seemed the bargain price of sixty dollars each.

I wonder if John contemplated returning home to Iowa instead. For well over a year, he had been separated from his wife, Elvy, and their six children. The youngest, Delila, had been only a few months old when John had set off, and she had died, at ten months, in his absence. He had left the family residing next to his sister-in-law Cyrena, who had remarried since William Lewelling's death, so at least John knew that Elvy and the children had companions in their grief. And it was too late in the year to go home by the Overland Trail. Travel by sea was now fairly fast, if you went by steamship and crossed at Panama or Nicaragua rather than sailing around Cape Horn. Maybe John planned to stay through another fall and winter simply as a favor to Henderson, or perhaps he delayed the voyage home because he hadn't made enough money to pay for it. John may have concluded that working for Henderson was the best way to accumulate cash—enough, perhaps, to bring his whole family to the Pacific coast.

For his part, Seth would continue keeping diaries, which doubled as account books. In these books he would occasionally doodle the words *State of Indiana*, often under his name. Unlike Henderson and John, he had never known another home. But he would never return to Indiana.

Seth may not have known it yet, but now he was going home—to his new home, in Oregon.

Chapter 7
Land of the Big Red Apple

> If every person settling on the goodly lands of the great Northwest will make a little effort to surround their homes with fruit and ornamental trees at first, what an amount of comfort and pleasure they will produce in a few years!
>
> –Seth Lewelling, 1889 Milwaukie Nursery catalog

John and Seth's trip to Astoria, by the mail steamer, took just a little over three days. They transferred to the steamboat *Willamette* and reached Henderson's place the next evening, on July 12.

Wedding Trip

Henderson had news that may have startled his brothers, though Seth expressed no surprise in his journal. Perhaps the plan had developed while the three were mining together. In any case, a month after leaving the diggings, Henderson had taken a new wife, Phebe Eddy Grimes. Now the two of them were planning to take a trip to New York, to shop at famous nurseries and perhaps to visit Phebe's family. They would bring along two of Henderson's children, probably eight-year-old Albert and six-year-old Levi, and they would return to Oregon with Seth's family. Perhaps the last was an offer Henderson made to convince Seth to stay in Oregon. If so, the tactic worked.

William Meek must have been Henderson and Phebe's matchmaker. Meek had spent his first winter in Oregon with Phebe and her husband, Ephraim Grimes; the three had probably developed a friendship on the Overland Trail. Meek had heeled in his trees on the Grimeses' provisional claim.

Phebe and Ephraim had raised three sons in Jefferson County, New York, near the eastern shore of Lake Ontario. In the spring of 1845 they left for Missouri, bringing along their then thirteen-year-old son, George.

While in Missouri they sold two parcels of New York land, but the sales were halted because Ephraim was reported to be dead. So the properties went into probate, probably to the advantage of the Grimeses' two other sons, who remained in the East. Perhaps waiting for payment that never arrived, Phebe and Ephraim delayed their overland crossing until the spring of 1847.

Once in Oregon, the Grimeses headed south, to the Santiam River, which they either forded or crossed by the ferry Milton Hale had just finished building downstream from today's Jefferson. They found or constructed a cabin "in the Forks of the Santiam"—a rough circle marked by today's towns of Jefferson, Stayton, Sweet Home, and Lebanon—where Ephraim filed two provisional claims.

In 1849 Ephraim truly did die, of an unrecorded cause. William Meek became the administrator of his estate. Phebe had to give up the family's provisional claims, because, as a widow, she was ineligible for a land grant under the Donation Land Claim Act of 1850. In the 1850 census she was living with Jason Wheeler, then twenty-six, who had been elected sheriff of the new Linn County two years before. Also in the household were Jason's nineteen-year-old bride and his younger brother. Phebe was probably keeping house, while her son George lived and worked elsewhere. At forty-seven years old in 1851, Phebe may have despaired for her future.

But Henderson was probably unconcerned that Phebe was beyond childbearing age. He had plenty of children. He may have felt he needed a mother for them, although the older ones were already caring for the youngest, and Hannah, in the middle, was in boarding school in Portland. Maybe he simply longed for a woman's companionship. Phebe may have eased any concern he had about her age by adjusting it. Although she died at forty-nine, her Milwaukie gravestone identifies her as forty-five at her death.

Phebe and Henderson were married in the Forks of the Santiam by Richmond Cheadle, a Baptist colporteur, a hawker of bibles and religious tracts. Back in Clackamas County, Lot Whitcomb and his son-in-law, William Torrance, signed the marriage affidavit.

Henderson's family had little chance to get to know Phebe before the two of them were off on their voyage. "H. L. & wife Started this morning for the States," noted Seth on August 23.

In Henderson's absence, Seth and John managed their brother's home and business both. Seth was "tending to the cooking," he wrote in his journal. He helped with the washing, too, and did whatever else needed doing. While John assisted Meek with marketing and selling trees, Seth sewed potato bags, dug potatoes, hunted for meat, worked at the mill dam, made a stable door, and sewed pants for himself and for Oregon Columbia.

Although the young shoemaker may have been new to horticulture, he labored avidly and skillfully in the nursery and orchard. The first day after arriving back in Milwaukie, he "Looked at the Orchard & Grafts" and noted "some verry fine Apples Pears Peaches Plums Cherries Raspberrys Currans Gooseberrys &c." Over the following months he spent many days grafting buds and cuttings, digging and setting trees, and rooting currant, gooseberry, and quince cuttings. He planted trees in the orchard, at the mill, and at Meek's cabin. He packed grafts for men who would operate the Milwaukie Nursery's branches: Alfred Stanton, a Friend from Indiana whose homestead was near Salem; Joseph Kelsey, who farmed along the Long Tom River near today's Monroe; and James Knox, who had settled near Albany, at the foot of the butte that still bears his name.

The Milwaukie fruit business began to attract substantial attention in the summer and fall of 1851, when many of the orchard trees bore their first, light crops and eighteen thousand grafted trees, averaging four feet tall, were ready for sale. On August 28, 1851, the *Oregon Weekly Times* took note of the thriving orchard:

> No doubt can exist in our mind as to the perfect adaptation of both our soil and climate to fruit growing, after visiting the admirable and extensive fruitery of our friends, Lewelling & Meek, at Milwaukie. . . .
>
> They carry on the horticultural business on an extensive scale, with scientific order and practical experience combined. . . . Their young and vigorous trees are bending over the grounds, the most beautiful specimens of Apples, Pears, Peaches, Plums, Nectarines, Grapes, Rhasperries, Gooseberries, Cherries, Currants, and many others which we do not now recollect. . . . We observed five of the pears growing in a cluster, which would not probably weigh less than a pound each.

> They have made extensive arrangement for furnishing the farming districts of Oregon and California with grafts for fall setting. They have 20,000 ready for setting this fall.

The nursery was already filling orders from California, reported the writer.

His hosts sent the reporter back to the office with specimen apples and plums—a way of wooing newspapermen that Henderson, Seth, John, and Meek would practice throughout their horticultural careers.

Despite his love of the "fruitery" and the clear signs that it would succeed, Seth had no plans to give up leatherwork. He bought new shoemaking tools in Portland, and he made some of his own—fingerboards, crimping boards, and boot trees. He made boots for himself and other people, and he made a halter for an ox. Although he is remembered today as a nurseryman and political activist, Seth would remain a shoemaker all his life.

But Seth's pet project after his return to Oregon was building a house—not a log cabin but a frame house, using, no doubt, lumber milled by Meek (the house was most likely on Henderson's claim, though I haven't been able to confirm this). The family probably helped with the work, including Henderson, before he left for New York. On August 9, Seth and his helpers "laid foundation & raised house." On September 3 they held a party in the new house, though Seth finished laying the floor only four days later, and later still built such necessities as stools, a drawer, and a partition. The house probably stood empty over the winter, while Seth tended to tasks such as pulling cherry trees "My last day's work at it being 3,000 trees," he wrote after one arduous day. In early 1852 he made finishing touches to the house: In January he bought a stove in Portland and made a bed tick, and in February he planted trees in the yard. Though he was still cooking at Henderson's in early March, his own house was now ready to live in.

Henderson and Company Return

Finally, in March 1852, Seth made plans for the arrival of his wife and children, whom he hadn't seen for two years. But first he felt obliged to visit his great-nephew, who was gravely ill. On March 21, the day before Clarissa and the children would return with Henderson and Phebe, Seth went to see twenty-one-month-old Andrew Jackson Davis Meek, who was staying with the Matlock family on their farm just south of Milwaukie.

Just after Seth arrived, the boy died. The next day the family buried him in the little Milwaukie cemetery, near his mother, his grandmother, and Captain Morse. That same evening Seth went to Portland to meet the steamboat bearing his wife and children, Henderson, two of Henderson's children, and Phebe. Seth did not note how Henderson took the news of his first grandchild's death.

Despite the fresh shock of Andrew's passing, Seth must have been overjoyed to greet Clarissa, Elva, Adeline, and Alice. "I had the satisfaction of accompanying them home," he wrote in his journal, in his ever understated style.

William Meek had more bad news for Henderson. Although no treaty with the Clackamas had yet been ratified, the federal government had decided to take 800 acres of the Luelling and Meek land claims for a public arsenal and ordnance depot. President Millard Fillmore, who had angered abolitionists like Henderson by signing into law the strict Fugitive Slave Act of 1850, had now issued the order to seize Henderson's and Meek's lands for the purpose of making war on Indians. A government surveyor had already mapped the area in detail.

Henderson and Meek had the task of preparing an affidavit in their defense. On July 19, they would present it to Judge Orville C. Pratt of the Supreme Court of Oregon Territory, summarizing their costs this way:

> These claims cost deponents in 1847–48 the sum of $1,850; they expended thereon in improvements in 1848, $1,200; in 1849, $7,500; in 1850, $13,000; and since then a large amount besides, making in all $30,000 or over. The clearing off and grubbing of their said land . . . has cost them at the high prices of everything in Oregon, full $500 an acre, and they have on said claims 25 acres and over thus cleared, etc.; their sawmill, also situate theron . . . has cost more than $12,000; they further say that they have growing on said claims an amount of valuable fruit of all the choice kinds and varieties obtained . . . an expense of many thousand dollars, which . . . would sell for $50,000 and upwards; and yet these deponents say that the actual value of their said nurseries, mills and other improvements is diminished by the aforesaid attempted reservation more than one-half which by the rule as aforesaid, to indemnify

> them, will scarcely allow an assessment of the twentieth part of their actual damages.

Henderson and Meek would win their case, although their rights to Elizabeth's and Mary's 320-acre portions—because the women died before their claims could be proven—would remain in doubt until 1875, when the matter was finally resolved in the families' favor. (The arsenal was never built; the territorial legislature informed Congress that Oregonians would fight their own Indian wars.)

But the battle over the arsenal was in the future. Now the travelers had adventure stories to tell. The mail steamer would have brought Henderson's family to Panama City in only nine to ten days. Traversing the Panamanian isthmus must have been harder, requiring riding on mules part way and in canoes the rest of the way, over the course of four to ten days, in total, and often in drenching weather. The trip home was hard and longer—three months, in total—even though the partially built Panama Railroad eliminated much of the water travel across the isthmus. But the Atlantic and Pacific steamship schedules weren't coordinated, and for various reasons the schedules were hard to keep. The San-Francisco-to-Astoria leg operated as a separate line, also without coordination. So Seth's and Henderson's families ended up being detained for a month at Panama and twelve days at San Francisco. They were all fortunate to have completed their travels without catching malaria, yellow fever, dysentery, or cholera.

But if the isthmus was hazardous it was also stunningly beautiful, and its strange fruits, to a nurseryman, particularly enticing. Bayard Taylor, who crossed the isthmus in 1849, described the extravagant scenery:

> All the gorgeous growths of an eternal summer are so mingled in one impenetrable mass that the eye is bewildered. From the rank jungle of canes and gigantic lilies, and the thickets of strange shrubs that line the water, rise the trunks of the mango, the ceiba, the coco, the sycamore, and the superb palm. . . . Every turn of the stream only disclosed another and more magnificent vista of leaf, bough, and blossom.

Like Bayard Taylor, Henderson fell in love with jungly Central America, so much that he would later try to make a home there.

At Chagres, on the Caribbean shore, Henderson's family caught another mail steamer, which stopped in Havana and New Orleans before continuing on to New York. They traveled, probably by steamboat, up the Hudson River to Newburgh, the site of Andrew Jackson Downing's famous Botanic Garden and Nurseries. Downing was a very different Andrew Jackson from Andrew Jackson Davis, but he was equally famous. With his brother Charles, Downing had written *Fruits and Fruit Trees of America*—no doubt a treasured reference in Henderson's library—and he was editor of *The Horticulturist and Journal of Rural Art and Rural Taste*, to which Henderson may have subscribed.

After completing their purchases in Newburgh, the family went on to Rochester, most likely by a train from Albany. In Rochester, whose byname was shifting from the Flour City to the Flower City, they visited George Ellwanger and Patrick Barry's Mount Hope Nursery, then the largest nursery in the United States. Perhaps they made a side trip north to Jefferson County to see Phebe's relatives; there Henderson may have met her younger sister, and his future wife, Betsey. Finally, they rendezvoused with Clarissa and her three daughters, either by taking a steamboat down the Ohio River to Indiana or by returning to New York City and taking a steamer to New Orleans, which Seth's family would have reached via the Ohio and Mississippi rivers.

The plants Henderson bought in New York—ornamental trees and shrubs as well as fruit trees—arrived in good health. They included apricots, almonds, and nectarines as well as peaches, plums, cherries, and many now-obscure varieties of apple and pear. According to Seth's count, the young apple, pear, peach, almond, and nectarine trees together totaled nearly two thousand, in fifty varieties.

One apple cultivar Henderson tried to obtain in New York was the Yellow Newtown Pippin, also known as the Albemarle Pippin. He had brought the regular, green Newtown Pippin from Iowa, but many thought the yellow type superior. The Newtown Pippin is a very old American variety, discovered in Queens, New York, in the late seventeenth or early eighteenth century and popularized in England and Europe through the efforts of Benjamin Franklin. The Yellow Newtown Pippin, from Virginia, may have sprung from a sport—a mutation—or from a seedling of the green variety, or its lighter color and softer texture may have resulted from different growing conditions or a later harvest.

Whether the two cultivars were distinct was a great subject of horticultural debate in the nineteenth century, and the controversy has yet to be resolved. In New York, Henderson had Downing personally point out the Yellow Newtown Pippin trees as they were dug to be sure he had the right cultivar. But the fruit turned out identical to that of Henderson's original Newtowns.

Henderson brought back from New York not only trees and shrubs but also starts of the Hovey strawberry, North America's first important strawberry cultivar. Sadly, the variety turned out to be pistillate, which means it lacked stamens and so remained fruitless unless a "perfect," or bisexual, strawberry was planted close by. The Milwaukie Nursery therefore had no strawberries to sell until 1858, and even then buyers were few. Strawberries were seen as puny, fragile, and sometimes bland fruits that grew wild nearly everywhere and so weren't worth adding to a garden. Strawberry jam, strawberry preserves, and strawberry pie were still practically unheard of.

With speedy propagation, the new fruit varieties would soon be available for sale. In 1854, the Milwaukie Nursery catalog would offer eighty varieties of apple, forty of pear, thirty-seven of peach, twelve of plum, and nine of cherry. With grafts from the new trees, other Oregon nurseries would soon expand their own offerings. Ralph Geer was soon producing forty-two varieties of apple, fifteen varieties of pear, six varieties of cherry, and five varieties of peach, and in 1856 Alfred Stanton would advertise sixty-three cultivars of apple, twenty-six of pear, nine of plum, and eight of cherry. Thanks largely to Henderson's voyage, the cultivation of grafted fruits reached its height of diversity in Oregon in the 1850s.

Other nurserymen soon contributed to this diversity. The advent of the mail steamships, supported by lucrative contracts with the U.S. government, made it possible to import plants from the East Coast to the Willamette Valley in less than four weeks. Like Henderson, P. W. Gillette had brought grafted trees via Panama in 1852. His came from his father's nursery in Ohio, and with them he established a nursery in Astoria (among his trees was the Peach Plum—a big-fruited plum that would prove popular in the Willamette Valley). In the same year John W. Ladd, of Howell Prairie, west of Silverton, imported and sold fruit trees from both Downing's nursery in New York and Thorburn's in New Jersey.

But no other Oregon nursery sold as many grafted trees as the Milwaukie Nursery.

After a brief respite with his family, Seth went back to grafting—peaches and cherries and apples, in the nursery, in the orchard, and on other emigrants' claims. On April 6 he added up the time he had worked for Henderson: seven months and seventeen days. He took a day off "on account of sore eyes," but then he resumed grafting.

Thanks in large part to Seth's unacclaimed work, the Milwaukie Nursery was winning renown, even in the Eastern states. On May 20, a letter in the *Indiana State Sentinel* about the wonders of Oregon described Henderson and Meek's business: "Some of these trees growed six feet, from the bud, in one season, and some of them formed quite a head. They bear at three years growth. Pears, peaches, cherries currents [*sic*], &c., all do as fine as the apple."

The Luellings weren't developing just a business, however; they were developing an industry. In the spring of 1852, they already had friendly competition. Ralph Geer advertised that he had eight thousand apple and one thousand pear trees, "comprising sixty varieties of Lewelling and Meek's selections." He offered one hundred three- to seven-foot apple trees for fifty dollars at the nursery or sixty dollars in Salem. The pear trees cost more, a dollar apiece.

John Departs

If Seth noted when John left for Iowa, the page on which this entry was written hasn't survived. Sometime in the spring of 1852, however, John headed home to Iowa. He would settle his affairs (and some of Henderson's), and return to the West Coast with his wife and children.

But John wouldn't come back to Oregon. Some writers have claimed he was disappointed he couldn't have a farm adjacent to Henderson's and share a fruit business with him as he had in Indiana and Iowa. Perhaps John felt that Meek had supplanted him. But plenty of other land was available nearby, and Seth's journal suggests no discord between John and Meek. It seems unlikely that Henderson and Meek would have refused to take on John as a partner. More likely, spending two cold, gray winters in Oregon gave John a clear preference for warmer, sunnier California. The Willamette fog may have aggravated his asthma, as the East Bay fog would do later. Or perhaps John simply considered that California would provide a bigger market for both fruit and fruit trees. Migration to Oregon was slowing; Americans were moving instead to California—which was, after all, now a state. For John, California was the place to be.

Back to Business

Seth and his family, meanwhile, settled in. Besides planting and sprouting, spading and hoeing, and budding and trimming for Henderson, Seth planted cabbages and potatoes for his family, built a dirt oven for baking, took his daughters to Portland, "clerked at Election," and even went to church—probably to Methodist services led by Clinton Kelly, who would hike through dense forest from his home in Oregon City to preach in Milwaukie.

In late July Clarissa came down with "the ague"—malaria—and Seth was soon sick, too. The intermittent fevers continued through most of the autumn. Seth's journal doesn't mention whether the children also got sick.

Between fevers, Seth continued to lead an active life. Perhaps feeling flush with all the money he had earned, he bought five ponies and, on September 19, a bigger house, in town. Built by Israel Mitchell on Front Street (now McLoughlin Boulevard), the house had two stories and two large downstairs rooms with movable partitions that allowed combining

Seth and Clarissa's house in Milwaukie viewed from the Willamette River. Courtesy of the Oregon Historical Society Research Library.

A closer view of Seth and Clarissa's house. Courtesy of the Library of Congress.

the two rooms into one. A man named Noah Hubler was leasing the building for use as a tavern, so Seth offered Noah a job in the nursery, and Noah closed the tavern. On September 26, Seth and his family moved into the Front Street house. He would live there for the rest of his life, and Noah would remain a valued employee for many years.

Henderson got back to work growing his business. The orchard produced just a little more in 1852 than it had the previous year. But in December Henderson was able to advertise in a San Francisco newspaper roots of his large- and purple-fruited "double-bearing" raspberry: It bore for six to seven weeks in summer and also produced a small crop in the fall (his East Coast acquisitions hadn't had much time to multiply, so he must have brought this raspberry from Iowa).

Now the Milwaukie Nursery reached its height of production. By the winter of 1852–53, the nursery had so much rootstock that fourteen men were kept grafting through the winter. Most were temporary workers, men who didn't remain long in Oregon, but among the bunch was Joseph Lambert, whom Meek had hired in 1851 to haul logs for the mill. In 1852, while Meek helped to organize and promote the fruit business, Joseph Lambert began managing the mill. That year sawmills at Humboldt

Bay began to dominate the California lumber trade; because of its long, straight grain and fire-resistance, redwood was favored over Douglas fir. With reduced demand for his lumber, Meek leased the mill to Joseph early in 1853. But the lumber business was so unprofitable that Joseph considered closing the mill and returning east. Instead, Henderson and Meek hired him to help with the fruit-tree grafting. Joseph would keep working for them through the 1854 harvest.

In early 1853, Henderson, Seth, and Meek made formal arrangements for branch nurseries, on the lands of Alfred Stanton, Joseph Kelsey, James Knox, and also Amos Harvey, whose farm was in Spring Valley, between the Eola Hills and the Willamette River. Seth later estimated that the men set out one hundred thousand grafts among the four nurseries. The Luellings were continuing the practice of expansion through partnerships that Silas Wharton had pioneered in the Old Northwest. By establishing branch nurseries, the men brought grafted trees closer to would-be customers whose claims were sprinkled throughout the Willamette Valley.

Henderson and Meek also extended their lands to the south by six acres, which they bought from Lot Whitcomb.

In February and March of 1853 Henderson's family was expanding and thriving along with his business. Alfred and Mary had their first child, Alfred William Luelling. Asenath—now living rather far away in Cowlitz County, in the new Washington Territory—gave birth to her second child, Howard Columbus Bozarth. In February Henderson's fourth child, Rachel, who would at some point start going by Hattie, married Seth William Eddy, at Henderson's house. Rachel was sixteen, Seth Eddy about twenty. A month later Hattie's sister Jane, two months short of fourteen years, married Seth's cousin Henry Welsh Eddy, who was twenty-three.

Henry and Seth were Phebe's nephews, each the son of a different brother. Henry came to visit his Aunt Phebe in Oregon in the spring of 1848, and he ended up staying. Seth apparently came sometime later. For their wedding, Henry took Jane back to the Forks of the Santiam, where he may have been living with Phebe's son George Grimes, who owned land in Linn County.

Perhaps Seth and Jane helped George, now twenty-two, to move to Milwaukie, because at about this time he did just that. He bought several lots from Lot Whitcomb and began running the Milwaukie Hotel.

Henderson, who had been named guardian of Ephraim Grimes's heirs and property, witnessed George's transactions and probably provided financial help.

At this point Henderson seems to have been fully engaged in his life in Oregon. He was turning Milwaukie into a leading nursery not only for grafted fruit but also for social and religious reform. On July 19, Henderson and his friend John Bonser, from the Overland Trail, advertised in the *Oregon Weekly Times* for "reformers,"

> those who have or wish to obtain knowledge of the unchanging Laws of Nature—Who have or wish to acquire a knowledge of A. J. Davis writings, and the sublime truth therein explained—to meet at Milwaukie on Saturday the 13th of August at ten o-clock A.M., to hold a free and social meeting, and take such measures as may be deemed proper, to promote the spread of knowledge. Come, true reformers. Let us see what can be done to awake Oregon from the sleep of formality.

Just fifteen days after this meeting, however, Henderson's life was again thrown into turmoil. After only two years and two months of marriage, Phebe died, the cause of her death unrecorded. The family buried her near Elizabeth and Mary in the Milwaukie cemetery.

The death of Henderson's second wife didn't slow him down. It may have only spurred his restlessness. Perhaps he was preparing for his next move when, on September 23, he signed a deed of sale to his stone house in Iowa and mailed it back to the buyer.

About the same time, Henderson elevated his brother Seth from hired hand to working partner. Seth began spelling his name *Luelling* to match his brother's. Their business, in the fall of 1853, was advertised as "the Milwaukie Nursery, H. & S. Luelling, Proprietors." Perhaps Henderson was anticipating that Seth would soon become the sole or leading owner.

Meek's work was limited, at this point, to care of the orchard and sales of its fruits. That work was substantial, because finally the orchard was producing "a good many apples." Seth helped pick one tree, he later remembered, "which bore 240 pounds, which Henderson took to San Francisco and sold for $1 per pound." The pears, peaches, and plums were bearing, too, and sold for $1.50 per pound. Much of the fruit was shipped to California, in boxes bound with strap iron as protection against thieves. "Very little of it sold for less than $1 per pound," Seth reported.

In fact, the fruit may have sold for much more. According to *California Farmer*, "Messrs. Meek & Luelling . . . brought about four bushels, or 200 lbs, from the sale of which they realized $500."

While Henderson was in California in late 1853, he didn't just sell apples. He also bought land. And he almost certainly met up with his brother John, who was already establishing himself as a Golden State orchardist.

Chapter 8
Stretching South

> Within the last five years, the planting of orchards has, in the United States, been carried to an extent never known before. . . . So many farmers have found their orchards the most profitable, because least expensive part of their farms, that orcharding has become in some parts of the west, almost an absolute distinct species of husbandry.
>
> —Andrew Jackson Downing, "A Few Words on Fruit Culture"

On January 4, 1853, John Lewelling debarked an ocean steamer in San Francisco with Elvy and their four sons, Eli, Elisha, Seth, and Silas. Eli, the eldest, would turn seventeen the next day; Silas, the youngest, was eight. With them also was Sarah, John and Elvy's nineteen-year-old daughter, and her husband Robert King. Sarah and Robert had married the prior June, probably soon after John's arrival back in Iowa.

The family had come to California down the Mississippi, across the Gulf of Mexico to Cuba, and then on to Nicaragua rather than the Isthmus of Panama. Crossing at Nicaragua shortened the trip by 750 miles, though it did not necessarily save the traveler any time. Cornelius Vanderbilt's first great money-making venture, the Nicaragua route carried California-bound travelers by river steamer up the San Juan River to the rapids at El Costillo. There the passengers would debark and walk around the rapids before boarding another steamer, which would carry them across Lake Nicaragua. Then they would travel by carriage twelve miles further, to San Juan del Sur, whose pretty Pacific beach must have served as a welcome resting spot for John and his family before they boarded the "old floating coffin S. S. Lewis" for a twenty-three-day sail to San Francisco.

A traveler who experienced this last leg of the journey in 1851 described the fare: "The potatoes gave out in three days; no fresh bread; the ship's biscuit was old, rotten and wormy, and was put in the oven every day to drive out and kill the insects; the fish stunk." Elvy, who was about three months pregnant upon the family's arrival in San Francisco, must have been particularly relieved to get off the boat.

John may have left his family in San Francisco—there were now several good hotels to choose from—while he arranged for long-term lodgings. He accomplished this quickly. Perhaps he had made preliminary plans before leaving Iowa, or even before leaving the West Coast. In any case, the family's next adventure would take them not to the Sierra foothills or the Napa Valley but to the lowlands on the eastern edge of the San Francisco Bay.

John at Mission San José

This country was dry half the year, but fertile. "The oats and clover range of these valleys exceed the account given by historians, which is hissed down as fabulous," wrote Enos Mendenhall to his brother a few months after John's return to California. "I have stood on the mountains and looked over the valley as far as I could discern, and it was one continuation of oats—beautiful as an oats field in the prairie."

From atop one of the ridges that parallel the eastern shore of the bay, Enos had gazed down on what had been the lands of the Chochenyo Ohlone and, subsequently, Mission San José. Established in 1797 in present-day Fremont (not in the pueblo of San José, thirteen miles to the south), the mission was among the most prosperous of the twenty-one established in California. Its fields and pastures extended northward all the way to today's Oakland. The pastures fed tens of thousands of cattle, horses, and sheep.

"I found several locations that pleased me well," Enos continued, "but I shall not buy land until the title is all settled in this country." John may have felt the same way. In portioning the arable parts of California into enormous land grants, the Spanish and Mexican governments had used metes and bounds—natural landmarks—instead of the rectilinear township-and-range system that the United States had applied in dividing up the West. Subsequent land sales, appropriation by squatters, and the requirement that land-grant recipients prove their ownership in court had rendered most land titles uncertain.

So John made a deal with a less cautious and more affluent settler, Elias Lyman Beard. Elias had arrived in California in 1849 from Indiana, where he had raised grain, run a sawmill and a stone quarry, helped

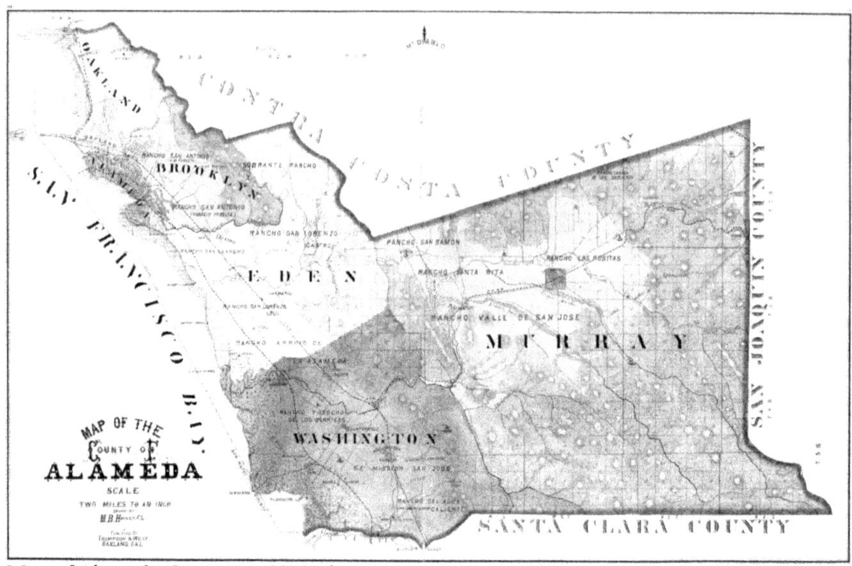

Map of Alameda County in 1878, showing Ex-Mission San José at the southern end. From Thompson and West, *Official Historical Atlas Map of Alameda County, California.*

construct the Wabash & Erie Canal, and packed and shipped pork. With another man, John M. Horner, Elias bought the thirty-thousand-acre Rancho Ex-Mission San José, which Governor Pio Pico had sold to Andrés Pico and Juan B. Alvarado in 1846. The rancho was called Ex-Mission because, after the Mexican government secularized all the missions, the church retained the San José mission buildings and the land immediately around them, for a time, while the rest of the lands were sold or given away. In common parlance, the *Ex-* was dropped; the area was called simply Mission San José. The Ex-Mission was in Washington Township, the southernmost township of Alameda County.

Elias began raising food for the gold miners, with great success. In 1852, he harvested 640 acres of grain and more than 180 acres of potatoes. Elias also took over the mission orchard, fifteen acres enclosed by high adobe walls and planted with vines, figs, olives, peaches, quinces, and pears. The pear crop, from 350 mature trees, was particularly impressive. A single tree yielded fifteen hundred pounds, for a gross income of $400, about $16,000 in 2024. And the gross receipts from the vineyard, in 1851, were $16,000, more than $640,000 in 2024.

Upon meeting John, Elias must have decided that he would like to expand the mission orchard with grafted trees and small fruits. Certainly he had land to spare for a man with John's skills. Elias offered to let John plant an orchard on shares, and advanced him more than sixty thousand dollars to do so. For seven years John would have a half-interest in the orchard.

John quickly placed an order with the Milwaukie Nursery. On February 20, Seth noted in his journal an accounting of a shipment to his brother in "San Jose Valley." In the order were 109 trees, including 50 of apple and 35 of assorted new varieties, priced at $1 to $2 each. There were also 40 gooseberry slips, 40 raspberry roots, 150 currant slips, and 24 currant "trees." And there were 1,500 "Cherry at 3 cts." These must have been cherry scions. It's unclear where John got the rootstock onto which he would graft them. Henderson had probably brought from New York mazzard (*Prunus avium*) rootstock—by then the rootstock of choice for sweet cherries—but the Milwaukie Nursery wouldn't yet have had enough of this stock to share. John himself probably brought cherry seeds from Iowa, but a year would pass before they could develop into seedlings ready for grafting. John may have also brought rootstock from Iowa, or someone else in the area may have already started a cherry nursery and had some seedling trees available for John. Wherever he got the trees, John probably cut up the roots to multiply the grafts. Clearly, John planned to grow a lot of cherry trees.

Up to this point cherries had been a rarity in California. Elisha Smith Capron, who published his *History of California* in 1854, listed cherries among the mission fruits, and other historians have duly reported that the padres grew cherries, but I've found no firm evidence to confirm these assertions. In 1852, a very small quantity of sweet cherries was reportedly sold in San Francisco. Perhaps they came from Monterey or from a young orchard recently established by a gold miner who had settled down.

Even if John's cherry nursery wasn't the first in California, it would soon be one of the biggest. In 1855 the entire Mission San José nursery and orchard covered seventy-one acres. The orchard included 300 cherry trees in six varieties, and the nursery 4,000 cherry grafts.

Currants were another new crop for California. Currants dislike heat and harsh sunshine, but on the foggy flatlands near the bay at least one variety, Cherry, would thrive. According to an article in the *Pacific Rural Press* (January 12, 1884), "it was in part the introduction of the cherry currant that made Alameda county famous and wealthy, and raised the price of her land from $60 to $400 per acre."

Seth's journal didn't specify which currant variety, or varieties, he sent to John. If he sent Cherry, John got more of the same plant straight from New York. In the fall of 1853, John, Elias Beard, and E. T. Crane, of San Lorenzo, sent one Captain Whalley, or Whaley, to visit Eastern nurseries. At Ellwanger and Barry's, in Rochester, Whalley was introduced to this currant cultivar, then popular in France but to that point a failure in the United States. Although other currants had performed poorly in San José, Ellwanger wanted the captain to try the Cherry. E. T. Crane ended up with four of the plants, John twelve, and Elias Beard more. A few years later Beard's currants had died, but Crane's were thriving, and John was propagating the plants by the thousands. Sales of currants for some years averaged two thousand to four thousand dollars per acre. By 1878 red currants were a drug on the market, but for years the currant business was extremely profitable.

John hadn't given up on apples and pears. Probably in part through Whalley's voyage, John built an extensive pear collection. In 1859 he would display at a horticultural society fair twenty-five pear varieties, only five of which Henderson had brought from New York. John planted new apple varieties, too, along with at least ten that Henderson had brought from Iowa (two of those, Red June and Carolina, probably came originally from North Carolina). In 1855 John's orchard included 5,700 apple trees of thirty varieties and 600 pear trees of thirty-four varieties, and the nursery contained 10,000 apple trees and 2,000 pear trees.

John's orchard included plums and peaches, too. Economic and environmental conditions would force him to specialize later, but his Mission San José stock was distinguished by its breadth. "The Orchard, in extent and variety, equals, and in maturity, excels any other to which our attention was directed," wrote a journalist in a review of orchard and nursery operations in the Bay Area and beyond.

Little is recorded of John's family life during this period. I don't know what sort of house the family lived in or whether the children attended school. Without a doubt, though, John and Elvy were shattered when, on April 10, 1853, their son Seth died of an unrecorded cause, only three months after the family's arrival in Oregon and two months short of his eleventh birthday. The following summer, however, brought new joy: On July 17 Elvy gave birth to another son, Arthur. And the next year Elvy and Sarah, mother and daughter, experienced the strange pleasure of undergoing pregnancy together. Elvy would give birth to her last child, Harvy John, on Valentine's Day 1855, the year she turned forty. Less than three weeks later, John and Elvy would become grandparents, when Sarah gave birth to Lewis Leroy King. Life at Mission San José was rich in babies.

Henderson by the Bay

After selling Oregon apples in San Francisco in the fall of 1853, Henderson searched for land for a California orchard of his own. He ended up buying several adjacent parcels in the east end of Alameda, today an island just off the Oakland shore but then, before the construction of a canal in 1902, a peninsula. The parcels cost him, in total, about $25,000. He returned to Oregon but left again for California in February 1854—apparently with trees, because when his daughter Rachel arrived later that year Henderson had an orchard as well as a house (she must have arrived in late spring, because, she noted, Henderson had many bearing strawberry plants at the time).

But the land titles proved unclear. By the time Rachel left, in early 1855, Henderson had lost his Alameda farm and bought one just across the estuary in what would become, in 1856, the township of Brooklyn—probably named for the ship *Brooklyn*, which had carried Mormons to

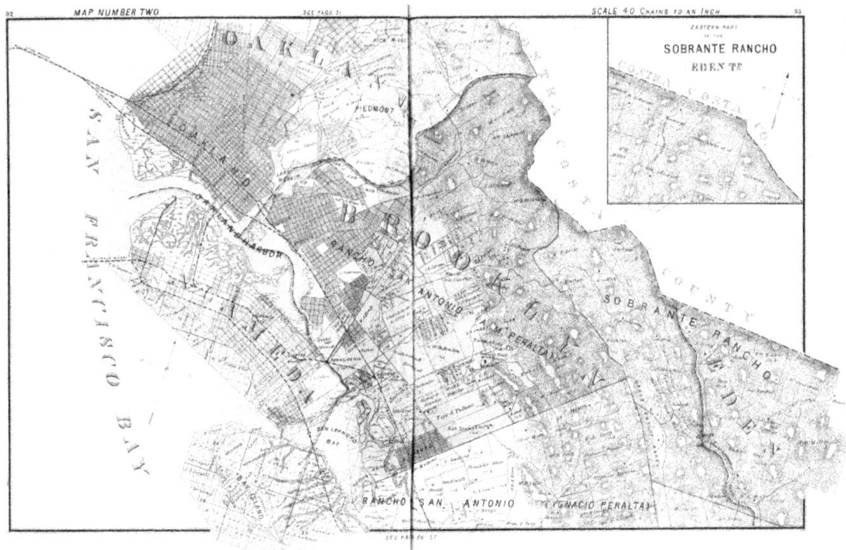

Brooklyn and Alameda in 1878. From Thompson and West, *Official Historical Atlas Map of Alameda County, California.*

Yerba Buena in 1846. The whole of Brooklyn Township would later be annexed to Oakland, but in the mid-1850s Oakland was just a small village by the bay.

Henderson's new estate, Fruit Vale, extended from today's Foothill Boulevard northeastward, on either side of Sausal Creek, to beyond where the creek emerged from a canyon. Henderson built a grand house at the foot of the canyon, at a spot known today as Dimond Park, next to an oak tree said to be "the largest but one in the United States," with a spread of ninety-six feet. About thirty years later the two words *Fruit Vale* would become one. Today's Fruitvale Avenue was once Henderson's driveway.

What little is known of Henderson's Fruit Vale years comes mostly from Franklin Rhoda, who grew up on a farm in Fruit Vale after the estate was divided. Rhoda became a minister, an orchardist, and, in the early twentieth century, the primary promoter of Henderson's memory. Fruit Vale, according to Rhoda, was about six hundred acres. It had been part of the much more extensive estate of Antonio Peralta, whose father had divided his Spanish land grant among his four sons. In 1855, Peralta sold what would become Fruit Vale to Lawrence Huerstel for $800, a bargain price. On September 18, 1856, Huerstel sold the tract to Henderson for $13,000, more than sixteen times what he had paid for it.

Alfred and his wife, Mary, decided to move with Henderson to California, taking with them their son, Alfred William Jr., whom they called by his middle name. Mary was pregnant with their second baby, Annie. Alfred and Mary bought 217 acres adjoining Henderson's land. It was Mary who suggested the name Fruit Vale for Henderson's Brooklyn estate.

Henderson may have encouraged Alfred and Mary's move by offering to buy the western half of their Oregon claim. In September 1854 Henderson and Meek paid $3,000 for that land, and combined it with the Luelling and Meek lands. (Alfred and Mary would sell the eastern half of the claim, in 1857, to a man named Thomas Kelley.)

In 1855, Henderson sold his half of the combined claims to his daughter Jane and her husband, Henry Eddy, for $15,000 (to afford the purchase, Henry borrowed $5,000 each from William Meek and Judge Orville Pratt). Henderson may have needed the money for his California land purchase, and the sale would keep the land in the family. For a time, Henry Eddy would take an active role in the Milwaukie orchard business.

Three months after that sale, in October 1855, Henderson returned to Oregon. This may have been in part a business trip; according to one source, Henderson would continue as a partner in the orchard operation until October 28, 1856. But Henderson had another reason to be in Oregon. Phebe's widowed sister, Betsey Ann Eddy Countryman, had arrived in Milwaukie from New York. She was probably staying with her nephew Henry and his wife, Henderson's daughter Jane. Jane and Henry were raising Henderson's youngest child, Eliza. But Levi, Albert, and Oregon—twelve, ten, and eight years old, respectively—still needed a mother. So, perhaps, did fourteen-year-old Hannah, who had left her Portland boarding school to join her father and brothers in California. Henderson had been single for more than two years. He wanted a woman to share his Alameda County home. So Henderson and Betsey Ann were married by Hector Campbell—Alfred's father-in-law, Milwaukie's first schoolteacher, and now a local judge.

Betsey Ann presumably returned with Henderson to California. But within months she was dead or gone away. Her fate is unknown.

Henderson and Alfred began transplanting trees from Alameda. They established an orchard and a nursery, and later a second nursery. Ultimately, in Rhoda's estimate, they would sell several hundred thousand trees from Fruit Vale.

With the Peralta hacienda very near to Fruit Vale, Brooklyn had a substantial Californio population and culture, including Sunday bullfights. But the area was changing fast. Soon other wealthy Americans would join Henderson, with fine houses, orchards, nurseries, shade trees, and lawns. Henderson would entertain them in 1858 at a Fruit Vale Fourth of July celebration.

At Fruit Vale Henderson would also take a new wife, his fourth. By mid-1857 he was married to Mary Ann Warren Lee. Like Phebe and Betsey Ann, Mary was a widow with grown children. She had been born in England and immigrated to Canada before coming to California, with her husband and three children, in 1855. Mr. Lee seems to have vanished from her life soon thereafter. For a time, Mary ran the American Exchange Hotel in San Francisco, according to her daughter Theresa's obituary. In 1857 Theresa was about twenty, her sister Mary Jane was about twenty-three—neither was yet married—and their brother George was thirteen. In March of 1858, at the age of forty-four, Mary would bear her, and Henderson's, last child, William Henderson Luelling.

In 1858 Henderson sold Meek, for $20,000, the remainder of his share in the Milwaukie business. Henderson may have needed the money for a new venture.

The Oregon Fruit Business

During the years that Henderson was establishing himself in California, first in Alameda and then in Brooklyn, he remained, in the eyes of many, the face of the Milwaukie orchard and nursery. But Seth, Meek, and others were running the business.

Despite the frenzy of orchard planting in Oregon, fresh fruit was still a rarity there. J. H. Settlemier, an 1850 emigrant who would become a nurseryman in his own right, couldn't remember seeing an apple in the territory before 1855. Arthur Miller remembered picking up an apple—a Sweet June—from the ground in the Luelling-Meek orchard, with another boy, in 1854. "We looked around very carefully to see if anybody saw us, and we cut it in two and ate it." As much as he savored his first apple in Oregon, he felt like a criminal.

Young Arthur must have been delighted when, the same year, Meek put his father, Henry Miller, in charge of a two-and-a-half acre apple orchard—formerly Alfred and Mary's orchard, I suspect—on a bluff over the river. Henry and Arthur "cultivated and plowed and watched the orchard to keep the people from stealing the fruit," and in return they got a third of that fruit. They sold six hundred to eight hundred apples on the streets of Portland for a dollar apiece.

Despite the rarity of apples in Portland, a dollar was a high price to pay for one. According to the *Oregonian*, the going price for an apple was three "York shillings," or pieces of eight—that is, 37.5 cents (about $14 in 2024)—or $4.50 per dozen. Even that was too much for most people. The *Oregonian* commented sourly: "Nobody but Lewelling would ever think of getting that price. We don't think he sells many even at that. Shylock had his day, and so will nurserymen in Oregon." Apparently many Oregonians simply waited, fruitless, for prices to come down further or for their own trees to come into production.

Californians, with their pockets full of gold, weren't so stingy—or so Oregon farmers imagined. "If a man and woman were passing Luelling's retail fruit stand in San Francisco at any time between 1849 to 1859, and the lady looked interested at the beautiful specimens," wrote the Salem orchardist John Minto in 1898, "she got her choice without regard to cost. Five dollars was sometimes paid for a single apple, and as late as 1856 Esopus Spitzenbergs, of average size, retailed from the stand at seventy-five cents each." But the fruit stand didn't actually belong to Henderson, Seth, or Meek, and the vendor almost certainly made higher profits than the farmer.

In any case, the Luellings and Meek sent ten times as much fruit to San Francisco in 1854 as in 1853—about forty bushels. The fruits were "contracted, on arrival, to George Hughes, at $1.25 per lb; but on delivering they were found to be damaged by heat in the steamer, and the sale was settled at 87 1/2c per lb, realizing about $2,500." The lower price might please an orchardist today, depending on transportation costs, but Meek and Henderson were doubtlessly disappointed. The experience must have reinforced Henderson's preference to grow fruit as close as possible to a major market.

The men also took note of their competition. As Seth later explained, "In the fall of 1854, quite a number of small orchards came into bearing, and the price fell." In 1855, reported *California Farmer*, "the receipts from Oregon amounted probably to some 1,500 boxes, prices ranging from 50c to $1 per lb. In 1856 the receipts amounted to several thousand boxes, sales ranging from 25c to 75c per lb." Pears, peaches, and plums brought more money; they "sold for $1.50 per pound when apples sold for $1." The rich would have their fruit at any price; even in 1856, a box of Esopus Spitzenberg apples netted the shipper $60, and three boxes of Winesap apples sold in Portland for $102. But the general trend was ominous.

Despite falling prices, the Milwaukie orchard business prospered for years. In 1859, the fifty-acre orchard was still "the source from whence is derived the major part of the winter [fruit] supply for the San Francisco market." By this time the business included a two-story, ventilated fruit house, thirty feet across by forty feet deep, in which perfect, hand-picked apples were stored on open shelves. Adjoining the fruit house was a packing shed, where the apples were put into boxes and the boxes set on "sliding-ways," down which they would slide straight onto the deck of a vessel in waiting. Meek and Eddy's was "doubtless one of the best arranged fruit-growing and fruit-packing establishments in the world."

The manufacture of fruit boxes was itself a new industry, spurred by the birth of the West Coast fruit industry. In eastern North America, since early colonial times, farmers had packed fruit, and many other kinds of produce, in barrels. Barrels had the advantage that they could be rolled—into and out of the orchard, and on and off carts and boats. Their main disadvantage is revealed by the phrase "bottom of the barrel"—fruit at the bottom was typically crushed or at least bruised. Barrels also required well-dried hardwood lumber and a cooper's skill in making them. Wooden boxes, in contrast, were "Neat, Light, Cheap," as one early manufacturer described them, and they were easy to carry and stack. Henderson, Seth, and Meek made their own boxes at first, using shooks—thin boards—from their own sawmill. In 1858 the business used forty thousand feet of lumber to make fruit boxes, and in 1859 sixty thousand feet. The size of boxes was eventually standardized so that three could be laid side by side across the width of the wagon box. John's son Elisha would patent his own fruit-box design in 1871, for cherries.

According to one historian, Meek distributed not only Milwaukie fruit but "nearly all the fruit raised in Oregon," to both Oregon and California markets, from 1855 to 1859. Large amounts of fruit went to British Columbia as well. Even though prices were dropping, 1856 and 1857 were the most profitable for apples. Meek "netted $45,000 in two years' business," more than $1.8 million in 2024.

More threatening to Oregon orchardists than the competition among themselves was rising competition with California fruit growers. Most Oregonians hadn't expected this; like many new Californians themselves, Oregon farmers didn't believe you could grow fruits and even vegetables, with or without irrigation, in a land where no rain fell for half the year. Seth and Meek may have taken this competition personally: Henderson and John were becoming their rivals.

Californians were already producing a bounty of summer fruits. Now their apple orchards were coming into production, and California apples ripened much earlier than the same cultivars in Oregon. For a time, Oregonians relied on sales of their winter apples—those that were harvested late and would keep through the winter—especially Newtown Pippin and the showy red Winesap. On February 28, 1857, the editor of the *Oregon Argus* predicted optimistically that

> more money will be brought into the country the next five years for fruit, than for any other one product of the country. Mr. Luelling informs us that the experiments made in fruit raising in California have induced the belief that climate is not well adapted to winter varieties. California and Oregon winter apples were sold at the same stands in San Francisco, and the Oregon fruit sold for enough more over the other to pay the price of shipment. While the California fruit seems to best ours in weight we excel them in flavor.

Yet prices for Oregon apples continued to fall. "In 1860," reported *California Farmer* (July 11, 1862), "the receipts amounted to about 86,000 boxes, sales ranging from 3c to 19c."

By 1861, Oregon orchardists were sending little fruit to California before November, because "the market being so well supplied with peaches, grapes, and other varieties that prices would not warrant the sending of early apples." Even in the winter, prices remained low. Much of the fruit arrived six to eight weeks late, because of flooding, and more was damaged by cold during transit, when the Columbia River was closed by ice.

Oregon farmers looked to the advent of railroads to solve their shipping problems. For this reason, William Meek and Lot Whitcomb became commissioners of the Oregon and California Railroad Company, incorporated in 1854. The railroad would eventually stretch from Portland to San Francisco, but it would reach Milwaukie on its way south only in late 1869.

The nursery as well as the orchard had competitors for the California market. On December 9, 1854, the *Oregon Weekly Times* noted that several thousand young fruit trees—"choice specimens"—were awaiting shipment by steamer. They were from nurseries run by Judge Ohey, General McCarver, and William Holmes as well as Seth Luelling.

Seth ensured his fruit trees would get special attention in the press, at least locally. In placing an ad for his trees, in 1854, Seth presented the editor of the *Oregon Weekly Times* with apples in eight varieties—each of them labeled, so the editor could name them in the paper.

The demand for trees, happily, outweighed supply. "Orders are continually arriving for fruit trees, for the California market," noted the *Weekly*

Times. And Seth was also supplying Washington Territory, which was split off from Oregon Territory in 1853. In 1854 he added a branch nursery at Hugh Pattison's place in Steilacoom, 140 miles away on the Puget Sound. Hugh had worked for Seth for a year, according to his daughter, before carrying off trees on pack horses.

Buying land in small parcels as he needed them, Seth also planted his own orchard. In 1861 a California newspaper quoted him on the start of his independent fruitery: Between 1854 and 1857, Seth said, he gradually planted five acres in orchard. Like his brother John, he kept careful accounts. In 1860, the orchard included "80 peach, 30 plum, 30 cherry, 120 pear and 540 apple trees. Among the orchard trees, I planted 140 currant, 140 gooseberry, 100 raspberry, 36 rods of strawberry, and 1 Lawton blackberry." That year the orchard produced 35,700 pounds of fruit, including 23 pounds from the single Lawton blackberry.

In the fall of 1857 Seth bought three more parcels, from William Meek and the Eddys. One of them was the original, forty-two-acre Milwaukie Nursery, on the shore of the mill pond. Seth used these parcels for his own nursery.

While continuing to grow mainly apples and pears, Seth experimented with new fruits. The big-fruited Lawton blackberry, the first widely cultivated blackberry in the United States, was one of them. Seth sent to New York for the single plant in 1858, and in 1859 he was selling cuttings he had rooted. He also ordered from New York several strawberry varieties, including Joseph Myatt's British Queen, a large-fruited, rich-flavored hybrid developed in England 1841. The next year he sold strawberries for seventy-five cents per pound. Unfortunately, the strawberry was still a little-known fruit in Oregon. "Up to 1860 I had no knowledge of another strawberry patch in the State for market," Seth later reported, "and the demand was so poor that I quit raising them." Seth also planted, about 1858, Oregon's first Italian prune orchard. Henderson had brought a German plum from Iowa, and it had become a favorite Oregon fruit. But the Italian prune proved so useful for drying and shipping, and so tolerant of neglect, that Seth's five-acre prune orchard eventually sparked a new industry in Oregon.

Seth must have sometimes found his nursery business lonely, because Henderson was just the first of his partners to desert him. Meek partnered with him only through 1857, which may have been the only year that Henry Eddy was also an active partner in the business. Then Henry Eddy left, too, probably to concentrate on his orchard. Beginning in 1858, a local man named Ross Merrick served as Seth's partner, but Ross, too, moved on about 1860.

That was the year, however, that Seth and Clarissa's first and only son, William Anton Lewelling, turned six. Seth was now training up a prospective heir to his nursery business.

John in San Lorenzo

While Henderson was trying to secure land with a clear title in Alameda County, John was looking for a parcel of his own. He chose Eden Township, in between Washington and Brooklyn townships. His purchase would land him, in 1855, just ten miles south of Fruit Vale.

John chose a site on the north bank of San Lorenzo Creek (or El Arroyo de San Lorenzo), which was named for Rancho San Lorenzo, a 26,722-acre estate granted in 1841 to Guillermo Castro, a career soldier in the Mexican army. The climate here was milder than that of Brooklyn, less windy and foggy, and the adobe soil was fertile, annually enriched by overflow from the creek. Lined with willows, sycamores, and oaks, the creek supplied water and sediment from the mountains before emptying into the bay at Roberts Landing, where William Roberts had erected a long wharf and warehouses and started a freighting business to San Francisco, a valuable piece of infrastructure for local farmers. Two other local businesses opened in 1853: a blacksmith shop and the San Lorenzo House, Albert E. Crane's hotel and tavern.

Until that year the area was known as Squattersville, for the weary gold miners who had settled along San Lorenzo Creek without bothering

Robert's Landing in 1878. From Thompson and West, *Official Historical Atlas Map of Alameda County, California.*

to pay Guillermo Castro for the land. John bought 40 acres from one of those squatters, Bob Farley, and soon after he bought the rest of Farley's land, for a total of 117 acres. But John was merely compensating Farley for his land improvements and inducing him to move on. He also bought a legitimate title to the land from Guillermo Castro—who sold it eagerly, because he had recently mortgaged his rancho.

John quickly began planting trees from the Mission San José nursery. In 1857 he advertised that San Lorenzo Nursery had fifty thousand one- to two-year-old fruit trees for sale—apple, pear, peach, plum, cherry, apricot, nectarine, fig, and almond. As the ad pointed out, the trees had been grown without irrigation, which meant that they should be especially hardy. They cost $.25 cents to $1.50.

John kept planting. He probably ordered more trees from Seth; in September 1858 he received an unspecified consignment on the steamship *Oregon*. That year, according to John's exact count, the nursery had 59,374 grafted trees and "about six thousands grape-vines, figs, gooseberries, currants, etc." Apple trees still dominated; they numbered more than thirty-seven thousand. (And the fruit was still much in demand. In 1859, according to his diary, Seth shipped John twenty-one boxes of apples. Presumably the brothers would share the proceeds.) Pears came in second, at more than fifteen thousand. Cherries, in twenty-five varieties, were a strong third, at 7,475. John found that cherries did "much better than was generally supposed several years ago," when they were grafted to Oregon bitter-cherry rootstock. Now, presumably, John's cherries were on mazzard or mahaleb rootstock. John also had small numbers of peaches, plums, nectarines, and apricots—no more than five hundred each. Because the peach trees were proving poorly suited to the climate, he would soon graft them to plums. He also had almonds, fifty varieties in 1859, and numerous European grape varieties as well as the American Isabella and Catawba.

By 1860, John had forty-eight acres of orchard and twelve of nursery in San Lorenzo. The orchard would eventually cover 117 acres and comprise "every variety of fruit and berry that thrives in the locality," and nuts, too—English walnut and American chestnut as well as almond. In his yard John planted a few orange and lemon trees, and even they produced well. The property was surrounded by "a beautiful hedge of Osage orange," whose spines were useful in keeping out cattle.

Alfred Luelling and Mary Campbell Luelling with their children. Courtesy of the Milwaukie Museum.

Like the Milwaukie Nursery, the Lewelling Nursery supplied other, smaller nurseries. In 1858 John sold one retail nursery nearly ten thousand three-year-old apple and pear trees.

John's business thrived so well that, in 1859, he was listed in the county assessor's book as among the forty-six richest persons in the county. With property valued at $10,385, however, John was near the bottom of the list, whereas his nephew Alfred, with sixteen acres in orchard and a worth of $13,700, was substantially higher up. (Henderson wasn't listed, because he had left the county.)

Despite the difficulties of establishing a home, nursery, and orchard in an unfamiliar country, John found time to take on civic responsibilities. In 1860 he was elected to the Alameda County Board of Supervisors and chosen its chairman. He would serve on the board for several terms, until his move to Napa. John was also appointed a guardian for the county, charged with protecting the well-being and finances of persons who couldn't care for themselves. His experience in leadership and service among Quakers easily translated to similar work for a broader, secular community.

Horticultural Societies and Fairs

The Yankee notion of advancing farming through collective effort spread westward from the 1820s on. Farmers shared ideas through journals, fairs, and voluntary organizations. Specialized journals—including *California Farmer* (1854 to 2013) and *Pacific Rural Press* (1871 to 1894)—were created specifically to serve farmers, and local and regional newspapers devoted much column space to agricultural news. Governments also supported farmers' interests, because what was good for the farmer was believed good for all.

In 1854, California legislators understood that gold mining wouldn't sustain the state's economy for long; the state's future wealth would depend on agriculture. So the legislature created the California State Agricultural Society and offered $5,000 for premiums awarded at the first state fair. That fair was held the same year, in the Music Hall at Bush and Montgomery streets in San Francisco. More than five thousand people attended. The next year, the society opened rooms in Sacramento "fitted up with a fine museum of natural science, and the full appliances of an Agricultural and Horticultural Reading Room." At the third state fair, in Stockton, more than fifty thousand people attended.

The Lewellings and their associates took full advantage of these developments. John Lewelling didn't get involved in the California State Agricultural Society right away. But Elias Beard became its first president, and Henderson and Alfred were both founding members. And the second state fair, held in Sacramento, featured a central display of "plates of Seckle pears, from Lewelling's Ranch, San Jose Mission." In 1856 the society sent a visiting committee to prominent fruit and flower nurseries, and John's was among those recognized. Four years later, John would represent Alameda County as a delegate to the California State Agricultural Society Convention.

Seth Luelling would also play a role in the California State Agricultural Fair. In 1859, he was among Oregon's delegates to the event. He entered apples, in both his name and William Meek's. Meek won first premium, Seth second, and Meek won another first premium for displaying the greatest number of varieties. Disregarding any concerns about temperance, Seth entered Meek's grape and currant wines and four bottles of his own wine. Of all the Oregon contributors, Seth had "the largest number of varieties of very fine fruit," though it had suffered from the ten-day trip by steamer—prolonged because Seth visited the Puget Sound along the way, probably selling apples and checking on his branch nursery at Steilacoom. After the fair, Seth visited Henderson and John and their families, and Elisha accompanied Seth on jaunts to San Francisco and Mission San José.

In 1857, "a large number of horticulturalists," perhaps frustrated by an emphasis on livestock at the state fair, met in San José to create the California Horticultural Society. They would hold their annual fair along with that of the Mechanics' Institute, an organization that promoted farming and manufacturing to bring wealth into California and keep it there. At the 1857 Mechanics and Horticultural Society Fair, held in San Francisco, exhibitors participated by invitation only. As one of the chosen fifty-eight, John presented apples, pears, plums, and peaches. He received a diploma—the highest honor—for his "magnificent display" of apples, in thirty-four varieties, a testament to his "skill and success as a practical horticulturist." He won second place for his six varieties of pears, which averaged a pound in weight (the biggest weighted 19.5 ounces). And he won a special premium for "Coe's Golden Drop—a very fine plum variety." The fair ran for three weeks and closed only because the State Agricultural Fair was about to open.

John would be an active member of the California Horticultural Society through its brief life. He became a vice president in 1858, and in 1859 he joined the committee on the names and synonyms of fruits, a group whose work was essential for sorting fair entries by cultivar for judging.

John exhibited again at the 1858 and 1859 horticultural society fairs, held in the Music Hall but apart from the Mechanics' Institute fair. In 1858, he won premiums for best specimens of summer apples, largest and best pear collection, best almond collection, and best currant jelly. At the third horticultural society fair he displayed not only thirty-four varieties of apple and twenty-five of pear but seven of plum, twelve of peach, three of nectarine, and two of apricot.

John didn't limit himself entirely to fruits. At the third California Horticultural Society fair, in 1859, he exhibited what the *Daily Alta California* (September 8, 1859) called "perhaps the most wonderful article" in the fair: a 115-pound "monster red beet." He had displayed it the prior fall, when it weighed just 42 pounds, and then he had put it back into the ground to produce seed. It had not, although it was "about four feet long and nearly a foot through." The reporter concluded that "California *beets* the world."

After 1857 the Mechanics' Institute held its fairs without fresh fruit exhibits. In 1859, however, Henderson Luelling participated in the Mechanics' Institute fair: He served as judge for "Preserved Meats and Vegetables, Pickles, Etc."

Alameda County created its own agricultural society in 1858. Henderson and Alfred were founding members; Henderson was vice president, Alfred a director. Two years later Alfred became a vice president and his uncle John was named a director. William Meek would also join the Alameda County Agricultural Society after his move to California. In 1866 he would become its president.

The Alameda County Agricultural Society held fairs of its own. At the county fair in 1859 John made "a very fine display of fruits," with eighteen varieties of grape, thirty-eight varieties of apple, twenty-three of pear, two of quince, one each of peach and prune, and dried fruits besides. Alfred exhibited, too, with thirty-four varieties of apple, eleven of pear, and an assortment of preserved fruits. In 1860 John won a premium at the Alameda fair for 'the handsomest and most prolific branch of cherries," with three hundred cherries along its two-foot length.

In 1860 the San Francisco Bay District Agricultural Society formed, and John was elected vice president for Alameda. The district held its first fair the same year. While Alfred won second place for his gooseberry jelly, John's fruit exhibit, with sixty-two varieties of apple, forty-three of pear, four of dried fruits, nine of almond, fifteen of cherries in spirits, and "cherry wine superb," topped the list in *California Farmer.* Besides winning premiums for his grapes and dried fruits, he also exhibited an enormous China Rose radish. It was "about a foot long, by six or eight inches in diameter."

At the Alameda fair John also won his first recognition as a fruit breeder, for the best seedling almond. This must have been Lewelling's Prolific. Although its fame grew slowly, by 1925 Lewelling's Prolific would be "one of the leading commercial varieties in California . . . grown in every district." It was liked for its heavy bearing and for the "sweet, pleasant flavor" of the kernels—although its large proportion of double kernels came to be seen as a shortcoming, since double kernels, in their yin-yang embrace, were considered deformed.

In 1858, California nursery growers formed a new kind of association—not for sharing knowledge but for regulating prices. High prices for pear fruit had inflated the demand for trees, until nurserymen were selling them for as much as six dollars each. Soon the market was flooded with high-priced trees. Hustlers bought up the leftovers, often labeling them incorrectly to suit demand, and peddled them by wagon. The growers who joined the association pledged that their trees would be sold only from their own grounds, at a price of two dollars for each year-old tree. John, who alone had grown a quarter of the trees for sale that year, was among the signers. So was Henderson. The "bootleggers" were forced out of business.

Oregon was a few years behind California in forming agricultural societies and fairs, but Seth Luelling was among the leaders of the movement. He was one of the growers who initiated, in 1857, what became the Multnomah County Agricultural Society. Several other Oregon counties formed horticultural societies in 1858, and that year Seth, Meek, and Henry Eddy were among the signers of a call for a "Pomological Convention." The following year Seth helped organize the Fruit Growers' Association of Oregon, with *Oregon Farmer* as its official organ. For a few years, according to one horticulturist, the journal's columns "were crowded with articles on fruit-growing, and the cards of nurserymen were numerous in its advertising columns." Seth served on a committee "to examine fruits in their proper season."

In 1861 the Fruit Growers' Association of Oregon merged with the Oregon State Agricultural Society, and the society held the first state fair, near Oregon City. Seth, for some reason, was not among the entrants; perhaps he was simply too busy. But he was certainly involved later, and by 1865 he was serving on the society board. At quarterly horticultural meetings around the state, members displayed fruits and flowers in decorated halls, read and discussed papers, and took excursions into the countryside. Seth regularly entered both fresh fruits and preserves in the annual fair, which the state began funding in 1864.

Henderson didn't join his brothers and son in exhibiting at the fairs. He may have been their mentor in the fruit business, but the pure joy that

John and Seth found in growing, propagating, breeding, and preserving fruits never seems to have infected Henderson. He was a businessman, and his business happened to be fruit. When he wasn't working, he dwelt in the realm of ideas. And Henderson had big ideas.

Chapter 9 Folly and Glory

> The road to the bottomless depths of humbug is well greased.
>
> —Frederick Marriott, editor, *California Mail Bag*

Henderson must have been delighted when, in 1858, regular ferry service began between Brooklyn and San Francisco. The city offered much stimulation for a reformist mind, especially one steeped in the wisdom of Andrew Jackson Davis. As early as 1852, spirit rappers, mediums, mesmerists, magnetic healers, and Spiritualist lecturers flocked to the city. In 1856 two brothers opened a store to sell Spiritualist newspapers and "clairvoyant medicines" and to arrange bookings for spirit mediums. By 1857 a Spiritualist congregation had formed around one Nelson J. Underwood, who lectured in San Francisco and Sacramento while purportedly in a trance, claiming he was learning from spirits to turn carbon into diamonds.

The Harmonial Brotherhood Colony

Henderson must have met E. S. Tyler soon after the latter's arrival in town early in the spring of 1859. "Dr." Tyler was "a middle-aged, benevolent-looking man, with a ferocious head of hair and a patriarchal pair of whiskers," according to a reporter for the *San Francisco Golden Era*. Tyler aimed to create a Harmonial Brotherhood community in the Central American wilderness. This got Henderson's attention. If Tyler succeeded, his community would far surpass the Harmonial Philosophy society that Henderson had tried to organize in Milwaukie. This new organization would be not a club but a colony, run according to Andrew Jackson Davis's principles.

Unfortunately, Henderson didn't take time to investigate Tyler's past. In Michigan, Tyler had been expelled from the Methodist ministry for having improper relations with an "adopted daughter." Then, while

Henderson Luelling. From Gaston, *Centennial History of Oregon*.

working as a blacksmith in Illinois, he had boarded a prostitute in his family's house, supposedly to reform her, but he got her pregnant instead. Next he left with his prostitute-turned-mistress for Kansas, where he shot somebody, possibly the mistress. Back in Illinois, he collected money for anti-slavery settlers in "bleeding Kansas," but he kept the money for himself. Then he went to upstate New York, where he lectured on Spiritualism, free love, and clairvoyance. With the wife of the family that boarded him, he fled to Berlin Heights, Ohio, and started a free-love commune there. At this point he began calling himself Dr. Tyler. With his new mistress, he tried to set up a water-cure establishment in a hotel in town, but he and his companions were arrested. He escaped to New York, where he advertised his services as a clairvoyant and "psychometric physician" and attempted to start the Equitable Emigration Association, with the goal of occupying one or more Pacific islands and experimenting with "Social Democracy." Attracting little interest in New York, he finally sailed for San Francisco.

There Henderson discovered him, and began to redirect his own life.

Henderson may never before have given much thought to free love, but the concept must have been at least vaguely familiar to him. It was fashionable among more radical reformists. For them, free love meant the freedom to enter and leave a monogamous relationship at will, without government regulation. At a time when laws regarding marriage, property, and divorce allowed men to turn their wives into near-slaves, free love attracted interest from feminists, who saw it as a defense against tyrannical, violent, and alcoholic husbands—and who sometimes failed to consider the vulnerability of mothers and children when fathers exercised the same freedom. To Andrew Jackson Davis, free lovers were advocates of reform in marriage and divorce laws, with the goal of securing each woman's control of her person, children, and home.

More likely than not, Henderson was already a free love advocate. He may have applied the philosophy—or had it applied against him—in his separation from Betsey Ann. He may have promoted free love to his children; his family was extremely rare in that two of his daughters would obtain divorces. Henderson may also have considered free love in regard to his current marriage to a woman who had no interest in founding a colony in the tropics and whose unmarried adult daughters may have presented a temptation to their stepfather.

To most people, free love meant more or less what it meant in the 1960s: sexual infidelity, if not promiscuity. Most who commented on it believed it to be an abomination, and even Spiritualists usually forswore it. Male advocates of the philosophy were thought disingenuous, and most probably were. So the press didn't look kindly on Henderson's Harmonial Brotherhood adventure. And only the press told the story; Henderson didn't defend himself in print or in any surviving letters. Still, the main events seem clear.

In the fall of 1859—probably even before Seth's visit to Alameda County, although Seth's diary doesn't mention it—Henderson sold nearly all of Fruit Vale, at a loss, to John Weller, then governor of California. *California Farmer* (February 17, 1860) judged Weller lucky: The "splendid farm and orchard" were "in a highly cultivated condition and one of the finest locations in Alameda County." With the money from the sale, Henderson bought a ship, the schooner *Santiago*, and hired a crew. After considering several possible places to settle in Latin America, Tyler and Henderson decided on Honduras, because the government there wouldn't require the immigrants to become Catholics.

Henderson brought along as many of his intimates as he could. Levi, Albert, and Oregon probably had no choice but to come along. Henderson's housekeeper joined the group, as did his personal secretary, a man named Brooks—and Brooks's wife and two of their children.

Some of the passengers were rather new acquaintances for Henderson. There was Tyler's wife, "who dressed in the extreme of the bloomer fashion." Another man was a debtor, who after boarding the ship hid himself from police officers by crawling under Mrs. Brooks's skirts. In total, the company included ten men, five women, and six or seven children.

Some people Henderson may have hoped would travel with him decided not to join the expedition. Alfred and Mary, who so far had four children (including an infant, born in August), declined to come along. The Brookses swore a writ of habeas corpus to compel their sixteen-year-old daughter to accompany them, but the girl showed the court a vial of strychnine and said she would swallow it if she were forced to get on the ship. The judge set her free. Henderson's current wife, Mary, refused to go as well. Finding herself and her children about to become homeless, she filed a writ *de lunatico inquirendo*, to require an investigation into her husband's sanity.

Santiago set sail on or about October 5—approximately five days after Seth left San Francisco for Oregon. To escape his wife and the authorities, Henderson hid himself before the ship left the wharf, and then took a yawl to meet the ship as it was passing through the Golden Gate.

Aboard the ship, the passengers soon began squabbling, mainly over food. Henderson had stocked provisions for the Harmonial Diet, a thing apparently of his own invention. Andrew Jackson Davis believed that everyone should eschew alcohol, opium, tobacco, and overeating, but that otherwise individuals should eat according to their instincts. The Harmonial Diet echoed not Davis's ideas but Sylvester Graham's. Sugar, coffee, tea, and animal foods were forbidden. "The principal food," according to a reporter, "consisted of coarse flour, apparently ground up with chaff, straw and all." The provisions didn't improve anyone's mood. Some dug into secret stores of coffee, tea, and salt pork, or sneaked them from the crew's larder. Others witnessed these infractions and complained. The crew began calling their passengers the Discordant Devils and their project Free Love Hell.

By the time the ship stopped on the Oaxacan coast, Henderson and Tyler could hardly stand each other. In the village of La Ventosa, Henderson bought "six or eight dozen" eggs. Tyler, unaware of the purchase, paid for them over again. The two men fought over ownership of the eggs, and their comrades took sides. The next day Henderson made a speech about the egg dispute, his words directed, he said, "by the most highest wisdom and came from the interior essence of his soul." Tyler, unimpressed with this Quakerish piety, swore that he would get even.

The ship sailed on to Tiger Island, a volcanic cone in the Gulf of Fonseca, Honduras. Neither Tiger Island nor any of the neighboring islands proved satisfactory for their needs, so the group sailed about sixty miles up a river on the mainland. But they had few supplies and nowhere to buy what they needed. The water may have been polluted. Although the company arrived in "the healthiest season"—with the least mosquito activity, presumably—several got sick and soon died. If malaria was the cause, no one treated it with quinine. "These radical reformers," wrote the reporter, "do not believe in medicines at all, but treat all diseases of what kind soever they may be with cold water. They took Mrs. C., while raging with the fever, wrapped her up in a wet blanket till she perspired profusely, and then threw cold water over her. The speedy result was her death." Now the colonists were short not only of goods but of people. Someone suggested they try to recruit a group of healthy German girls "to improve the stock."

But the colony was breaking up. Tyler and his wife "had seceded; others had left, and several were waiting every opportunity to get away." Two of Henderson's sons and the Brooks family, parents and children, were ailing. The group set sail for the coast.

On the way back to San Francisco, in July of 1860, the ship was wrecked at Mazatlán. Fortunately, the passengers survived. They made their separate ways home.

Henderson was now a laughingstock, throughout California and beyond; an article about "the Free-Love Colony" had been reprinted around the country. Although other members of the company were identified only by initials, Henderson was named and described. His failure was ridiculed as proof of "the folly and wickedness" of the "pestilent doctrine" of free love.

So Henderson went under cover. In the 1860 census he was listed as Henry Lewelling, born in England and living adjacent to Alfred and Mary, their four children, and their six laborers. I'm amused to think of Henderson putting on a British accent for the census taker. With him, "Henry" reported, lived seventeen-year-old George, a native of western Canada. This was probably George Lee, Mary Warren's son by her first husband.

Levi, Albert, and Oregon are all missing from the 1860 census. Perhaps they were in transit to homes of their older siblings. (In the 1870 census, Levi would be living with his sister Rachel and her husband, Seth Eddy, and Albert would be living with Asenath and her husband, John Bozarth.)

Theresa Lee, Mary Warren's younger daughter, was in Stockton with her new husband, C. C. Calvert, at the time of the 1860 census. Her obituary, written in 1911, said that Henderson Luelling was her first husband. Could it be that Theresa was Henderson's free-love wife during the voyage to Honduras? Did their relationship perhaps begin even earlier? Could Theresa have been William Henderson's birth mother? This is all a mystery. Perhaps the obituary writer erred.

Henderson never recovered his fortune, but he retained some of his spunk. His rambling itch got the better of him again in 1862, after the discovery of gold in what would soon be Idaho Territory (it would be carved out of Washington Territory the following year). There, gold was found first along the Clearwater River, in 1860, and then along the Salmon River, in 1861. In the spring of 1862, fifty-three-year-old Henderson visited Milwaukie with Alfred and Albert. The three "started to the mines," according to Seth's diary, on May 4. (John's son Eli may have gone along or left separately, because Alfred returned with him.) Seth didn't record their winnings, but they missed the Idaho mother lode, in Boise Basin. That was discovered by George Grimes, Phebe's son, about three months later. (Gold didn't make even George Grimes rich. He was murdered within a few days of the discovery—by Indians, supposedly, or perhaps by one of his own party—and buried in a prospect hole.)

Back in California, Henderson maintained a low profile, keeping his name out of the newspapers and the city directories. He could have found plenty of work in the orchards in and around Fruit Vale, especially before Alfred and his family moved back to Oregon, in 1862 (the same year as the gold-mining trip to Idaho). But at some point Henderson returned to merchandizing. In 1866, he was a storekeeper in Brooklyn Township. In 1868, he was living and working as a merchant in San Francisco.

Henderson's abandoned wife, Mary, raised their son, William Henderson, with help from her own family if not from the elder Henderson (the 1870 census shows Mary and her youngest child sharing a house with Mary's daughter Theresa, her husband, and their children). Somehow, Henderson retained the respect of both mother and child. Mary didn't divorce Henderson until 1876, and she went by Mary Luelling until her death, in 1893. She called her youngest child Henderson, not William. As an adult, he went by "Henderson W. Luelling" or just "Henderson Luelling."

Strangely, by 1866 Henderson the elder was calling *himself* "William Henderson Luelling." Was he still trying to disguise his identity, or was he honoring his brother William, who had died in 1847?

The Birth of Cherryland

While Henderson was trying to create his utopian community in Honduras, William Meek was dreaming of a new life in California. Meek had visited California in the summer of 1854. He probably had business in San Francisco, but he also visited his in-laws, Sarah Stone's family. Silas Stone and Susannah Ward Stone had come west in 1853, in a wagon train led by their son Albert. They brought with them the five youngest of their eleven children and, presumably, Meek's daughter, Sarah Charlotte, who turned eight in 1854 (she would later be known as Lottie). The family settled in the San Ramon Valley—or, more specifically, in what became known as Stone Valley, east of the Oakland Hills and west of Mount Diablo. Silas Stone became alcalde (mayor) for the area.

Though Sarah Meek could have had no memory of her father, he took her back to Oregon. Once there, instead of keeping her with him in Milwaukie, he lodged her in Salem with a Mr. Willoughbey, who must have assumed responsibility for her education. Today Salem is an hour's drive from Milwaukie, but in 1854 the trip must have taken days, so Meek couldn't have seen his daughter often.

In the fall of 1855, Meek drafted a letter to Fidelia Stone, now a young woman of twenty-two, who had cared for Sarah in her infancy. He expressed his longing for Sarah—or, at least, his guilt at having abandoned her for a second time. "The rainy season is now on hard and the worst task is getting her home from Mr. Willoughbey, and another thing she is most to small to travel with much without another's company." And then he told Fidelia he was coming to California again, with Sarah, and confessed his desire for a wife:

> It is now four years lacking a few days since the death of my companion and I have not even kept company with any lady since. Neither do I intend to until I see you or hear that you are married. . . . I feel duty bound to you and Mary Anne for your cares and troubles towards my only child my dear sweet one, and on my return to Oregon I shall feel much disappointed if one of you does not accompany me home.

The letter was a rough draft, so perhaps Meek amended the last sentence in the final version. Or maybe Fidelia was unfazed by the news that Meek would be as happy with her younger sister's lifelong companionship as with her own. In either case, when Meek went to California in January 1856 Fidelia married him, and she accompanied Meek and Sarah back to Oregon. This wife, Meek's fourth, would stick around long enough to bear five children and outlive Meek by eleven years. Their first two children, Horry and Silas, were born in Milwaukie.

But the family didn't stay in Oregon long. Perhaps Meek anticipated better money-making opportunities in California. Still, his orchard business was thriving. Meek now co-owned, with Henry and Jane Eddy, a farm of 1,600 acres. According to the *Sacramento Daily Union* (June 18, 1859),

> There are fifty acres of orchard and nursery grounds. Forty thousand feet of lumber were used last year for making fruit boxes. . . . This year their business will require sixty thousand feet of lumber. From 36,000 to 38,000 bushels of fruit were raised last year, 800 of which were cherries, pears, and plums. The gross sales last year, above all freights and commissions after the fruit left Portland, were $30,000. The year before they were $20,000.

Maybe the reasons for leaving Oregon weren't financial at all. Perhaps Fidelia missed her parents and siblings, and Meek wanted a new adventure. Perhaps letters from Henderson lured Meek to California. In any case, in August 1859 he offered his share in the farm to Henry Miller

William Meek.
From Wood, *History of Alameda County, California.*

and Joseph Lambert, the husband of Henry's daughter Clementine. Lambert and Miller paid Meek $500 down, and Meek held the mortgage for a balance of $24,075. It would take them eight years to repay the loan.

Other Oregonians owed Meek money, too—about $25,000, in total, including the $5,000 loan to Henry Eddy. Meek arranged with a local bank to manage his financial affairs. For a time he was discrete about his wealth; in the 1860 census, he would report a personal estate of only $1,000.

When the 1859 harvest season was over, Meek and his family sailed to California and moved into a house beside the Stones'. Fidelia's brother Lysander Stone, who had accompanied Meek on the Overland Trail and then left Oregon to raise cattle in Colusa, California, moved in with his parents at about the same time. Together the two friends searched for farmland, probably with recommendations or referrals from John or Alfred. Lysander bought a 250-acre parcel on the present border between Oakland and San Leandro. Meek chose land in San Lorenzo, right across the creek from John Lewelling's.

Meek bought 400 acres to start, from Henry Walker Crabb, who would later grow grapes, along with John, in St. Helena. Soon thereafter

Meek bought 1,600 acres more. He would ultimately own 3,000 acres in the area. At first he grew grain—wheat, barley, and corn—and raised sheep and dairy cattle. But after several years he was again harvesting fruit. In 1864 he would have 260 acres in orchard. Meek would follow John's example in emphasizing cherries and currants; in 1864 he would have 4,200 cherry trees and 225,000 currant plants, along with 3,000 plum trees. That year he would also sell 20,000 almond trees and plant 7,000 more. He would also raise tobacco, citrus, and race horses. He would have sixty to seventy-five horses working a single field at a time. Horticulture would be Eden Township's leading industry, and Meek would be the "first farmer" of the township, not in time but in land and wealth.

For a while, John and Meek would share fame as San Lorenzo cherry and currant farmers. As another cherry grower later remembered, "More than three fourths of all the cherries in the State were grown in the vicinity of the little Town of San Lorenzo . . . and the greater part of these in the orchards of Messrs. Meek and Lewelling." "The San Lorenzo fruit district," according to the *Daily Alta California* (June 23, 1873), "has more cherry trees and current bushes than any other equal area in the State or the United States." The *Los Angeles Evening Star*, on September

San Lorenzo in 1878, when Eli, not John, operated the farm. Meek's driveway and house are indicated at the lower right. From Thompson and West, *Official Historical Atlas Map of Alameda County, California*.

Meek's house and farm in San Lorenzo. From Thompson and West, *Official Historical Atlas Map of Alameda County, California.*

17, 1880, referred to "the mammoth yield of the famous orchard of Meek and Lewelling," as if Meek and Lewelling were partners.

By this time, however, the Lewelling of San Lorenzo was Eli, not John. In 1885, Eli and Meek would be among the first farmers to ship cherries, and gooseberries and currants as well, to New York by rail. When Californians understood that they could raise fruit, even soft fruit, for the entire country, a rash of orchard planting followed. (Seth Lewelling's Oregon nursery would benefit from the tree-planting boom.)

Today a large subdivision of Meek's former estate is the unincorporated community of Cherryland. It includes Meek's Italianate mansion—it cost him $20,000 in 1870, plus $5,000 for the furniture—and the grounds immediately around it, now maintained as a wedding venue by the Hayward Area Parks and Recreation District. Meek landscaped the grounds with plants he bought from Seth Luelling.

I don't know how much John and Meek and their families socialized together or cooperated in business. Certainly they could visit easily, by crossing the little wooden bridge over San Lorenzo Creek, just in front of Meek's house. In any case, they shared a graveyard; the San Lorenzo

Meek's house in 2022.
Photo by the author.

cemetery extended into both their adjoining parcels. The Lewellings interred fifteen-year-old Silas there in 1860, and in 1862 the Meeks buried near him their own Silas, or "Siley," who was just three years old. In 1864 John and Meek donated the land to the San Lorenzo Cemetery Association, along with money for care of the graveyard. The three-and-a-half-acre parcel would accommodate two generations of Meeks, Stones, and Lewellings, along with San Lorenzo farmers and farmworkers from as far away as Ireland, Portugal, Denmark, China, and Japan.

Chapter 10
Seth

> In the whole range of cares and pleasures belonging to the garden, there is nothing more truly interesting than the production of new varieties of fruit.
>
> —Charles Downing, *Selected Fruits*

From 1854 on, Seth Luelling kept small, leather-bound annual diaries. He used them mainly for tracking business transactions. He recorded hours his employees worked, sometimes with long rows of close vertical tally marks, and what kinds of work they did—hoeing, spading, "grubbing" (uprooting stumps), grafting, digging up young trees, making cider or sausage, and so on. He noted purchases and sales and shipments. Seth recorded loans to neighbors and friends and amounts he borrowed himself. He made notes on the weather ("I heard the Frogs hollow to Night for the first time Since the turn of winter."). He noted when he began budding trees or harvesting fruit or working on the mill race, and whose shoes or boots he made or mended.

Seth also recorded personal information, including houseguests, letters received and sent, hunting outings, and books ordered and read. Although the entries are brief, and although they almost never impart emotion, reading through the surviving diaries provides a touching portrait of one Oregon farmer's life from the 1850s through the 1870s.

1855 to 1861

In the spring of 1855, Seth noted, he painted a cradle. He did not say whom the cradle was for. But about six weeks before, Clarissa had given birth to her last child and only son, William Anton. Seth would call him, in his diaries, first Willey and later Willie. When Willie was ten, Seth would build him a playhouse.

Seth Luelling. From the *Eighth Biennial Report of the Oregon State Board of Horticulture*, 1905.

Seth grew vegetables for the family. He planted garden peas and noted when squirrels and birds dug them up. He experimented with uncommon crops for Oregon: Mexican peas (chickpeas), Japan peas (soybeans), and snake (Armenian) cucumbers. He grew popcorn and tobacco, and potatoes between the rows in the orchard. He yoked his goose and put it in the garden, probably to eat the grass. He noted one day in June 1868 as "a fine day for killing weeds." Seth designed his own hoe and filed for a patent on it.

Seth picked berries, probably the wild *Rubus ursinus*, or trailing blackberry, then as common as the invasive Himalayan blackberry is today. He may also have encountered *R. laciniatus*, the Eurasian evergreen or cutleaf blackberry, which birds were already spreading through the Pacific Northwest.

In 1859 Seth acquired from a man in Oregon City Scotch broom, a shrub now considered a noxious weed on both U.S. coasts. He probably sold it widely.

The same year, Seth planted filberts, today a major crop for Oregon. They did not lessen his taste for native hazelnuts. One year he noted when he and Willie went “hazle nutting,” filling their socks with the little wild nuts. He used hazel shoots, too, as stakes for young trees.

In 1859 or earlier Seth began keeping bees. He was among the earliest beekeepers in area, but not the first: Various people had brought honeybees to Oregon during the 1850s, and in 1858 the state had 338 hives. He noted when the bees swarmed and when he caught swarms. In 1864 he mentioned hunting for wild bees; honeybees must have naturalized by then. He built an observation hive.

Seth undoubtably valued bees more for their wax than for their honey. He needed plenty of wax for grafting. He mixed his own grafting compound, probably by heating the beeswax with rosin and either linseed oil or tallow. Henderson and their father had probably used the same recipe.

Seth went fishing and hunting, even after becoming a vegetarian (his workers probably ate the prey). He made a trap for catching trout. He hunted with Henry Eddy, William Meek, and Ross Merrick, and on his own. He killed deer and grouse. One time he killed a “wildcat”—a bobcat—and had the skin tanned. In 1874 he was selling deerskins as well as skins from his own flock of sheep.

Along with work, there was entertainment. In 1859, Seth went to the circus, twice. The second time he took his children.

Seth and Clarissa welcomed house guests. They included, in 1859, William Mills and his wife, Rachel Fisher Mills—the same Rachel Fisher who had journeyed from Iowa with Henderson and his family—and Henderson’s daughter Asenath and her husband, John Bozarth.

Seth was a strong believer in education. He voted, in 1859, to support the building of a new schoolhouse. For many years, he served as a trustee of the new school. He even cleaned the stovepipe. In the evenings the schoolhouse served as a community education center.

At a meeting at the Milwaukie schoolhouse in April 1860, Seth made a list of seven Harmonial Philosophy books, which he subsequently ordered from Andrew Jackson Davis himself. “Exciting times,” he wrote in his journal. I don’t know whether Seth read any of Davis’s books while Henderson was in Oregon, but now he and Clarissa were becoming ardent Spiritualists.

Disasters, Natural and Familial

On December 5, 1861, Seth noted the “highest water in Willamette ever known by whites.” The Willamette flood was part of a rare weather event that inundated California, Nevada, Utah, Idaho, Arizona, and Sonora over the winter of 1861–62. California suffered most; the Central Valley became an inland sea for several months, and in San Lorenzo John's orchard was under two feet of water for a time. But damages were substantial in Oregon, too. The flood destroyed whole towns, such as Champoeg; carried away mills, a bridge, a foundry, warehouses, a hotel, and houses from Oregon City; and covered the second floor of Milwaukie's Standard Mill, which had been built in 1858 and was already famous for its pure white flour.

For Seth's family, more troubles followed. His sixteen-year-old daughter Elva became very sick, perhaps from water contamination resulting from the flood. The year before, she had married William Bradbury, partner with Henry Eddy and Joseph Kellogg in the Standard Mill. William Bradbury must have brought Elva home to her parents so they could care for her. On January 3, 1862, Seth noted that Elva suffered about thirty seizures, which were probably caused by dehydration or meningitis. Although he failed to note it in his diary, she died the same day. (William Bradbury would later marry Henderson's daughter Hannah, after her divorce from her first husband.)

About a month after Elva's death, her younger sister Alice became sick, also with fever and seizures. Alice hung on for two months, with her father at her bedside much of the time, before she sank away entirely on May 1. She was twelve years old. Later Seth would name his Sweet Alice apple for his youngest daughter.

While Alice was dying, Willey came down with measles. Fortunately, he recovered.

Seth's journal doesn't describe Elva's funeral, but Alice's was thoroughly Spiritualist. Mrs. Butler, a well-known medium from Portland, presided. She "gave a beautiful discours while in a trans state," Seth noted.

The middle daughter of the family, Addie, probably stayed well for a time only because she was at boarding school in Portland, although she came home briefly to see Elva just before she died. A month after Alice's death, however, Seth brought Addie home sick. Happily, Addie, like Willie, got well.

Shaken by the deaths and near-deaths of their children, Seth and Clarissa dove deeper into Spiritualism. On June 29 Seth "heared a Spiritual lecture." In August he and Clarissa held a circle at their house. That evening a Mr. Conkrite prophesied about the ongoing Civil War, as Seth wrote in his journal:

> He says that Richmond will not be taken. that Ohio will be invaded by the South. that Lyncoln will be assassinated by a parince. . . . that Boston will be utterly distroid. that neither North nor South will conquer that England will acknowledge the South in less than 6 months & then the whole world will go to war. that the hardest fighting will be at San Francisco. . . . that Queen Victoria will fly to Newyork & will marry in Newyork. that Lyncoln & McClelland are Both illegitimate children

Although Seth recorded the prophecy in unusual detail, he noted no opinion about it. Perhaps he decided to reserve judgment until he could check whether the man's statements proved true. If he thought Conkrite a little crazy, this didn't put him off Spiritualism. Mrs. Butler visited the house in November, and the following September Seth, and probably Clarissa, went to a camp meeting, probably the Spiritualists' meeting in the yew grove at Woodburn Station.

In becoming Spiritualists, the Luellings weren't extreme among Oregonians. As W. G. Lawson, a Salem lawyer, wrote in 1860 to the *Banner of Light* (the longest lasting and most influential of the many Spiritualist journals published in the United States),

> Oregon for many years has been developing mediums, and distributing the literature of Spiritualism. I estimate the number of Spiritualists at about one-fifth of the population that can vote. There are two societies in the State doing well. But our greatest progress in in private circles. I venture to state it as a fact, that every one, once known as a free-thinker, and all who do not belong to some orthodox church, are now confirmed Spiritualists.

C. A. Reed, another Salem Spiritualist, wrote to the *Banner of Light*, in 1867, even more triumphantly: "To-day I may venture to affirm that nearly one-half the people [in Oregon] are believers in the essential doctrines of Spiritualism." However much Lawson and Reed may have exaggerated, being a Spiritualist in Oregon, in the 1860s, was only mildly eccentric.

Going Vegetarian

At about this time, Seth and Clarissa adopted for their household a severely restricted diet. The new regimen must have begun sometime after Christmas in 1863, since Seth noted that dinner that day featured roast pig (perhaps at this point Christmas felt holier than other days). The diet was much like that prescribed by Sylvester Graham except that it allowed milk and sugar. Although Seth did not give up hunting or fishing, he and Clarissa used no animal food except milk. When the family cow was dry, they drank water; apparently they swore off alcohol as well as meat, butter, eggs, fish, and oysters. (Yet in the fall of 1864 Seth bought fifty gallons of wine from a neighbor. Perhaps he planned to distill it and sell the spirits? A recipe for grape brandy is tucked into the diary.) They also banned spices, tea, coffee, baking soda, and baking powder from the house. They no longer made vinegar from their apples, because, Clarissa believed, "a substance which would eat its way through the bottom of a tin can would eat its way through a human stomach." They spurned refined flour as well. Although Seth had once raised his own wheat, now he would buy a wagonload each year and have it ground between stones at Philip Foster's Eagle Creek mill, seventeen miles from Milwaukie. Clarissa made breads, pies, and cakes from flour with every particle of its bran. The couple did indulge in sweeteners; Seth bought both sugar and corn syrup by the barrel. Perhaps sugar and syrup, in their minds, retained some of their old medicinal reputation.

The regimen included daily, early-morning cold shower-baths, "with water freshly pumped from the kitchen well." The baths were followed by "a vigorous rubbing" with a coarse linen towel "beside a glowing stove." Even while camping at the state fair, Seth and Clarissa didn't skip their shower-baths; they bathed in a shed beneath a watering can. Sylvester Graham would have thoroughly approved.

According to a November 3, 1876, article in *Willamette Farmer*, the family had practiced this regimen for thirteen years, and during this period they had been free from disease, "while all were more or less ailing previously." Seth hadn't mentioned in his diaries, in the early 1860s, that either he or his wife was sickly, except to note that he gave Clarissa "an Emmettick" while Alice was dying. But Clarissa told the reporter that she had been an invalid, unable to get "permanent relief from doctors or medicine." Seth said he had more strength and better health in 1876 than he had had thirteen years before. Although a boarder left in 1873 because she "could not Stand the diet," Seth and Clarissa would carry on this regimen for the rest of their lives.

1863 to 1870

Seth and his family continued taking evening classes at the Milwaukie school. They attended, at various times, Spelling School, Music School, and Reading School. At Reading School in 1864, Seth "read the 1st peace that I ever Read in public."

The couple spent other evenings socializing with neighbors, and often stayed the night at a friend's house before coming home. They went to parties and danced all night (I wonder when and how these former Quakers learned to dance). And they participated in more and more Spiritualist circles—in their own house, at the schoolhouse, at the Butlers', and in other homes in Milwaukie and Portland. In late 1864 Seth again recorded visions described during a circle: The warship *Atlanta* would be sunk in a storm, and Captain Stephen Kearny would battle and defeat the Mormons at Salt Lake. In 1866 Seth attended at least twelve circles.

Family members and friends were always welcome to join the circles. Henderson's son Levi, visiting in 1864, was "influenced," during a circle, "by 4 diferent spirits to talk." Fidelia Meek attended a circle in 1866, and the next winter Hannah Luelling, now divorced from her first husband, Walter Wood, and visiting with her brother Oregon Columbia Luelling, was influenced while participating in a circle at Seth and Clarissa's ("but they could not control her Speech," Seth noted; apparently Hannah experienced glossolalia). In a circle in 1868, William Meek's daughter, now called Lottie, "was influenced for some time." Hector Campbell attended at least one circle that year. In an 1869 circle both Willie and Alfred were influenced.

Seth enjoyed other pastimes, too. Outside of the circles, he visited neighbors to chat, to greet a new baby, and to see, at Jane and Henry Eddy's house, a new sewing machine. Seth bought his own sewing machine later the same year. He sewed Willey's pants and made Mother—he usually called Clarissa Mother—velvet slippers. He taught Willie how to make shoes. Seth spent days, in 1868, skating on the Standard Mill pond, whose ice, by January 19, was a foot thick.

The same year Seth "went to see first dirt moved" on the Oregon and California Railroad, which would pass close by his house in Milwaukie. Beginning the following year he would be able to ship trees by rail to Portland. But construction of the remaining track was slow. Three more years would pass before the railroad would reach through the Willamette Valley to Roseburg. The railroad wouldn't reach the California border until 1887.

Like his father and his brother Henderson, Seth was a healer. Some people came to the house to be doctored. Often Seth visited the sick and injured, including a man who fell off a scaffold at the Standard Mill.

Industrialization brought many such accidents. Seth noted when Henderson Eddy, Jane and Henry's eldest, fell into the vat at the tannery and nearly drowned. He noted when the "plank kiln caught fire at New Mill & it took all hands in town to Save it from utter distruction."

Seth wrote and received many letters. He corresponded occasionally with his brothers and with Meek, after the latter's move to California. Seth often wrote his nephews Eli and Elisha, in San Lorenzo, especially after Addie went off to school in Oakland, California, in 1866. During the several years that she studied at the Female College of the Pacific, Elisha apparently served as a guardian to his cousin, though Addie was already twenty years old on her arrival and Elisha only six years older. Seth frequently sent Elisha money, apparently for Addie's schooling, room and board, or both.

Some of their California relatives paid Seth and Clarissa long visits. In 1866 Elisha stayed for several weeks before accompanying Addie back to California. Only a few days after Elisha and Addie left, Hannah and Oregon Luelling, Henderson's children, arrived. They stayed for two months.

Seth and Clarissa's house was roomy enough, and the nursery and orchard earnings scant enough, that they took in paying boarders—employees, their spouses, and people who simply needed a place to stay for a time. Among them was one Mary. In 1868 Seth bought a "bathing tub"—a zinc- or copper-lined wood-encased bathtub, for $211—more than $4,600 in 2024 dollars, although assembly was required. Seth soldered and painted the tub just in time for Mary to take a tepid bath in it after giving birth. Her attentive landlord noted when Mary took a walk in the garden the next day. Two months later Seth babysat while Mary took a trip to Portland.

Henderson's son Levi Luelling, in 1868, apparently arrived as a houseguest but became another of Seth and Clarissa's paying boarders, and a farm employee as well. Seth made Levi a pair of boots.

Seth looked out for not only Henderson's children but also his grandchildren. When Andrew Eddy, Rachel and Seth Eddy's son, commenced some sort of higher education, at age twenty, Seth paid for three months of his schooling and gave him twenty-five dollars more "for his Pony & Rigging." The next year Seth hired Andrew.

Seth continued to enter fruit at the state fair, which after its first year was always held in Salem. Before the coming of the railroad, exhibiting at the fair was a full week's work—at a busy time of the year, during the apple and pear harvest and at prime planting time for trees and shrubs in Oregon. Seth had to gather and load the fruit, travel to Salem, guard the exhibit for days, and collect his premiums before heading back to Milwaukie.

Seth exhibited preserves as well as fresh fruit. Upon arriving home from the fair in 1868, he prepared for the next year's fair by making seven kinds of jelly. Two and a half weeks later, he completed *twenty-four* kinds of jelly. Seth even made cranberry jelly, though his diaries don't mention growing cranberries. He also baked bread to exhibit at the fair.

By 1870 Seth was canning whole fruit—plums, raspberries, and gooseberries—in water or syrup. Seth didn't mention taking his canned fruits to the fair, but he sent jars to Addie and Dale.

Seth and Clarissa happily ignored the old Quaker prohibition against music. In 1866 Seth bought Addie a melodeon, a kind of pump organ, and paid for her music lessons. In 1870 he rented a piano. This was just over a month before Addie married and left for California with her husband, James Dale Smith, so perhaps Seth or Clarissa intended to learn to play. Seven years later Seth would buy them a piano of their own. It would be shipped around Cape Horn, and it would cost Seth a thousand dollars.

The day after Addie and James's wedding, Seth turned fifty.

Paradise Lost

Horticulture, in Oregon, got harder. Between 1860 and the early 1890s, the Oregon fruit business collapsed. California farmers had been importing thousands of young trees and root grafts and multiplying them into millions. By 1859, California had nearly forty professional nurseries. Now the state was an exporter of fruits—not only to the Eastern states, but also to the Northwest. "California sent us apples, pears, cherries, plums, prunes, apricots, grapes, and berries a month or two earlier than we could produce them," wrote James R. Cardwell, a Portland dentist who apparently cared more about horticulture than about teeth. Steamers left Portland for San Francisco with only a few boxes each of the late winter varieties—Newtown Pippin, Winesap, Red Cheek Pippin, Genet, and Red Romanite. With no long-distance railroads and with ocean shipping both expensive and unreliable, Oregon orchardists seldom shipped even dried fruits. Nurserymen could no longer afford to advertise, so in 1863 the *Oregon Farmer* ceased publication.

Fruit prices fell so low in Oregon that each year thousands of bushels rotted on the ground, and thousands more were fed to livestock. Many farmers neglected their orchards; they stopped pruning, stopped mending fences, let the weeds and brush grow, and let the cattle and pigs have their fill of the fruit. This was before the spread of blights and pests through the Willamette Valley. Fruit farming fruit would get even harder.

While less committed farmers fled the fruit business, Seth Luelling was a holdout. He never stopped growing apples. But he did stop propagating the more finicky cultivars. Whereas in 1854 the Luelling and Meek catalog included eighty varieties of apple, in 1870 Seth listed only thirty-seven (his fellow horticulturist Henry Miller believed that the list was still too long, and that only twenty-four varieties had proven excellent for the region).

Seth also concentrated more on other fruits. In late 1863 he shipped eighty-two boxes of pears to San Francisco and only fifty-eight boxes of apples. He planted more cherries and peaches and plums, including, the Italian prune, the Peach Plum'(or, more likely, George Walling's seedling Late Peach Plum, with its finer, greenish-yellow flesh), and, eventually, his own Golden Prune. He planted mahaleb and mazzard cherries for rootstock in 1860, though he was still digging wild cherries in late 1863. The list of cherries in his catalog approximately doubled from 1854 to 1870.

Seth also experimented with more exotic fruits. He was grafting persimmons, according to his diary, in 1872, soon after the Japanese persimmon was introduced to California. In 1877 he noted that he "wrote to Iowa for persimmon trees." Perhaps he planned to graft Japanese persimmon scions onto American persimmon rootstock. He also sold almond trees—including Lewelling's Prolific, his brother John's creation—although almonds have never produced reliably in Oregon, because the trees bloom too early in spring.

And Seth became known as a fruit breeder.

The Black Republican and His Cherry

In 1860, Seth eyed an accidental cherry seedling and decided to let it grow up. Several years later, the big, black, firm fruits convinced him that the tree was a keeper. He thought the seed came from a Black Eagle cherry tree, but otherwise he didn't know the parentage. Calling the tree Black Republican, Seth set about propagating it.

This wasn't the first time Seth had selected a seedling tree as a new cultivar. He had already propagated the Luelling cherry, which he would sell in substantial quantities from 1870 on. Likewise of unknown parentage, the Luelling was a large black cherry with solid flesh. The Black Republican had the same qualities, but it was even bigger and firmer.

Seth wanted the new variety to get noticed, fast. So in 1864 he arranged for three other nurserymen, in Vancouver, Lake Oswego, and East Portland, to graft scions of the new cherry to rootstock and to introduce the Black Republican to the public. They would give him half the proceeds of sales, about five hundred dollars in total.

The editor of the *Portland Daily Bulletin* described the big, sweet new cherry in 1870: "Many of the cherries shown us were three and a half inches in circumference. The skin is black (wherefore the name) and the pulp firm, of a reddish color, and cuts like an apple—no juice flowing from it when the knife passes through. When the stem is pulled from a cherry, no juice comes from the cavity left."

Seth sent a pound of the cherries—forty-four fruits—to Philadelphia's Centennial International Exhibition in 1876, along with six pears. He won the world's premium for the finest and largest of both cherries and pears. The cherry's offspring, Bing, would eventually be recognized as both bigger and better than the Black Republican, but only marginally so (both were taken for plums at the Trans-Mississippi Exposition at Omaha in 1898).

The Black Republican cherry. From the US Department of Agriculture Pomological Watercolor Collection.

Because the Black Republican was firm and long-keeping, it was an excellent shipper, and it was widely planted in California as well as Oregon. Seth ended up making more money from the Black Republican than from any other new fruit tree he introduced. (His brother John, however, was not entirely impressed with the Black Republican, which in 1879 he ranked fourth among cherries, with the Black Tartarian at the top of the list.)

The name of Seth's new cherry left little doubt about his political views. Clearly, the term *Black Republican* made Seth bristle. Democrats and No-Nothings used it from 1854 on against Radical Republicans, War Democrats, John C. Frémont, and anyone else who supported the overthrow of the Confederacy and the immediate abolition of slavery. Asahel Bush, editor of thc Salem *Statesman*, used the term to associate

Republicans and anti-slavery Democrats with blackness in two senses, with Negroes and with evil—the evil, to Bush's mind and many others, of racial equality and interracial marriage. Like most Oregonians, Bush opposed extending slavery to Oregon, but he also scorned abolitionists. Most of all, he aimed to keep Black people out of Oregon. He promoted his views through vitriolic editorials.

Bush and his Democratic "Salem Clique" dominated Oregon territorial politics. They called their critics within the party "soft" Democrats. Like many others on the lower Willamette, Seth was probably one of these softies. But although Seth was civically engaged before the Civil War, regularly clerking in elections and managing the Milwaukie school, his political activities were limited. They certainly were not radical. Seth may or may not have attended the first Republican gathering in Clackamas County, in January 1857, but he wasn't a delegate to Oregon's first statewide Republican convention, held in Albany the following month. It is easy to understand why. Seth must have known that the new party wasn't wholly opposed to slavery. Although some of the convention delegates were abolitionists and general social radicals, most were not. The Republicans' primary goal was taking power from the Salem Clique. Although the party also sought to establish a "free State constitution for Oregon," universal emancipation was not an objective. That the convention failed to nominate candidates further discouraged would-be supporters.

That year, 1857, was one of political turmoil. Oregon men had thrice voted against joining the Union, but after the U.S. Supreme Court declared, in *Dred Scot* v. *Sanford,* that only a sovereign state could prohibit slavery, voters overwhelmingly agreed, in June 1857, to hold a constitutional convention. The draft constitution outlawed slavery. In a separate clause, though, it also banned Black people from entering the state, from owning property, from making contracts, and from bringing suit. Convictions about race had changed little since 1849, when the territorial legislature had banned free Black people. That law would be rescinded five years later, after white citizens filed petitions to allow their Black neighbors to stay. Still, in November 1857 more Oregonians voted in favor of the exclusion clause than in favor of statehood itself. Congress would ratify both the constitution and the exclusion clause fifteen months later, making Oregon the first and only state to begin statehood with a constitution that excluded people of African descent.

In the meantime, Seth presumably stuck with the Democratic Party. He may have done so because Clackamas County Democrats were unusually progressive. In 1858 they nominated candidates through a direct primary election, forty-six years before Oregonians made the direct primary law. The same year, a group calling themselves the National Democrats boycotted the regular Democratic convention in Salem and held their own convention in Eugene. Their goal wasn't to abolish slavery but to defeat the Salem Clique. Regardless, Bush labeled the Nationals Black Republicans. The National Democratic candidates in Clackamas County repudiated their party's platform and adopted the Republican Party's in its place. Through most of the state, in fact, the Republicans and the National Democrats functioned as a coalition in 1858. Seth probably saw no reason to change parties.

In the spring of 1859, the Oregon Republicans began organizing as a permanent and independent party opposed to the Democrats. To strengthen their cause, they firmly renounced abolitionism. Thomas Dryer, the editor of the *Oregonian* and a longtime Whig, endorsed their platform and joined the party himself. He condemned both

> the ultraists for and the ultraists against slavery. Each branch of this class seems to have set up a Congo Negro as a fit subject or idol of their worship. We are none of this class and we speak for the Republican party of Oregon by authority, when we say that they do not compose either branch of this class.

Some of Dryer's readers were no doubt swayed by his words to join the new party, but Seth could not have been impressed.

After the war Seth occasionally attended precinct meetings and county conventions. These were Democratic, not Republican, gatherings. He joined Milwaukie's Grant Club, in 1868, to support the presidential candidacy of Ulysses S. Grant, of the National Union Party, which at this point was, in fact, the Republican Party under another name. In Oregon, however, Republicans had come to dominate an increasingly corrupt state government, with which Seth would later find much fault. William Anton Luelling, Seth's son, *did* involve himself with the Republicans, in 1878, if not before. But I've found no evidence that his father ever joined the Republican Party.

The Black exclusion clause of 1857 was never enforced, and in 1865 the legislature voted down a bill that would have authorized sheriffs to deport Black residents from their counties. Still, the exclusion clause was at least partially responsible for the fact that Oregon's Black population increased by only seventy-five in the 1850s, while California's increased by four thousand.

Seth was irritated enough by discrimination against Blacks to order, in 1864, the anonymously written pamphlet *Miscegenation: The Theory of the Blending of the Races*. The source of the coinage *miscegenation*, the pamphlet was fully in favor of racial mixing, mainly as a means of improving white bloodlines.

Seth's stepdaughter, Florence Olson Ledding, later explained that in naming his new cherry Seth determined to make *Black Republican* "a term of honor." He would make anti-abolitionists "relish Black Republicans." He "saw his critics literally eat their words."

But new fruits take years to make an impression. By the time the Black Republican cherry became popular, the Civil War was long over, and in Oregon racist sentiments were mostly directed at Chinese residents, who were many times more numerous in the state than Black people. The cherry's curious name had little sting—except in the South, where the Black Republican cherry was sold as the Luelling or, later, the Lewelling.

A year after introducing the Black Republican, Seth selected another promising cherry, also probably a seedling of Black Eagle. He called the new variety Lincoln. Now no one could doubt Seth's political leanings—though admiration for the once accursed Emancipator became the norm after his murder. Few, unfortunately, took to his namesake cherry.

Oregon legislators found more ways to oppress non-whites, with laws that included a poll tax in 1862 and a ban on intermarriage in 1866. With the end of slavery, however, West Coast reformers shifted their focus from injustices against Black people to other concerns. When a "colored man," John "Setin," came to Seth's house to ask for a job in 1871, Seth hired him on the spot, for an entire year. Men with faces like John's were a rarity in Oregon; of 90,923 Oregonians in the 1870 census, only 346 were identified as Black or mulatto. Before or after John Setin's hiring, Portland's small Black community must have come to known Seth as a reliable ally, because in 1885 a twelve-year-old Black runaway from the city would take refuge at Seth's farm and refuse to return home. He was among friends at the fruit farm, well-fed and well-clothed. Clearly, Seth was happy to help individual Blacks in need. Yet fighting for Black rights was a pursuit of the past, for Seth and the rest of the Luellings.

The Scientific Farmer

Seth introduced other fruits. In 1860 he originated his own grape variety, the Luelling. With very large, black sweet fruits, it proved "a most valuable acquisition to the list of grapes adapted to the climate of western Oregon and Washington."

Like the Luelling, Black Republican, and Lincoln cherries, the Luelling grape was probably a happy accident. But Seth soon began developing new fruits deliberately and systematically.

He was particularly proud of his Golden Prune. In 1875 or thereabouts, he planted 200 seeds of Italian plums. One of the trees that grew up had fruit with golden instead of blue skin, and the Goldens were half again to twice as large as the average Italian plum. They were easy to peel, freestone, and excellent for eating fresh, for canning, and for drying. The tree bore abundantly, too; Dale Smith, Addie's husband, later said his production averaged four hundred pounds per tree. Unfortunately, Golden Prune trees died young in the Willamette Valley. But they grew vigorously in eastern Oregon and proved so cold-resistant that they were favored in South Dakota. They grew well in California, too, both for Dale Smith in Pleasanton and for Leonard Coates in the Napa Valley.

Seth's other creations included a cultivar of gooseberry about which nothing seems to be remembered, a "mammoth" rhubarb that did not go to seed, the sweet apple—Sweet Alice—named for his daughter, and a small pear, called Mother's Favorite (for Clarissa, no doubt), which children liked to eat dried whole.

Seth was a student and teacher of horticulture. He read *Oregon Farmer* until it ceased publication, subscribed to *Willamette Farmer* when it appeared, and bought at least one subscription to the latter for a friend. He deliberated with his fellow horticulturists in meetings of the Oregon State Agricultural Society, and he took leadership roles in the organization. And, like John and Henderson, he trained dozens, possibly hundreds, of people to graft, to prune, and to raise excellent fruit.

Through some of the men he trained, Seth helped spread the art of horticulture beyond Oregon. Besides teaching Hugh Pattison and regularly sending him grafted trees, he trained Ezra Meeker of Puyallup through the summer of 1865, and grubstaked him with 1,500 trees. A third Washingtonian, J. M. Ogle, of Puyallup Nursery, was one of Seth's best customers and a frequent correspondent.

Seth was a constant experimenter, as a journalist later described:

> If, upon bearing, the fruit of a young tree did not please him, he would plant another by its side and graft the tops together so as to form one tree, in hopes that the fruit thus produced would be better than the first. It is stated that in this way he grafted trees together until there was one with 14 trunks and but one top; another with 13 trunks, and many with a lesser number of trunks.

In Seth's orchard, too, were trees that bore several kinds of fruit at once, through multiple grafts, and trees whose trunks were braided together.

Seth's breeding methods are revealed in a story he liked to tell. A prominent woman came to tour his orchard. Unbeknownst to her, Seth would bag blossoms that he had hand-pollinated, and after removing the bags he would tie strings of various colors by the clusters, to indicate fruit to be saved for later planting. The visitor reached for a marked cluster of luscious cherries and popped them all into her mouth, exclaiming over their deliciousness. Seth gently asked for the pits. He heard later that she called him "the stingiest man I ever heard of."

Seth gave his crops meticulous care. He spread manure in his orchards, and he enriched the soil with blood meal and bone meal. After the woolly aphid invaded, he corresponded with a manufacturer of a new insecticide.

Seth was unafraid to invest in new equipment. He spent $500 on a large brick and iron fruit dryer designed and built by H. S. Jory, an 1847 emigrant who had settled in the South Salem Hills. After putting the dryer to use, Seth said "he would not take $500 bonus to have it removed."

The skill, discipline, and creativity Seth applied to his horticultural work brought him continued recognition as an orchardist as well as nurseryman. In 1871, the *Sacramento Daily Union* noted that "Lewelling Orchards in Oregon" was shipping cherries to California. The *Daily Alta California* observed the same summer that a five-foot branch of a Royal Ann cherry from Seth's orchard, weighing seven pounds and bearing 354 cherries, was exhibited at a San Francisco drugstore. In his 1889 fruit catalog, Seth boasted: "At the Oregon State fair of 1876 and 1877, I received gold medals for the greatest number of varieties and best exhibit of fruits. I have received the first premium at the Oregon State Fair for the best exhibit of fruits, seventeen years successively." He didn't mention that his fruits had also won prizes at multiple world's fairs.

The Spiritualist and Reformer

In April 1864 Seth wrote in his journal a list of "Books I wish to get," which he subsequently ordered from Andrew Jackson Davis. Along with a book of poetry, the pamphlet on miscegenation, and a collection of Thomas Paine's works were a book on the historical Jesus and one on New Testament apocrypha. Seth always maintained his interest in Christianity; for him it bore no inherent conflict with Spiritualism. He was happy to send Addie to attend St. Mary's Academy, a Portland school run by nuns from Quebec whom he paid partially in fruit. And he would often record in his diary that he had gone to hear a visiting preacher preach. Spiritualism, for Seth, was inclusive—although he had no patience for religious rules such as the ban on work on Sunday.

Also on Seth's list, of course, were explicitly Spiritualist books: an autobiography of a medium, a Spiritualist guide to women's rights, a book on psychometrics (the study of the ability to learn about someone or something by touching inanimate objects), two copies of Andrew Jackson Davis's guide to Spiritualist Sunday schools (*The Progressive Lyceum*), and five copies each of five of Davis's lectures. Seth was not only studying Spiritualism; he must also have been proselytizing.

Seth's appetite for Spiritualist writing persisted. He ordered more books from Davis that fall. In 1868 he subscribed to the *Banner of Light* and the *Spiritual Light*, a short-lived publication from San Francisco. In 1870 he ordered three pamphlets by Spiritualists other than Andrew Jackson Davis.

When the New Era Spiritualist camp opened, in 1876, near Canby, Oregon, Seth and Clarissa became regular attendees and contributors. So did Alfred; in 1882, he would serve as secretary of the camp.

Seth, Clarissa, and Willie attended Spiritualist lectures and public séances as well as more intimate circles. Among the stage mediums were several described by Emma Hardinge in her *Modern American Spiritualism:* the "sweet little lady" Mrs. C. M. Stowe, who lectured at the Milwaukie schoolhouse; Ada Hoyt Foye, "the celebrated test rapping medium," who converted Emma Hardinge herself to Spiritualism; Dr. J. P. Bryant, "the renowned healer," and Benjamin Todd, "a brave eloquent and fearless lecturer," who spoke in Milwaukie in 1867 and visited the Luellings with his wife in 1871. (Apparently Benjamin Todd was also a bookseller, because Seth ordered several books from him in 1868, including three by Andrew Jackson Davis.)

Not all of the lectures the Lewellings attended or sponsored were specifically about Spiritualism. One concerned phrenology, the study of bumps on the head as signs of personality and character. At least two of the lectures concerned temperance—a subject of renewed interest for Seth, perhaps, since his adoption of a restricted diet. The most frequent topic was probably women's rights. In August 1871 Seth went to Portland to fetch Abigail Scott Duniway, the publisher of the *New Northwest* and Oregon's leading suffragist, along with "Mrs. Gordon"—almost certainly Laura de Force Gordon, a California suffragist, a newspaper publisher, and a lawyer as well as a Spiritualist. Gordon lectured at the Milwaukie schoolhouse; perhaps Duniway did, too. And a month later Seth and Willie, and probably Clarissa, attended two of Susan B. Anthony's lectures in Portland. For Seth and Clarissa, as for many other Spiritualists, faith was inseparable from the quest for societal reform.

In 1872 Seth placed an order with W. E. Jones, a Portland merchant of Spiritualist and other "progressive" publications. The order included a biography of Victoria Woodhull, a Spiritualist and advocate for women's rights and free love who had been nominated that year as the first female candidate for the U.S. presidency. Also included in the order was the famous spirit photograph of Mary Todd Lincoln, with the ghost of her husband standing behind her, his hands on her shoulders. Spirit pictures were photographers' tricks, but they had special appeal for Spiritualists—especially when the spirit portrayed had once been an enlightened reformer. Seth himself, after his death, would be the subject of some darkroom dabbler's spirit picture.

Willie

Seth and Clarissa must have had great hopes for their son, William Anton. As a young teenager he had worked regularly for his father; at fourteen, Seth noted, Willie grafted 400 trees in a day. Then he went off to school in California at Livermore College. Addie's husband, James Dale Smith, had bought Livermore Collegiate Institute from its founders in 1874 and renamed it. He and Addie together taught their students, who probably never numbered more than fifty and who included two of Henderson's grandchildren, Rachel's and Hannah's daughters, as well as their cousin Willie.

Willie finished school with seemingly unclear ambitions. He lived for a time in Oregon's Washington County—probably with his cousin Alfred—where he became an officer for both the Oddfellows and the Good Templars, the latter devoted to promoting abstinence from alcohol. He may have planned for a time to make his career as a lawyer; he took a case to trial at least once, defending a man in an assault-and-battery case.

But in the summer of 1876 Willie was back in Milwaukie, working as his father's partner in the nursery business. His bride and former schoolmate, Mary Harlan, joined him the following year. Willie continued his straight-laced activities: He joined Eugene Thorpe in the Milwaukie Templars' lodge; he and Mary put on a concert to raise money for a sidewalk to the train depot; and Willie took a seat on the committee on credentials at the Clackamas County Republican Convention.

In January 1877, Seth took Willie to Oregon City for a sitting with a local medium, Mrs. Pattison (I suspect she was the mother of Hugh Pattison, who ran the branch nursery at Steilacoom). In a Spiritualist sitting, the medium shares messages from her client's dead loved ones. Perhaps Willie wanted to hear from his sisters Elva and Alice, or get some spirit's opinion on his upcoming wedding. But Mrs. Pattison may have disappointed him. She may have confused details of the past or foretold a sad future. In any case, by March Willie was completely disillusioned with Spiritualism. He and his friend Eugene L. Thorpe began traveling the state giving lectures to expose Spiritualism as fakery. They engaged the Reed Opera House, in Salem, for the purpose. Although Seth didn't mention these events in his journal, he and Clarissa must have been mortified.

Apparently the family worked out their differences. The father-and-son partnership continued, and Willie began winning a reputation as a horticulturist. In the fall of 1877, he gave the opening address at the Oregon State Fair.

In the spring of 1879, Mary Harland Luelling gave birth to a son, Lorin Leroy. Seth and Clarissa must have been delighted to see the Milwaukie Luelling clan growing again.

Summer Frolic

In 1878 Seth took another trip to California, this time with Clarissa. It was their first, and only, long vacation, and it lasted the whole summer. They spent nearly the whole time with family members. Seth kept a special journal just for the trip.

The Bay Area had been thoroughly transformed since Seth's first visit, in 1850. Not only did steamboats now ply the bay in all directions, but railroads lined both sides of it, from San Francisco to San Jose (the accent on the *e* of that city's name had largely vanished) and from San Jose to Oakland. The latter route passed through the junction at Niles, today part of Fremont. From Niles, the route of the first transcontinental railroad ran east through Stockton, passing through Livermore, at the eastern edge of Alameda County.

Seth and Clarissa first visited Addie and Dale at Livermore. The Smiths' only child, Duncan Lewelling Smith, turned four in 1878. Dale and Addie played the piano and sang for her parents, and they all attended a Livermore College dance. Seth and Dale together went to bathe in Sulphur Springs, south of Livermore.

With Addie, Dale, and Duncan, Seth and Clarissa took the train to San Lorenzo. Seth and Clarissa stayed at the Meeks' home, the others at Lottie and her husband's cottage on Meek's estate. They spent an evening with John's son Eli and his mother, Elvy, who was visiting from St. Helena. After they passed a second night at the Meeks' and one at Eli's, Oregon Columbia came to visit them from Oakland. Then Seth, Clarissa, Addie, Dale, and Duncan went to San Jose to see Henderson's daughter Rachel, or Hattie, now divorced from Seth Eddy and living with her second husband, Henry Charles Wilson. Henderson visited briefly that evening, and the next day Seth and Clarissa went to Henderson's home. There they met his fifth wife—or sixth, if you count Theresa Lee.

Seth didn't record the new wife's name in his journal, but she was Rubie Rosella Cadwell, a woman Henderson's age. She had come from

Illinois, where she lost all three of her babies and subsequently, in 1853, her husband. In 1864, she moved to California with her widowed eldest brother, Orren Cadwell, and one of Orren's sons. Orren's siblings, nieces, and nephews soon followed, until nearly the whole Cadwell clan had resettled in the San Francisco Bay Area. When Rubie met Henderson, she and Orren had long shared a household.

As descendants of Caleb Rich, the first American-born Universalist preacher, the Cadwells were unconventionally religious. Orren's brother Caleb Cadwell, who owned a farm in the Santa Cruz Mountains, was, like Henderson, an ardent follower of Andrew Jackson Davis. Through Caleb's will—he would die in 1883—he would try to create an organization of San Jose Spiritualists and fund a meeting place for them.

The Wilsons, Smiths, and Rubie must have all been Spiritualists, or at least willing partakers, because at Rachel's house the family held circles two evenings in a row. The second was attended by a Mr. Shortridge, whose lectures Seth and Clarissa had attended in Oregon, and Shortridge's wife. "Heard numerous raps," Seth noted.

Seth never reported, in his diaries, whether any spirits he heard speak through mediums were family members. I wonder if, during these circles with Henderson, someone was influenced by the spirit of Levi Luelling. The preceding December Levi had been visiting his wife's family in Hillsboro, Oregon, when he went for a stroll, stood against a tree, and shot himself with a pistol through the head. Domestic troubles were said to be the cause of his distress. He died, leaving his wife of three years and a child. The entire Lewelling clan must have felt haunted by his death. But, then, plenty of other Lewelling spirits were available for mediums to channel.

Seth, Clarissa, Addie, Dale, and Duncan took a train back to Livermore, but soon they were off again, to camp at Los Gatos and travel on to Santa Cruz County. They picked blackberries in Felton, visited the lime kiln there—you can still hike to its ruins—and picnicked at Big Trees, now Henry Cowell Redwoods State Park, where the biggest tree was fifty-three feet around. At Soquel, they bathed in the sea. They toured the tannery in Santa Cruz and Spreckels's beet-sugar factory in Watsonville. They saw a beached whale.

They visited Eli again before moving on to see John, by boating across the bay to Vallejo before taking the California Pacific rail line that now extended to Calistoga. In St. Helena, John and Elvy's son Harvy took them for a buggy ride. John showed them his old place as well as the new, and they visited the resort at White Sulphur Springs and the St. Helena water works.

They passed some days in San Francisco before returning to the coast of the Monterey Bay. Stopping again at Rachel's on the way, they headed to Camp Capitola, California's first seaside resort, near Santa Cruz. They spent at least a week there, bathing in the sea and fishing. At Camp Capitola Seth saw, for the first time, the woolly aphid, which in California had become a serious pest of apples. The little insects "hung in festoons." Two years later he would notice woolly apple aphids in Oregon, and soon they and other pests would make apple culture very difficult in the Willamette Valley.

After leaving Camp Capitola, the family attended the Oakland Fair—apparently Seth was not an exhibitor—and then spent another night at the Meeks' before traveling to Cloverdale, in northern Sonoma County, to attend a wedding. Seth's description of the last part of the trip is lost, if it ever existed, but he and Clarissa couldn't have returned home before late September.

Painful Passings

If Seth continued keeping annual diaries, they didn't make it into the Oregon Historical Society's collection. Perhaps he stopped writing, or perhaps the diaries were lost. Maybe he destroyed them. In any case, the next years must have been hard ones for Seth.

In September 1878, thirty-one-year-old Oregon Columbia Luelling—who now went by O. C.—seems to have lost his head. He vanished from the Oakland hardware store he had been managing, leaving the business short of $15,000. Indicted for embezzlement, he fled to his namesake state. After the new year he returned, gave himself up to the Alameda County court, and paid his bail. Later the judge set aside his indictment on grounds that certain members of the grand jury were prejudiced against him. The case never went to trial. But O. C. had undoubtably brought shame on the family.

While O. C. was on the lam, his father was burning weeds, along with his brother-in-law Orren Cadwell, on a rented lot in San Jose. Henderson was preparing to cultivate the parcel, though what he planned to grow went unrecorded. Orren left him to do some chores at home. When

Orren returned about forty-five minutes later, Henderson was lying dead in the burned stubble, his clothing on fire. He had been having dizzy spells for several years and had recently fainted on the street. An inquest determined that he had had a heart attack before falling into the burning weeds. He was sixty-nine years old.

Henderson was buried at the immense and beautifully landscaped Mountain View Cemetery in Oakland. But his grave was left unmarked. Perhaps too little money remained in his estate to pay for a headstone.

About this time, probably in the summer of 1879, one of Seth's employees, Willard Harvey, drowned while bathing in the Willamette River. Seth had the disquieting experience of finding the body.

In late August of the same year, Willie died of typhoid fever. If Henderson's and Willard's deaths shook Seth, Willie's must have devastated him. Seth was undoubtably proud when the Oregon State Agricultural Society honored Willie as "a young man of pure moral character . . . whose whole life has been intimately connected with horticulture." But now Seth was again without a business partner, and he and Clarissa had lost their only son. Addie was their only surviving child. Willie's wife, Mary, was left to raise Lorin Leroy on her own. The boy was not yet five months old.

In his distress, Seth decided to sell off all his nursery stock, 150,000 fruit trees. With orchards to manage and his own fruit store in Portland, he was overwhelmed. "In consequence of the death of my son, he explained in a newspaper ad, "having no one to assist me I have determined to close out that part of my business as soon as possible."

It was about this time that Seth resumed spelling his last name *Lewelling*. With two of the Luelling men he cared most about gone, he may have yearned for greater connection to John's family in California and to his Lewelling relations back east, both those still living and those departed (but still living!).

Exactly when Seth resumed his work as a nurseryman I don't know, but more blows came the following year. Alfred's daughter Annie died of brain fever at twenty-five. And in December 1880 William Meek died, at sixty-three years old. Unlike his friend Henderson, this "highly esteemed pioneer" was buried with acclaim. Meek was remembered for his integrity, for his ardent support of the principles of the Republican Party, and for his sunny smile. In San Lorenzo, stores closed for the day, and flags flew at half-mast.

Two years later, in December 1882, Seth lost Clarissa. The cause of her death was unrecorded. She was buried near Willie in the Milwaukie cemetery. Addie and Dale came to Milwaukie for Clarissa's funeral, or soon afterward. They helped the bereaved Seth make a plan. He would lease out his Oregon nursery and orchard lands and move to California, where he would start a new nursery. Dale rented for Seth six acres in Pleasanton—"one of the best pieces of land in Alameda County"—near Addie and Dale's home in Livermore.

Seth arrived in California in late February 1883. The following winter Dale advertised a new nursery, Smith & Luelling's. The nursery offered fourteen thousand Oregon Champion gooseberry plants as well as prune, plum, apple, pear, apricot, and peach trees.

But by late spring of 1884 Seth returned to Milwaukie, leaving Dale to run the branch nursery in Pleasanton. Perhaps Seth had gotten homesick. He may have missed his Spiritualist friends, one in particular.

During his stay in California, Seth was probably on hand for yet another funeral—that of his brother John, in late December 1883. But I am getting ahead of myself. John's last chapter is a full one.

Chapter 11
John

> Human happiness is the acme of earthly ambition. Individual happiness depends upon general prosperity.
>
> —Preamble to the National Grange constitution

John Lewelling suffered with asthma, and apparently it had gotten worse since his move to San Lorenzo. The frequent fogs seemed to aggravate the disease. He must have remembered his trip into the warmer, drier Napa Valley years before, in 1851. The climate there, he figured, might be better for his health. So in 1864 John, Elvy, and their two youngest sons, Arthur and Harvy, moved to the valley. They bought a farm of 163 acres near St. Helena and left Eli in charge of the farm in San Lorenzo. The transition must have been gradual; as Henderson had done between Indiana and Iowa and between Iowa and Oregon, and as John himself had done between Oregon and Mission San José and between Mission San José and San Lorenzo, John used one farm to provide the young trees, seeds, and scions for the next, and to furnish the income needed until the new farm became productive.

Last Transplants

On the new farm, called Oak Grove, John planted 500 apple trees, 1,800 almond trees, 35,000 European grapevines, and smaller numbers of plums, cherries, and apricots.

John's plums included the German Prune, or Luelling's German, which Henderson had brought from Iowa. It was among a few varieties of plum to "succeed admirably" in the Napa Valley, wrote John's fellow orchardist Leonard Coates in 1882.

Apples would be a minor crop for John. Because of imported pests, the trees were getting hard to grow well in California. The woolly apple aphid, which sucks on both limbs and roots, had recently reached the

John Lewelling. From Palmer, *History of Napa and Lake Counties, California.*

state from its homeland back east. Codling moths had arrived either direct from their Asian homeland or from the Eastern states, where their larvae had long tunneled through the centers of apples and pears. And San Jose scale, a tiny sucker that feeds on a variety of fruit trees and berries but is especially ruinous to apples, came from China in the 1870s on flowering peach trees imported to the San Jose area. By the 1880s, John's apples were mainly the Golden Russet, which Henderson had brought from Iowa, and Rall's Genet (the Never Fail), because neither of these varieties was bothered by woolly aphids.

I don't know why John didn't plant a large cherry orchard. Perhaps he was avoiding competition with his sons in San Lorenzo, or perhaps he no longer wanted to contend with the difficulty of keeping cherries fresh from farm to market. Maybe he perceived that cherries were losing market share to apricots, which by 1880 were being canned and bottled and shipped to London. Maybe he simply wanted to concentrate on grapes and almonds, crops he expected to do well in the Napa Valley.

In 1868, John bought 184 acres more, from a man named L. H. Murray. The new parcel was just across the county road (today's State Route 29) from Oak Grove, and the land extended to the foot of the Mayacamas Mountains. The county road, and the railroad that ran beside it, now crossed John's lands.

On the west side of the railroad John planted 1,600 almond trees and 50,000 vines, of about twenty-four varieties, mostly European. By 1877 John would be one of two principal almond growers in the upper Napa Valley; that year he raised ten thousand pounds of them.

In 1870 John bought another 190 acres. This parcel was adjacent to the Murray place to the west. It was hill land, unsuitable for planting, but it would serve as a hunting ground, and its three springs would provide plentiful water for John's vineyard, orchard, and household.

John named the Murray place, with its extension into the foothills, Deer Mount. In 1870 he built a twenty-room, redwood Gothic Revival house on a rise on the property. He furnished the house with modern amenities, including running water and a cistern to provide soft water

John Lewelling's house and farm in St. Helena. From Smith and Elliott, *Illustrations of Napa County, California.*

John Lewelling's house and farm in St. Helena. From Smith and Elliott, *Illustrations of Napa County, California.*

for washing hair and clothes. John designed the area around the house according to the naturalistic principles of Andrew Jackson Downing, with rare ornamentals such as palms, a Southern magnolia, camellias, pomegranates, ginkgoes, a weeping cypress, and century plants. A long lane lined with almond and walnut trees led to the house from the main road.

John's St. Helena homestead was soon considered among the most beautiful in the valley. He must have thought it so himself, because in 1878 he paid as much as a thousand dollars to have it included in Smith and Elliott's *Illustrations of Napa County, California*, one of many books published during the 1870s to flatter the vanity of wealthy farmers, whose payments covered the books' production costs.

Over the years John continued to develop the property. He built redwood barns. He installed a tank for mixing cow manure with water, to create a slurry to spread over the orchard floor and the vineyard. He dug fishponds, and in 1881 he enlarged the ponds and dug a well to supply them with their own water source. In 1879 he planted 200 orange trees.

John Lewelling's house today. Photo by the author.

Over the coming years, John would replace trees as needed, probably trying new varieties now and then. After giving up his San Lorenzo Nursery, he ordered trees from his brother Seth. In 1874, Seth noted in his diary, he sold John 150 apple trees, 2 pear, 20 plum, 2 peach, and 9 cherry, along with 12 grapevines.

Losing Children, Gathering Grandchildren

Despite John's success as a farmer, the early years in St. Helena were hard ones. In 1865 John and Elvy lost Sarah, their daughter and eldest child. Her husband, Robert King, had died the year before. Now Sarah and Robert's three children—Lewis Leroy, Clinton, and Elva King—who had all been born in California, were orphaned in Iowa, to where the Kings had returned about 1859. At Sarah's death, Elva, the youngest, was only five years old, and Lewis Leroy, the eldest, was ten.

John sent Elisha and Eli to bring the children back to California. Raising them became a family project. At the time of the 1870 census, Lewis Leroy and Clinton were living in Eden Township with Elisha, or "E. D." (his given name, he had apparently concluded, was too close to his brother Eli's). Elva was probably living with John and Elvy.

And then E. D. died. Elisha had been a successful fruit farmer in his own right; he had nine Portuguese and two Chinese workers, besides his nephews, living with him in 1870. E. D.'s life had been full of promise. He entered California College, the predecessor to the University of California, in 1862, the year the school opened. As an incoming freshman, he gave a speech on "Prospects in California." He joined the Republican Party, and in 1868 he was appointed to the Alameda County committee on credentials. The next year he ran for a seat in the California Assembly, not as a Republican but as an independent. He won. During that session a bill was introduced to make E. D. a member of a Board of Forest Commissioners, which would have the power to appoint a state forester. E. D. was to serve with Leland Stanford, then a banker, a former governor, a winery owner, and the president of the Southern Pacific Railroad, and H. N. Bolander, a botany professor, the superintendent of public instruction, and the president of the State Horticultural Society. Some of E. D.'s fellow legislators must have thought very highly of him to include him on the proposed board.

But the governor never signed the forestry bill, and E. D. had no further opportunity to promote tree planting in California. His first year in the legislature was his last. Not yet thirty-two years old, he died of tuberculosis in the spring of 1872, at a soda-water spring in Lake County, California, about forty miles north of his parents' home.

Before he died, E. D. probably spent time in St. Helena with John, Elvy, and his two youngest brothers. This might explain why the following year Arthur B. Lewelling, nineteen years old, died as well. The two share a headstone at the San Lorenzo Pioneer Cemetery.

John and Elvy were left with only two children, Eli and Harvy John. Eli, by this time, had built a fine house in San Lorenzo. He would marry, but not until he was fifty-one years old. He and his wife, Carmen Mina Madden, would have no children. Before their marriage in 1882, what had been John's San Lorenzo farm was auctioned, with all its equipment and livestock. Because no bids were sufficiently high—Eli wanted $100,000—he eventually offered the land for sale in four- to fifteen-acre parcels. Eli continued to farm elsewhere in San Lorenzo; in 1885 he had "perhaps the largest apple orchard in the county." He also bought and sold land for profit, not only in Eden Township but in Oakland, San Francisco, and St. Helena. He would own 260 acres of Alameda County farmland at his death at age ninety.

Eli Lewelling's farm in San Lorenzo in 1878. From Thompson and West, *Official Historical Atlas Map of Alameda County, California.*

John and Elvy's youngest child, Harvy, was seventeen when Elisha died. Harvy would work alongside his father and prepare to take over the St. Helena farm at John's death.

Patron of Husbandry

Life must have grown merrier for John and Elvy, not long after Arthur's death, when they joined the Grange. The National Grange—the Patrons of Husbandry—was formed in Washington, D.C., in 1867. By 1873 California had 104 local Granges. That year the movement swelled. It was the year of a European stock market crash, after which U.S. railroads couldn't borrow money; the year of the Coinage Act, which banned the production of silver coins, despite the West's great investment in silver mining; and the year of a financial panic that resulted in the closure of hundreds of banks. For farmers, crop prices fell while production expanded. Farmers couldn't get loans, and they blamed capitalists for charging too much for shipping, warehousing, and supplies such as grain sacks. To address these complaints, the California Farmers' Union held its first convention in the spring of 1873. But apparently the farmers concluded that they didn't need this new organization; rather, they needed to expand and strengthen the Grange. The week after the Farmers' Union convention adjourned in San Francisco, the California State Grange formed in Napa. The Farmers' Union evaporated.

For John and his family, the Grange had clear appeal. The organization had no political or religious tests for membership. Women and teenagers were welcome to join. The Grangers' ideal was cooperation for mutual betterment, and their goals were practical. They included securing more favorable shipping and storage rates, establishing banks that would lend to farmers at reasonable rates, and arranging for purchase of farm implements, supplies, and machinery direct from manufacturers. Across the country, Grangers pooled their money. They invested in trade unions, elevators, warehouses, packing houses, grist mills, factories, and transportation services. The Grange provided its members with arbitration services and fire insurance. The organization supported progressive legislation, including, eventually, women's suffrage.

And Grangers knew how to have fun. In August 1874, in a meeting at his own house, John was elected Worthy Master of the St. Helena Grange. "With a face in which you can read the ten commandments," reported another Granger to the *Pacific Rural Press*, John thanked his fellows for the honor and "promised to take good care of our symbolic farm." After the installation, the party began:

> Bro. L. might have been seen looking through a bay window, down his nearly mile long almond-shaded avenue, at a long dark line of something approaching. He looks and wonders till his splendid mansion is surrounded by carriages full of "brave men and fair women" . . . fifty-three in number. . . . The invaders kept possession of the Master's citadel . . . regaling themselves at the sumptuous board, interchanging happy thoughts while the young folks "tripped the light fantastic toe," to the music of the piano, till the approaching Sabbath morn.

John and his family took active roles in the Napa County Grange and the state Grange as well as the St. Helena Grange. When the state Grange put on its Feast of Pomona in 1875, John provided fruit. That same year he was elected Chaplain of Napa County's Pomona Grange, which meant he led rituals and organized funeral services. Elvy was elected Flora, one of the three Graces, who represented both agriculture and feminine virtues. The next year, when John was reelected master of the St. Helena Grange, Harvy, almost twenty-one, was elected Gatekeeper; his job was to ensure that only certified members were admitted to meetings. As Napa's representative to the state Grange, in 1879, John urged farmers to attend the state fair and exhibit there. In 1875 John was elected treasurer of the new California Grangers' Business Association, which formed to concentrate and centralize the buying and selling of farmers' "necessaries" and products. The association opened a three-story warehouse and office on Market Street in San Francisco. And in 1876 John became vice president of the Grangers' Bank of California, whose stock was owned by more than fifteen hundred Patrons of Husbandry. In 1882 he became president of the bank. He was also one of its largest shareholders.

John's experience in the Grange must have given him the confidence, in August of 1882, to became a founding director of the Bank of St. Helena. A month previously, "about twenty substantial citizens" appointed a committee of five "winegrowers," as they called themselves, to solicit stock subscriptions in the new bank. The goal was to make agricultural loans available at fair rates. As the Grange taught, farmers would help farmers through this new local bank.

Growing Vines

When he arrived in St. Helena, John hadn't grown grapes on a large scale before, and he apparently didn't plan to make grapes into wine. He wanted to take advantage of the Napa Valley's relatively hot, dry summers by drying grapes into raisins. In 1872 he planted muscat grapes (which may have been any of several varieties, all bearing the same strong scent), and he harvested some the same year. As an article in the St. Helena *Star* described, he dipped the ripe grapes in boiling lye water and then dried them on scaffolds. The lye dip sped drying, made the skin more transparent and tender, and, John believed, improved the flavor of the raisins. They sold well in San Francisco. The next year he produced a ton of raisins, though wet fall weather kept him from drying them as thoroughly as he would have liked. To ensure proper finishing, he concluded, he needed a dry house. He built one in 1874, with two furnaces, and patented the design. He also had a concrete bed constructed for drying grapes. Painted black, it was not only cleaner than the earth; it was also hotter. That year he produced three tons of raisins, and the next year four. In 1876 John expected to produce at least ten tons of raisins, mostly muscat but also Malaga and some other varieties. He was now the Napa Valley's authority on raisin production.

John also sold grapes fresh, shipping them in rail cars chilled with ice. In 1881 he shipped to Chicago Flame Tokay grapes, a pink-fruited cultivar that was immensely popular until it was supplanted by the hybrid Flame Seedless.

And John also made wine.

Making Wine

It wasn't long after his move to St. Helena that John joined the pioneers of today's Napa Valley wine industry. Any Quakerish concerns about temperance were, for John, long a thing of the past; in San Lorenzo he had made wine from cherries, and probably from other fruits as well.

Before statehood and for some years afterward, California winemakers had relied on the Mission grape, which missionaries had introduced from Spain to Mexico in the sixteenth century and then carried north with them from mission to mission. The Mission grape did not make particularly good wine. So, beginning in about 1852, French farmers in the Santa Clara Valley began introducing other European grapes (one man is said to have saved his cuttings during a long voyage by inserting the ends into potatoes). In 1858, Frank Stock, of San José, planted grape cuttings his father had sent him from Germany. The varieties included Riesling, Sylvaner, and Traminer. Gradually, California wines grew diverse and refined.

In the Napa Valley, viticulture began relatively late. It was George B. Crane who first predicted that "the light, gravelly land" of St. Helena would be ideal for growing wine grapes. He grubbed out manzanita and chamise and, in 1859, planted twelve acres of Mission grapes. Two years later, he bought cuttings of various cultivars from Frank Stock in San José. An unlabeled package, sold at half-price, turned out to be Riesling.

Charles Krug was the valley's first winemaker. A former German revolutionary, he came to Napa Valley from Sonoma, where, in early 1858, he had bought a parcel of land from his friend Agoston Haraszthy, planted twenty acres of vines, and made his first batch of wine from Haraszthy's grapes.

Haraszthy is today remembered as the founder of the California wine industry. With the support of San Francisco investors, he eventually expanded his Buena Vista vineyards to six thousand acres. He showed Californians that grapes could grow well in their state without irrigation. He won the governor's appointment to a commission studying how to promote the improvement of the grapevine in California, and in this role he brought back cuttings of 380 grape varieties from France, Germany, Switzerland, Spain, and his native Hungary. He published a book, too, on grape growing and wine making. Before all that, though, he inspired his friend Charles Krug to take up wine making. Haraszthy apparently mentored Krug as well.

In the fall of 1858, on the request of another grape grower, Krug made twelve hundred gallons of Mission wine, using a small cider press, on a ranch near Napa City. Each year he made more wine, on various Napa Valley ranches, until in 1864 his own vineyard produced enough to allow him to make wine from his own grapes. That vineyard was north of St. Helena, on land he acquired in 1860 as his wife's dowry.

Until about 1880, the Napa Valley wine industry wasn't particularly profitable. A rush to plant vineyards began in 1861, and by 1867 the local market was glutted with wine. Securing customers elsewhere wasn't easy.

Wine drinkers outside the state were unfamiliar with the California product, and they didn't trust it. Among the few Easterners who had tasted California wine, many knew only the Mission variety. Even better varieties became poor wine when fermented in wooden barns without proper equipment or skill. In addition, a nationwide depression from 1873 to 1879 hurt sales of all wine. As a result, good Napa Valley wine was commonly sold under foreign labels, and wine from the extensively planted Mission grape was often made into vinegar, brandy, port, or angelica wine (a sweet, fortified wine invented by Franciscan missionaries in southern California).

In response to this situation, St. Helena winegrowers formed a club in 1875. John Lewelling was a founding member, along with Charles Krug and George Crane. Among the other founders were Henry A. Pellet, George Crane's winemaker; the appropriately named J. C. Weinberger; and Henry Walker Crabb, John's former neighbor in San Lorenzo, who followed John to St. Helena a year later. These men and ten others became the St. Helena Vinicultural Club.

Perhaps inspired by fellow club members, John soon acquired his own wine cellar. In 1876 he bought out Joseph Ghisletta, who had built a fine stone cellar on the south side of Spring Street. Almost immediately, John added a fermenting room to the building.

The St. Helena Vinicultural Club met regularly, to refine their skills and knowledge in growing grapes and making wine, brandy, and regional versions of sherry and port. They evaluated grape cultivars, and they phased out the inferior Mission vines quicker than growers in other area. They gave new growers cuttings of European grape varieties at no charge. They worked with the State Viticultural Commission to have local soils and products analyzed and to hold lectures on viticulture and enology. Their goal was to make St. Helena a center of superior wine making.

With his decades of horticultural experience, John was soon a leader among the winegrowers. Other members asked his opinion about when and how to graft, how much to prune and when, whether to stake vines, when to apply sulfur, and how best to root and plant cuttings. The men discussed how cuttings should best be shipped from the East and from Europe. John judged, from his experience, that the Isthmus of Panama route was fatal to seeds and cuttings both, probably because of the heat. At other meetings, John shared samples of his Catawba wine, and he described his experience with black-knot fungus.

According to the wine historian Charles L. Sullivan, the depression in the Napa Valley wine industry broke in January 1877, when John received an unsolicited and unexpected order from a Philadelphia merchant for all the wine he could send. In 1879, the St. Helena winegrowers produced nearly one million gallons of wine. Charles Krug, who supplemented his own grapes with those of other growers, had the highest production: 225,000 gallons. John Lewelling tied with another grower for seventh place among producers; each produced 45,000 gallons. Prices were up, and the winegrowers buoyant.

The winegrowers used government support to secure and expand their markets. They lobbied the U.S. Congress to keep the duty on French wine high—at forty cents per gallon rather than the twenty-five cents the French requested. They petitioned Congress to require labeling artificially carbonated champagne as "sparkling wine." They appointed a committee to write a bill to prevent the adulteration of wine.

In 1878, the winegrowers decided to build a bonded warehouse near the railroad depot. Here they could store brandy, in accordance with the law, without paying taxes on it for as long as three years. John was appointed to the committee to prepare plans and estimates and to buy a parcel of land. The stone building was completed in September of the same year, and John was among the directors and stockholders. Initially forty by sixty feet, with a capacity of 25,000 gallons, the building was lengthened to forty by one hundred-and-thirty-five feet in 1881, doubled from that size in 1882, and finally, after John's death, tripled from the 1881 footprint in 1889. Until the year he died, John served as proprietor of the bonded warehouse.

In 1880, the winegrowers began constructing another building, the St. Helena Viticultural Hall, as a home for their meetings and records. John led the committee charged with finding a site and raising funds. The group filed articles of incorporation, sold shares to fund the project, and hired a contractor. On John's suggestion, they added a second story to the building, to house a Grange hall (membership in the two organizations, no doubt, overlapped substantially). In late August of the same year the winegrowers' building was complete. The winegrowers held their first meeting in the new hall, and the St. Helena Grange—with John as Overseer—celebrated with a harvest feast upstairs.

Fighting Phylloxera

Also in 1880, the winegrowers talked with ever-growing concern about a newly discovered pest, phylloxera. A tiny, aphid-like insect that sucks the sap from the roots and leaves of grapevines, phylloxera is native to eastern North America. It causes only minor harm to the grape species with which it has evolved, including *Vitis labrusca*, the fox grape, whose aroma most Americans know from the Concord variety; *V. riparia*, the cold-hardy riverbank grape, with tart, herbaceous fruit; and *V. rupestris*, a bushy, black-fruited plant found mainly in the Ozarks. But when phylloxera attacks the Old World grape, *V. vinifera*, the insect deforms and girdles the roots, cutting off the flow of nutrients and water to the vine and inviting fungal infections. Because of phylloxera, Easterners had had no long-term success in growing European grapes.

While Easterners had tried again and again to grow *V. vinifera*, plant lovers in England and continental Europe had experimented with American grapes. Phylloxera, unfortunately, can hitch a ride across the ocean on grape cuttings. After decades of trading cuttings across the Atlantic, grape growers inevitably introduced an American pest to Europe. The damage first manifested itself in southern France in 1863. In a land densely planted with vineyards, the insect spread fast. California's vineyard-planting craze was due in part to farmers' bets that they could profit from their French counterparts' loss. By 1889, in fact, about three-quarters of European vineyards were destroyed.

But phylloxera showed its face in California—at Haraszthy's Buena Vista vineyard—only a few years after making itself known in France. Many Californians assumed the insect arrived on cuttings Haraszthy had brought from Europe in 1861. Damage from phylloxera, however, becomes obvious only about fifteen years after the initial infestation. So the insects may have started sucking at Buena Vista vines even before Haraszthy bought the vineyard, which had initially been planted in 1832. Californians had long been growing Eastern grapes, especially *V. vinifera–V. labrusca* hybrids such as Catawba and Isabella. Phylloxera may have taken a relatively short trip over the Rockies rather than coming by way of Europe. The insect may have been introduced multiple times, in multiple ways. However phylloxera established itself in Sonoma, the Buena Vista vines sickened, and production declined. Haraszthy's investors fired him.

Early in 1880, phylloxera was found in a vineyard in Glen Ellen, ten miles from Buena Vista. Until this time the pest had spread slowly, probably because California vineyards and growing areas were farther apart than their European counterparts. Besides, no one in California had seen the winged form of phylloxera; the dry summers were thought to keep it from developing. It seemed obvious that flying phylloxera would travel faster and farther than crawlers—although crawlers, in fact, can be carried by the wind as well as accidentally transported by humans. In any case, the St. Helena winegrowers' first priorities now were to keep phylloxera out of the Napa Valley as long as possible and to learn to manage it when it appeared. It seemed only a matter of time before the insect would arrive over the Mayacamas Mountains. So the winegrowers appointed John and two other men to check vineyards from Yountville to Calistoga for phylloxera.

In 1881 the Phylloxera Committee found infected vines at J. C. Weinberger's estate, north of St. Helena. They couldn't see the insects, even with a large microscope, but the damage was obvious. Weinberger's vineyard was treated with a method developed in France: Carbon bisulfide was injected into the soil. The treatment helped, but it was not a long-term solution.

There was, to this point, almost no tradition of grafting grapes. Grapes are propagated soon after the vines are pruned in winter. You simply take a short cutting and push it into the earth. If rains continue for several months, the cutting roots and grows. The entire new plant is genetically identical to the parent. But some of the winegrowers already knew how to graft grapes, because they had joined better varieties onto their Mission vines. And in the 1870s Henry Crabb had begun experimenting with grafting to phylloxera-resistant V. *riparia* rootstock. Now Crabb's approach seemed the answer to phylloxera. They winegrowers considered which species had resistance to the insects, and they made plans to import phylloxera-resistant cuttings when needed.

At Deer Mount, John had also experimented with grape grafting. In March 1883, he demonstrated to the group exactly how to graft against phylloxera.

Endings

In 1880 John began leasing his vineyard to Nestor DeGouy. The Lewelling vineyard was by then among the largest in the St. Helena area, with 110 acres. That year Nestor produced 58,000 gallons of wine from John's grapes, and brandy as well. The following year, Nestor produced 60,000 gallons of wine, and in 1882 he advertised wine vinegar.

Although John was no longer producing wine himself, the year 1883 seemed the height of John's horticultural career. He had successfully led the revival of the California Horticultural Society, serving first as its chairman pro tem and subsequently as vice president (the first incarnation of the society had died by 1860). In a visit to Napa City in June, John reported that "he had never seen a better season" for his orchards and vines "since coming to the State." The following month, he and his workers were picking five hundred pounds of apricots a day to fill a contract for five thousand pounds. In early fall he was sick, so sick that the doctor was sent for, but he recovered enough to go on working. In September, in

John Lewelling's bust, which still stands by his now vacant house. Photo by the author.

the middle of the grape harvest, John forsook his characteristic modesty to place on his grounds near the house a marble bust of himself, on a marble pedestal illustrated with scenes of fruit cultivation and harvesting. In October John and his employees harvested ten tons of almonds from twelve hundred trees.

On October 27 John introduced to the St. Helena winegrowers his own grape cultivar. The vigorous vine bore abundant, large, loose bunches of thin-skinned, juicy, seedless white grapes with a "taste much like Green Reisling [*sic*]." President Krug suggested the grape should be named for its discoverer. "Mr. Lewelling blushingly bowed to the compliment," reported the *St. Helena Star*, "but said that if the grape were to be named after him he would like to have added, in view of its enormous bearing power, the word 'Prolific.'" Apparently John didn't know that his brother Seth had already introduced a grape called Luelling, which would later also be known as Lewelling. And so John's grape acquired the same name as his almond and nearly the same name as Seth's grape.

"We are glad to have the name of our venerable and honored friend, John Lewelling, of St. Helena, fixed upon a new and promising grape," wrote Edward J. Wickson in *Pacific Rural Press.* Samples would be sent to Eugene Hilgard, professor of agriculture at the University of California.

In late November, John represented Napa County at the third annual Convention of California Fruit Growers in San Francisco. Despite the gravity of the discussions—about pests, pricing, supply and demand, and so on—for John this must have been a happy reunion with scattered colleagues.

On December 6, a rash appeared on the inside of John's left leg, just above the ankle. It was, he knew, erysipelas, also known as St. Anthony's fire. He had had the disease once before, as a young man, and it had nearly crippled him. This time his leg swelled painfully. The bacteria had invaded his lymphatic system. John died at a half hour after midnight on Christmas morning, 1883. He was seventy-three years old.

On Christmas afternoon, someone draped John's bust in mourning. Early the next day his body was carried by train from Vineland Station to San Lorenzo, with an escort committee of male Grangers and female companions for Elvy. On the train's arrival in San Lorenzo a funeral was held, and John was buried in the family plot. In St. Helena, the Grange hall was draped in mourning for thirty days.

Newspapers published not just obituaries but eulogies for John. He was praised as "an affectionate husband and father, a kind and hospitable neighbor, and a true friend whose friendship was deserving." He was called "a sterling good man, this loyal and devoted Patron of Husbandry, this pioneer horticulturist, whose deeds will live long after him in the many departments of his enterprising work." To his superior judgment, in "a great measure," was ascribed "the reputation and standing of the wine industry of Napa." The California Horticultural Society declared him to be "the Father of California Horticulture."

John didn't live quite long enough to see Napa Valley wines win renown. But in 1889 they did so, nationwide and even in Europe. That year the *New York Tribune* published an article praising Napa Valley winemakers. The same year, California producers won twenty-one medals at the Paris International Exposition, and eleven of the medals were for Napa Valley wines and brandies. The Easterners' prejudice against California wines was finally defeated.

Fortunately, perhaps, John also missed seeing the devastation of California vineyards by phylloxera. In 1892 the ruined vineyards of St. Helena were being torn up and replanted on V. *riparia* rootstock.

More tragedies followed for California winegrowers. The 1906 earthquake spared the Napa Valley but destroyed forty million gallons of stored wine in the Bay Area. And in 1920 came the final blow: Prohibition. Winegrowers could sell their grapes fresh or make raisins, syrup, or in some cases, holy wine, but they couldn't sell table wines. So commenced a long dry spell in the Napa Valley.

Another Spiritualist in the Family

John Lewelling, like his brothers, practiced Spiritualism. I have found no record of his attendance at séances or of his book purchases, but after his death his friend John Allyn wrote the *St. Helena Star* to point out that John's religious practices were missing from his obituary. John Lewelling, John Allyn maintained,

> was a firm believer in Spiritualism. . . . Fifteen years ago he told me that he never engaged in any enterprise without consulting his guardian spirits. This he did not by the help of medium, but through his own organism. He would sit entirely by himself and if he felt impressed that he was in accord with the teachings of higher spirits his undertaking was sure to be successful.

His Spiritualism sounds like a solitary form of Quakerism, with spirits taking the place of the Inner Light.

John Lewelling presumably also believed in Summerland, Andrew Jackson Davis's afterlife of beautiful houses, lecture halls, music, gardens, and spirits living in harmony with one another and nature. And how exactly did John imagine his life in Summerland? John told his friend that "in spirit life he expected to follow the same occupation he had in this—that of raising and perfecting fruit."

Chapter 12
Pests and Politics

> About six years ago Mr. W. S. U'Ren was brought to our house by a friend of Reform. . . . Good government being to us what religion is to most people, we looked to this man as its high priest.
>
> —Sophronia Lewelling

In the late 1870s, pests and blights struck Willamette Valley orchards. Before their arrival, James R. Cardwell remembered, "the fruits of Willamette Valley were uniformly large and free from insect pests or fungus blights, consequently made a superlatively fine showing, stood handling and transportation much better than the fruits of this valley to-day, kept much longer and better." That blissful time lasted fewer than thirty years.

Invading Hordes

The enemies were various. According to Cardwell, "The first codlin[g] moth was discovered in box of early apples from California, in 1882; did not become a pest until early in the '90's, when the woolly aphis and the whole aphis family [aphids] came with the San Jose scale and other pests, all from California." The fungal disease apple scab, which had migrated along with the apple from its native central Asia, also reached the Willamette Valley in the late nineteenth century.

But none of these plagues had a name or distinct identity, as far as Oregon farmers knew in 1879. That's when the Oregon State Agricultural Society first held a general discussion about "the Apple Blight." Members alternately described damage from aphids, fungus, and sunscald, and Seth himself opined that the blight must be the same one affecting gooseberries, peaches, and grapes. The following June the discussion continued, just as helplessly. Members complained of trees bearing little fruit and of flying insects filling the air. In response to insect damage one man broadcast salt. Joseph Lambert bored holes in trees and filled them with sulfur, copper, or saltpeter. One man "suggested that the apple may have to go through a course of diseases in its young days the same as human beings." Another blamed the climate. George Settlemier advised pruning with an ax. Henry Miller figured that "both the vegetable and animal kingdom suffered from the development of evils as a new country was opened up."

Henry Miller was right: Pests followed the fruit. Modern transportation sped their migration. So did the practice of selling grafted trees; seeds did not usually carry insects or diseases, but trees and scions and fruit often did. And Oregon's abandoned and neglected orchards nurtured the invaders.

To defeat the fungi, apple culture began moving over the Cascades into the drier Hood River Valley, in Oregon, and into the Yakima, Wenatchee, and Okanogan valleys, desert or near-desert areas of eastern Washington. These orchards required irrigation, but at least the apples weren't defaced by scab.

Seth and a shrinking number of Willamette Valley fruit farmers persevered and adapted. In 1885, Seth helped to found the Oregon Horticultural Society, which was partially supported by the new Oregon State College. Thenceforth Oregon fruit growers would have access to scientific advice about pests, diseases, and other natural challenges.

The biggest threat to horticulturists, however, wasn't nature but the economy.

Alfred

The U.S. economy was going from bad to worse. The Panic of 1873 initiated the country's first Great Depression, also known as the Long Depression. It lasted until 1879—or much longer, depending on which economic historian you ask. Fortunately for Seth, the nursery business recovered quickly; after 1875 sales of fruit trees gradually increased. But as farm production increased prices fell, while interest rates and shipping costs rose. In 1882 commenced another economic downturn. The country began to recover from that one only in 1885.

In Oregon as in California, the Patrons of Husbandry struggled against railroads, monopolists, and capitalists. The Oregon State Grange formed in 1873, the same year as its Californian counterpart. By 1875 there were 177 local Granges in Oregon. The Oregon Grange engaged in cooperative business activities and lobbied in the legislature, but with no great success. Membership declined in the late 1870s and 1880s.

Seth stayed away from the Grange through this period. His stepdaughter, Florence Ledding, later said that the organization was too conservative for the family. It was not, however, too conservative for Alfred Luelling, long the lone Granger of the family. It was Alfred who would eventually bring Seth into the Grange.

When Alfred and Mary sold their farm in Brooklyn and moved their family back to Oregon, in 1862, they settled near Hillsboro. Following his father's example, Alfred decided to farm with a friend. He formed a partnership with William Mills, the husband of Rachel Fisher, the Luellings' companion on the Overland Trail. The two men became serious cattle and sheep breeders, winning premiums in the Oregon State Fair for their French merino sheep and buying a "Spanish ram" at the California State Fair for $800—about $15,000 in 2023. Alfred also planted an orchard, for which he ordered fruit trees from his uncle Seth, according to Seth's diary.

Alfred soon involved himself in local and statewide civic affairs. In 1870, he became an incorporator of the Astoria and Salem Railroad, which presumably would have run through Hillsboro if had ever been built. He became a Mason. He was elected chief marshal of the state fair pavilion in 1872, taking over the job from his uncle Seth, and reelected in subsequent years. He was an officer in the Oregon State Agricultural Society in 1873 and 1874 and president of the Washington County Agricultural Society in 1874. In 1875 he became clerk of Washington County. The next year he chaired a county convention of the Independent Party, which promoted reform and opposed monopolies.

In 1878 Alfred and his family moved to Multnomah County. Alfred's civic activities continued, leaning left. Alfred and Mary returned to Hillsboro to host Abigail Scott Duniway, publisher of the *New Northwest*, when she spoke on women's rights and suffrage there. And the couple joined the Grange.

In 1884, Alfred was secretary of the Pomona (county-wide) Grange of Multnomah. He arranged for the Multnomah Grange to meet in Milwaukie, just over the county line. The Multnomah Grange met there twice, in both March and October. Presumably the idea was to recruit locals, who might start a local Grange. But no record exists that Seth or any other Milwaukie residents attended either meeting.

In May Alfred became Worthy Overseer of the Oregon State Grange, and both Alfred and Mary were elected delegates to the annual session of the State Grange.

Soon thereafter, Alfred and Mary moved back to Milwaukie, where he was appointed a notary public. I don't know whether Alfred returned so he could provide his uncle with help and companionship, but the two spent much time together. Alfred may have partnered with Seth in the nursery business for several years. Alfred was probably a frequent participant in Spiritualist circles at Seth's house, and he and Seth both became officers in a statewide Spiritualists' organization when it formed in 1886. Alfred also gradually drew Seth into politics.

But it wasn't until 1894 that Seth joined Alfred in the Grange. The reasons were political.

Sophronia

Alfred was one of three people who were very close to Seth in his late years. Another was Sophronia Vaughn Olson. When Seth and Clarissa first encountered her, Sophronia was a young widow who had only recently arrived from Nebraska. She and Clarissa became fast friends after meeting at the New Era Spiritualist camp, and Sophronia often visited the Lewellings' home. I suspect that Seth and Sophronia exchanged letters during his year in California, and that their growing intimacy encouraged him to return to Milwaukie.

In 1885, about three years after Clarissa's death, Seth and Sophronia married. She was only thirty-two, thirty-three years younger than Seth. Fourteen-year-old Bessie Lambert, Joseph Lambert's daughter, wrote in her journal on April 5 that "the boys have shivereed them every night since they came home from Salem. They haven't been able to get the couple out yet."

Sophronia brought with her into Seth's home her daughter Florence, who turned eight that year.

Besides being a Spiritualist, Sophronia was a reformer. For a time she had been a neighbor to Abigail Scott Duniway, founder of the women's suffrage movement in Oregon, and under Abigail's influence she herself had become a strong advocate for women's rights. After marrying Seth, Sophronia began holding Sunday afternoon salons, to which she invited fellow reformers and intellectuals. They included Oregonians such as

Sophronia Vaughn Lewelling. Courtesy of the Milwaukie Museum.

Abigail Duniway; Ernst Kroner, a Portland architect and Populist; and J. D. Stevens, who recited Shakespearean verse. National reformers visited, too: Thomas Mills, a Socialist writer and publisher; Mary Elizabeth Lease, a Populist orator from Kansas (and an irritant to Governor Lorenzo Dow Lewelling, Seth's nephew, who in 1893 removed her from her position as president of the Kansas Board of Charities); and Susan B. Anthony.

Sophronia, happily, was still young enough to produce babies. In 1886 she gave birth to a boy, whom the couple named Seth. But the baby died at eleven weeks. Two years later she gave birth to another son, Don Vaughn Lewelling. Seth now had a child to cheer his old age, and some consolation for the loss of Clarissa and all her children—including, in 1890, Addie, who died at forty-three (she was buried in the San Lorenzo cemetery, near her uncle John and various cousins). Seth's last child—the only one to outlive him—would grow up to call himself Don Llewellyn.

After Don's birth, Sophronia continued to devote herself to political work. Motherhood couldn't slow her down.

Bing

Seth would once more express his political leanings, gently, through the name of a cherry cultivar. His lasting fame, moreover, would derive not from the Black Republican cherry or the Luelling grape or even the Golden Prune, but from the Bing cherry. This is only in part because the variety has been considered, for a century and a half, one of the best sweet cherries in the world. The cherry's name, more than its qualities, has made its breeder unforgettable, because the name reflects Seth's peculiar regard for a Chinese farmworker, a man who otherwise would have been entirely forgotten in the land of his extended sojourn.

Chinese migrant workers, mostly from the province of Guangdong (also known as Canton or Kwangtung), at first came to North America's western shore for gold. As gold takings declined and the Chinese faced harassment, violence, and discriminatory fees and taxes, they turned to railroad, reclamation, factory, domestic, and farm work. Wealthy white people favored the Chinese as laborers and servants, because they were generally hardworking, quiet, neat, clean, and reliable.

By 1866, more than three-quarters of California's farmworkers were Chinese. Some would spend the off-season in urban Chinatowns and return to the same farms when needed, year after year. Some Chinese rented land, usually as sharecroppers, and planted their own field crops and orchards. Many Chinese farmers came with horticultural expertise; they had been vegetable farmers or orchardists in China.

Between 1870 and 1880, according to the U.S. Census, Chinese residents in the United States increased from 63,199 to 105,465, over 40 percent. More than 83 percent of them lived on the West Coast. During the Gold Rush, few ventured beyond California. But eventually Chinese workers spread up the coast to Oregon and Washington. They traveled in groups, often from the same village. Many worked under contract to Chinese labor bosses. By 1880, they composed more than 5 percent of Oregon's population.

John Lewelling and William Meek both hired Chinese workers. St. Helena had its own little Chinatown. As John Lewelling's descendant Doug Wight pointed out to me, a fruit harvester carved on the column supporting John's bust could well be, with his flat-topped cap, a Chinese man. But few records survive of these farmworkers' lives (although we do know that one accidentally set fire to a fence he and others were building on John's farm).

In Oregon, Seth hired his first "Chinaman"—the label was considered polite enough at the time—to work as a cook in 1862. Seth began hiring Chinese farmworkers in the spring of 1870, when he brought one, and then another, home from Portland. He hired more Chinese the next year. To two of them he gave a place to sleep in the grafting shop and a year's contract. The Chinese did whatever work was needed—grubbing out stumps, repairing the dam, hauling manure, digging seedling trees, peeling chittum bark, tending the fruit-drying house, and grafting trees. Sometimes the Chinese toiled as a team; sometimes they labored alongside white employees; and sometimes they worked solely with Seth, who was never a boss to relax while other men did his work. He hired more Chinese over subsequent years—eighteen of them in less than a week in 1872—and paid them as well as his white workers.

Seth first hired Bing in 1873, and set him to work hauling manure. Bing was about twenty-seven. In 1875 Seth gave Bing a year's contract, for $275. In 1875, 1876, and 1877, the two renewed the contract at the same rate. None of Seth's yearly diaries have survived beyond 1877, but Bing must have stayed with the Luellings, at least on and off, until the 1880s, when Seth's stepdaughter, Florence Olson, met him.

In a Federal Writers' Project interview conducted in 1939, Florence described Bing as unusual among the West Coast Chinese in that he came not from Guangdong but from Manchuria. He was close to six feet tall, or even taller. She said that he regularly sent money to his wife in China, who, without her husband around to father children, had adopted six or seven boys. The adopted sons would carry on the traditionally required ancestor worship. Bing, who liked to sing "Old Black Joe" "over and over again in a low minor key," talked often about his family and his desire to return to China to see them.

As Florence told the story, the Bing cherry got its name while Seth and Bing were working alternate rows in the orchard and discovered a seedling tree with excellent fruit. Someone said Seth should name it for himself, but he already had the Luelling. According to Florence, he replied, "I'll name this for Bing. It's a big cherry and Bing's big, and anyway it's in his row, so that shall be its name."

The Burlingame Treaty of 1868 had allowed free migration and emigration between China and the United States. (The treaty was the work of Anson Burlingame, U.S. minister and subsequently special envoy to China, who had visited Seth in 1859 and who would in 1869 send him a peach tree, two flowering cherry trees, and several shrubs from China.) But in the 1870s the United States entered a long economic depression, and Chinese immigrants got the blame. Thousands of white workers idling in San Francisco formed "anti-coolie clubs," called for boycotts of goods not labeled "made by white labor," and attacked Chinese residents. In July 1877, a rally to support strikers in the Eastern states triggered an anti-Chinese riot that lasted for days. Twenty laundries were burned, the windows of a Methodist mission were smashed, and four people were killed. An Irish immigrant, Dennis Kearney, was inspired by the riots to form his Workingmen's Party of California and continue the anti-Chinese agitation. In 1878 the Workingmen successfully fought for a state constitutional convention, which resulted in revisions that forbade government agencies and corporations from hiring Chinese and permitted municipalities to impose discriminatory requirements on Chinese residents and even to evict them. Some people suggested that white children should replace Chinese workers in the orchards.

Under pressure from California, Congress subsequently passed, in 1882, the first Chinese Exclusion Act. It forbade Chinese laborers from coming into the country, although merchants, professionals, diplomats, and students were permitted entry, and laborers currently residing in the United States could go to China and come back with a Certificate of Return.

The bank failures of 1884 spread panic throughout the nation and, in the Northwest, heightened resentment against the Chinese, who were said to steal jobs from white people by working cheap. They did indeed work cheap. In 1881, half the employees at the Oregon City woolen mills were Chinese. While the white workers made \$1.25 to \$1.50 a day, the Chinese workers made \$.90 to \$1.00. Chinese workers were paid \$.86 a day for railroad grading, whites \$1.75 a day (and white men ate twice as much, noted *Willamette Farmer*). Chinese got \$14 an acre for grubbing and clearing land, and "a more intelligent class" earned \$3.50 per week as house servants, taking the place of white girls.

Hostility to the Chinese was already well established in Oregon. The Oregon Constitution of 1859 forbade Chinese from owning mining claims or real estate. In 1870, Chinese workers refused to take jobs at the Salem woolen mills because they were afraid of "receiving violent treatment from mobs."

Yet the Portland area had been a relatively safe place for Chinese people. This was largely thanks to Harvey Scott, editor of the *Oregonian*, who consistently argued for the economic benefits of foreign as well as American labor and who supported an exclusion act but opposed violence against Chinese people. As a result, Portland had, in 1880, 9,515 Chinese residents, according to the U.S. Census. This was the second largest Chinese population among U.S. cities. When a Tacoma mob drove out its Chinese residents, on November 3, 1885, many of those expelled resettled in Portland.

Following the Tacoma riot, anti-Chinese violence continued in the region. Mobs ran most of the Chinese out of Seattle's Chinatown on February 6, 1886, and attempted to put them on a steamship bound for San Francisco. On February 7, Tacoma rioters again expelled the city's Chinese residents. On February 8, a mob in Olympia harassed their Chinese neighbors but failed to force them out of town.

Soon thereafter, on February 22, the attacks spread to Oregon. In Oregon City, members of the Knights of Labor and the Anti-Coolie League marched Chinese woolen-mill workers to the river and forced them onto a steamboat to Portland. In Portland, meanwhile, thirty-five hundred people paraded through the streets with signs reading, "Slavery must not exist here in 1886" and "The Chinese must go." Armed white men broke up a Chinese woodcutters' camp in Albina, then a nearby village. When the same Chinese were found cutting wood on Mount Tabor about ten days later, a mob drove them across the river to Portland.

Through this time of terror, according to Florence, Seth had his Chinese workers sleep in his house rather than in outbuildings. Anyone who came for his Chinese employees would have to take on the whole Luelling family.

On October 1, 1888, the federal Scott Act took effect. By declaring Certificates of Return void, the act trapped twenty thousand Chinese outside the United States with useless reentry permits. Some reached American ports before being turned back.

A spirit photograph of Seth and the ghost of Bing, with the ghost portrayed not as a farmworker but as a mandarin. Photographer unknown. Courtesy of the Milwaukie Museum.

Florence told her interviewer that Bing left in 1889 or 1890. Perhaps he actually left in 1888, before the Scott Act was passed, and then couldn't use his Certificate of Return. Perhaps he really did leave the country in 1889 or 1890, and didn't know the rules about returning. Or maybe he simply decided to stay in China. In any case, he never returned to Oregon.

Seth introduced the Bing cherry less systematically than the Black Republican. Although the Bing took first premium at the most magnificent of world's fairs—the 1893 Columbian Exposition in Chicago—the cherry wasn't widely appreciated for a long time, according to the horticulturist H. M. Williamson. But by 1905 the Bing was "fast supplanting its parent, the Black Republican. . . . It is without question one of the largest and best cherries grown, and the commercial fruit-growers of the Pacific Northwest owe a large debt of gratitude [to Seth] for originating this cherry."

The Farmers' Alliance

By 1890, reformers were fed up with the concentration of wealth and power that marked the Gilded Age. In Oregon, they fretted over the "ignorant, illiterate, lazy, [and] politically and personally immoral" men who dominated the state legislature. In that year, the Farmers' Alliance took over the Oregon Grange's political role.

The Farmers' Alliance had developed in the 1870s in the Midwest, High Plains, and South. In the South, the Alliance had fought the abuses of the crop-lien system, which left farmers in chronic debt. The Alliance also supported governmental regulation or takeover of the railroads, the establishment of a graduated income tax, the direct election of U.S. senators, and the use of silver as legal tender. "Free silver," advocates believed, would relax the money supply and thereby boost crop prices and make credit more available.

This, perhaps, was an organization radical enough for the Lewellings—or, I suspect, for Sophronia as well as Alfred. When the Alliance made its appearance in Oregon, the Lewellings immediately took leadership. The first Clackamas County Alliance meeting was held in the Good Temperance Hall in Milwaukie in the fall of 1890. At that meeting, Alfred was elected chair of the new Milwaukie Farmers' Alliance. Meetings continued at the Good Temperance Hall until it burned, after which the Alliance met at Seth and Sophronia's house. With the dividing wall open, the big living-dining room held about fifty people. The members discussed railroad rates, the shortage of currency, and the control of the legislature by monied interests. They brought relevant books they were reading, discussed them, and shared them.

Interest in the Farmers' Alliance spread so fast in the Willamette Valley that on July 25, 1891, the *Lebanon* (Oregon) *Express* published a "Farmers' Alliance Extra." On the front page appeared the Oregon State Alliance platform. It called for abolition of national banks, an increase in circulating currency, the free coinage of silver, the nationalization of the railways and other monopolies, the closing of saloons, a graduated income tax, small government loans to citizens, pay that Union soldiers had lost through the contraction of currency, fair renumeration for the "toiling masses," and "harmony and good will to all mankind." The platform comprised plenty of planks to appeal to social radicals.

U'Ren

Seth and Sophronia's Spiritualist activities continued. People came from as far as Portland to join the circles. One of them was Mrs. Laure Durkee, the wife of a former professor at the University of Oregon. On the Lewelling's grounds were several outbuildings that were used as housing for farmworkers. "On several occasions," writes the historian Thomas McClintock, Mrs. Durkee "brought to the Lewellings young men who were destitute and the family would help them get on their feet. They would be given one of the cabins and would take their meals with the family." In or about 1891, Mrs. Durkee brought William Simon U'Ren to one of the Lewellings' circles. He was broke, sick with asthma, and recovering from tuberculosis. He would become Seth's third close companion of his late years.

Born in 1859, U'Ren was the son of Cornish immigrants to Wisconsin. Apparently his parents added the apostrophe to the family name to prevent an embarrassing mispronunciation. U'Ren's father, a luckless farmer and blacksmith, moved the family frequently. They settled, briefly, in Colorado, Wyoming, and Nebraska. At seventeen U'Ren left home to work in the Colorado mines, and at nineteenth he became a blacksmith in Denver and attended night classes in business. Subsequently he read law, gained admission to the bar, and volunteered for the Republican Party, which he learned, to his dismay, was staging anti-Chinese riots to garner law-and-order votes. U'Ren served briefly as newspaper editor in the mining town of Tin Cup, and then, feeble with tuberculosis, traveled to Hawaii to work on a sugar plantation and either recover his health or die. After a year in the islands, he ended up in Oregon, where his parents were living.

Somewhere along the way U'Ren read Henry George's *Progress and Poverty*, the gospel of the single-tax movement. He immediately became a disciple. "I went just as crazy over the single-tax idea as anyone else ever did," he reported at the first Single Tax Conference, held in New York City in 1910. The idea was this: Taxing land according to its true value, with all improvements exempted, would discourage speculation and deliver farmers from misery.

From the single-tax idea U'Ren launched himself into struggles for other democratic legislation. Oregon seemed especially needful of this work; the state's government was reputedly among the most corrupt and

William Simon U'Ren. From Gaston, *Centennial History of Oregon.*

inefficient in the United States. U'Ren later remembered that votes were bought for two and a half dollars, that "repeaters" (repeat voters) were bused from one Portland polling place to another, and that the legislature elected U.S. senators during "forty days and forty nights" of debauchery. U'Ren worked with the lawyer Edward W. Bingham to establish the "Australian ballot," or secret ballot, in Oregon elections. The legislature passed the measure about the time U'Ren met the Lewellings.

U'Ren quickly became close to the family. He began attending Farmers' Alliance meetings, the Lewellings' salons, and more of their circles. During one circle, Sophronia said many years later, U'Ren pretended to come under the influence of Seth's son William Anton, then about twelve years dead. "HYPNOTIZED HER HUSBAND," read the *Oregonian* headline. U'Ren denied doing any such thing, though he freely admitted being a Spiritualist. Perhaps U'Ren reminded Seth of Willie. For whatever reason, Seth liked U'Ren so well that he hired him as secretary for the nursery business.

At one of the Farmers' Alliance meetings, Alfred presented a copy of *Direct Legislation by Citizenship, Through the Initiative and Referendum,* by James W. Sullivan, who had served as labor editor for Henry George's weekly *Standard.* "I read the book through before I slept that night," U'Ren later recalled. "I forgot, for the time, all about Henry George and the single tax. . . . The one important thing was to restore the law-making power where it belongs—into the hands of the people. Once give us that, we could get anything we wanted—single tax, anything." From then on, Sullivan's "Swiss System" of direct legislation was the main topic of discussion at Milwaukie's Alliance meetings.

At a meeting attended by two Swiss natives, the Milwaukie Farmers' Alliance decided to organize to bring direct legislation to Oregon. They asked the state executive committee of the Farmers' Alliance to invite the state Grange, the Oregon Knights of Labor, the Portland Federated Trades, and the Portland Chamber of Commerce to join in forming the Joint Committee on Direct Legislation. Every one of the organizations except the Chamber of Commerce accepted. U'Ren became not president but secretary for the new organization. As Edward Bingham had taught him, he could work most effectively from the back seat.

Alliance leaders in Milwaukie and elsewhere soon began to organize a People's, or Populist, Party in Oregon. In joining the Populists, Seth may have drawn inspiration from his nephew—and Alfred from his cousin—Lorenzo Dow Lewelling. Just a baby when his father died, this youngest son of William Lorenzo Lewelling had worked as the superintendent of the Iowa Women's Reform School and as a newspaper editor before moving to Kansas, where he became a Congregationalist and a butter wholesaler. Although he was little known in Kansas when he arrived at the state's Populist convention in 1892, Lorenzo Lewelling took the opportunity to make a speech. He must have displayed the inspirational power of both his father and his namesake, the preacher Lorenzo Dow, because his speech so moved the crowd that within a day he was voted the Populist candidate for governor. He would win the race, barely, and become the nation's first Populist governor. He would soon make *Lewelling* a household name nationwide.

The Oregon Populists held a party convention, in Oregon City in March 1892, on the day after the statewide Farmers' Alliance convention so that Alliance delegates could easily attend both events. Most did, and soon "the same men held offices in both groups." The Lewellings, U'Ren, and J. D. Stevens, who was also living in the Lewelling household, all joined the People's Party at this point (J. D. Stevens was later described in one newspaper article as "the man who attempts to convert the world to Socialism on the street corners of Portland"). They and their followers made sure that direct legislation took a prominent place in the Populist platform. The new party had such widespread appeal that in November Oregonians would elect a Populist presidential elector and five Populist state legislators.

In late 1892, Seth invited U'Ren to become a partner in the nursery business, with a three-year renewable contract. U'Ren would join Seth and another partner, Edgar A. Hansee of Sellwood. Although U'Ren had no money to contribute to the business, he was to receive a third of the profits. This was an extraordinary opportunity for a destitute young man.

Only a few months later, however, the Panic of 1893 struck, and the American economy foundered again. The market for fruit trees collapsed. J. H. Settlemier, a fellow Oregon nurseryman, described how the panic affected his own business: "There was no sale for nursery stock of any kind. The Woodburn nursery had to dig and burn block after block of the very finest trees that were getting too large for sale. . . . The firm sunk $38,000 before the tide turned to a paying basis."

Seth was already advertising, in his 1893 catalog, "Prices Lower Than Ever Before Anywhere." And they probably were: he was offering one-year-old trees for ten to fifteen cents each, and two-year-old trees for ten to twenty cents. Now he couldn't sell trees even at those prices.

U'Ren suggested that the Milwaukie partners shut down the business. But Seth would not, nor would he agree to U'Ren's leaving the partnership. It was perhaps at this point that he gave U'Ren a share in all the family's taxable property—including buildings, accounts, household furnishings, horses, cattle, and 347.5 acres of land. The land was in 61-, 21-, 240-, and 1.5-acre farm parcels, plus the twenty-four blocks of Lewelling Park, a residential addition to the city of Milwaukie. The total assessed value of the land was $11,500, or about $397,000 in 2024 dollars. The tax bill and receipt for all of this were issued jointly to Seth and Sophronia Lewelling and William U'Ren.

Despite a fruit-tree-planting boom, in California, Oregon, Washington, and Idaho, that peaked in 1892, Seth's finances had been in trouble even before the economic crisis. At the Oregon Historical Society is a box of Seth's correspondence from late 1892 and 1893. Much of it concerns monies owed. In November 1892 the Oregon State Horticultural Society asked Seth to pay his late dues. In December he was denied a loan on some of his orchard property. On January 17 his bank, Ladd and Tilton, wrote him about three past-due notes, for $500, $1,000, and $2,000—a total of about $120,000 in 2024 dollars. Nine days later, lawyers wrote Seth about a past-due note for $650 that had been placed in their hands for collection.

Apparently the same day he received the collection notice, Seth wrote his bankers, "Gentlemen: We need $150.00 Will you honor our checks for that amount, and oblige us." Ladd and Tilton—or Ladd, Tilton, or an employee—replied in a handwritten note at the bottom of Seth's letter. "Not unless you have funds to your credit to meet same. There is to your credit this morning $25.19."

Merchants who had given Seth credit pleaded with him. In February a hardware company sent a statement of Seth's unpaid purchases from 1892. The same month, a machinery company requested a "long since" due $4.80. Seth paid the latter, but closed the account. The following June, the debt-collecting lawyers informed Seth that he still owed nearly $300 on the $650 note.

Meanwhile, Seth was receiving troubling notes from J. T. Chute, who ran Seth's nursery at Canby. On April 24 Chute wrote, "Our hay is not going to last only this week what will we do about it." He added a postscript: "And we are out of meat also tell me what to do." On May 26 he informed his boss, "Frank White was here this morning and he says that he will give you between three and four days to get his pay here or he will collect damages."

Over the preceding months, Seth and Sophronia had been spending to a risky extent. In 1892 Seth had invested $1,000 in an interurban electric railroad—the nation's first—to connect Milwaukie with Portland and Oregon City. The line began operating the following year, and it was a boon to the area. But the investment was one that the family could ill afford. So was Sophronia's purchase of three lots in Summerland, a Spiritualist resort founded near Santa Barbara, California, and named for Andrew Jackson Davis's conception of the Spiritualist afterlife. The couple had also invested in Pruneland, an agricultural subdivision near

Canby, for which in July 1893 Seth owed $97.60 interest on a $1,200 note (Seth's Canby nursery was probably on Pruneland parcels). In addition, Seth and U'Ren had also given financial support to new reformist publications, *Freedom: A Radical Review*, published from 1891 to 1893, and the *Northwest Reform Journal*, published from 1890 to 1894 (while Alfred joined like-minded men in founding the short-lived Populist *Farmers' Journal*).

According to U'Ren, when he joined the partnership "there was an indebtedness against the property of between $5000 and $6000." Soon it would be $28,000. Seth and his partners closed the nursery at Canby.

Fruit sales that year failed to raise Seth out of debt. Low prices were one problem; another was the difficulty of shipping soft fruits long distances. Lindsay and Company, of Helena, Montana, wrote to complain of the condition of Seth's strawberries: "They were a little over-ripe, or else, had been picked in the rain." The crates weren't the best sort, Lindsay groused, and they should have been covered with manila paper rather than tissue. Four days later Lindsay sent a telegram: "Strawberries very bad condition. Better not ship sure loss." Harris Brothers, in Tacoma, also sent a telegram: "Market busted stop shipments until we advise." Ed Adams' Sons wrote from Tacoma as well: "The Raspberries are a total loss—they being mashed. We don't think it adviseable to ship raspberries unless in pint boxes." Lindsay, in Montana, wrote Seth again in July: "Ship no more cherries no sale other fruit to cheap will write."

Where was Seth's secretary and newest partner during these challenging times? Sometimes, at least, he was at his desk in Seth and Sophronia's house. U'Ren had the authority to sign Seth's name to all checks and other documents concerned with the nursery business, Sophronia later reported. Perhaps Seth never saw much of the correspondence he himself ostensibly carried on in 1893.

Unfortunately, U'Ren had little time to put the nursery business in order. He was now secretary of the Populist State Committee as well as the Joint Committee on Direct Legislation. In both organizations, U'Ren's job was to run a public information campaign about the initiative and referendum, or "I. & R.," in preparation for the 1894 election. Through the joint committee, he sought the support of other parties besides the Populists. He convinced the Democrats, though not the Republicans, to make I. & R. a plank in their platform.

Meanwhile, the Lewellings and their Milwaukie neighbors also worked hard for the cause. They bought and distributed 1,000 copies of Sullivan's book. Then the Direct Legislation Committee designed an eight-page pamphlet explaining the I. & R. The printers' union printed it, and the women of Milwaukie stitched each copy together. In the winter of 1893–94, two-thirds of the homes in Milwaukie (about twelve) took part in the project. They prepared fifty thousand pamphlets in English and, for Oregon's many German-speaking residents, another eighteen thousand in their language. The Alliance members sent copies of a similar piece to newspaper editors and persuaded the editors to insert them into their papers. By these means they circulated four hundred thousand printed pieces about the I. & R. from 1892 to 1898.

I didn't find printers' bills in the box at the Oregon Historical Society, but the expenses must have been substantial. Sophronia, in 1908, claimed that the educational campaign cost Seth four thousand dollars plus U'Ren's hotel and transportation expenses. U'Ren countered that the Lewellings provided "possibly a few hundred dollars" to promote the I. & R.

Although Seth, in his seventies, was too busy and probably too tired to travel much, other members of the Milwaukie Alliance—especially Sophronia, Florence, U'Ren, Alfred, and J. D. Stevens—addressed meetings near and far about the I. & R. Among the gatherings they visited were other Alliance groups, teachers' groups, and Granges.

The campaigners may have figured that they would have more influence within the Grange if they all became Grangers themselves. Besides, with the rise of the People's Party, the Farmers' Alliance was vanishing away. So, in January 1894, the Milwaukie Alliance members founded their own local Grange, with Alfred as first master. Not all the founding members were considered radicals, but most must have had reformist inclinations, because the Alliance activities continued through the Grange. Florence Ledding later said that getting the members to endorse the I. & R. required two rounds of voting. Still, the Pomona Grange of Milwaukie was among the first, if not the very first, among Oregon Granges to endorse the reforms.

Wherever they went, the I. & R. advocates took petitions along. These petitions asked the legislature to call a constitutional convention that would make the I. & R. part of the state constitution. J. D. Stevens walked all over Clackamas County, "eating and sleeping at farmhouses and talking for the cause wherever he found an audience," and gathering signatures. When U'Ren delivered the petitions to the legislature in 1895, they bore fourteen thousand signatures—out of a total electorate of eighty thousand.

But in the legislature the motion lost by one vote. U'Ren was furious. He went "out from the Legislature to punish the members who had broken their pledges," he explained to an interviewer later. Apparently he meant that he publicized their wrongdoings. Alfred gently convinced him to stop this. From then on, said U'Ren, "our policy was to publish, not a man's delinquencies, but his promises."

On July 1, 1895, Seth suffered a stroke. It partially paralyzed him. He was now helpless either to run his business or to work in the I. & R. campaign.

Faced with defeat in the legislature and the crippling of his close friend, business partner, and benefactor, U'Ren remained tenacious and even optimistic. He considered that the I. & R. could be passed in another way than by holding a constitutional convention. Oregon, in fact, already had a sort of referendum law. If the I. & R. were passed in two consecutive legislative sessions, the proposal could be submitted to the electorate for a vote.

On February 21, 1896, Seth died. His funeral, held at his house, "was attended by nearly every resident" of Milwaukie, reported the *Oregon Courier* (February 28, 1896). "His body was followed to its last rest" in the Milwaukie cemetery, according to the *Oregon City Enterprise* (February 28, 1896), "by a large number of sorrowing neighbors and pioneer friends from far and near." The Milwaukie Grange performed "the beautiful service of that Order."

Seemingly unfazed by Seth's death, U'Ren decided to run for the legislature himself. In 1896 he became a Populist candidate for the Oregon house of representatives. On May 22, 1896, the *Oregon City Enterprise* ridiculed him as

> virtually a carpet bagger, being a comparative recent arrival in the state of Oregon, and as he is not a taxpayer, he is not identified with the interest of Clackamas county any more than to hold down a soft job as manager of the Lewelling nursery at Milwaukee [*sic*], which by the way has gone fluey under his alleged management.

> He would like to be governor of Oregon . . . , consequently he would give all his old clothes and half the populist party to get elected to office.

U'Ren was now suspected both of crippling the Milwaukie Nursery and of lusting for power. He was maligned, too, for hurting the Populists through his incessant emphasis on the I. & R. over the "free silver" question. But the Lewellings, J. D. Stevens, and other Milwaukie Populists canvassed for U'Ren, and he dazzled the crowds in a series of debates in his district. Although the majority of Clackamas County voters were Republican, the entire Populist ticket won in the county.

The I. & R. would finally win the voters' approval in 1902, after twice passing in the legislature. It passed in the legislature only because of a deal U'Ren made with other legislators, in 1897, to prevent John Mitchell's election to the U.S. Senate and to keep the Oregon House of Representatives from organizing. By taking a seat on the credentials committee and then failing to report to a meeting, U'Ren and other anti-Mitchell legislators prevented the House from organizing and kept Oregon from electing a U.S. senator. This was the start of Oregon's infamous "Hold-Up Session." No legislation was passed during U'Ren's one term in office, and no House member was paid. But U'Ren ensured that enough Republicans would support I. & R. in 1899 and 1901 that the measures would go to the ballot. When Oregonians finally got the chance, they voted overwhelmingly in favor of the initiative and referendum process.

In 1903 a circuit court declared the I. & R. unconstitutional, but the Oregon Supreme Court upheld the laws. Oregon's initiative and referendum system has remained popular ever since.

In 1897, however, U'Ren's fellow Milwaukie Grangers were upset by his scheming in the legislature. The "Moses that was to lead the people of the state into peace, plenty and comfort" seemed to be undermining democracy instead. Learning of the full indebtedness of Seth's estate turned Sophronia even more against U'Ren. The sheriff sold much of the estate to meet creditors' claims. Sophronia was able to keep only the house in Milwaukie and twenty-two acres of land—and that through help from Florence and a relative in California. U'Ren, the negligent nursery manager, got the blame. As a final injury, Sophronia had to hire a foreman to do the nursery work U'Ren was shirking.

U'Ren moved out of the Lewelling home in late summer of 1897. Sophronia, Florence, and J. D. Stevens went to war against him. On November 1 Sophronia filed an affidavit of all she had witnessed of U'Ren's alleged corruption, including his display of "a large roll of bills," which he had "drawn on his share of the Salem business." In January 1898 Florence and Stevens presented formal charges against U'Ren to the Populist County Central Committee in Oregon City while displaying letters that U'Ren said had been stolen from his home. At the next meeting of the Central Committee, U'Ren refused Stevens entrance, and the two hit each other in the face.

U'Ren was exonerated by the central committee, and he was never prosecuted for any crimes. But when he campaigned for a seat in the Oregon Senate in 1898, he later recounted, "Mrs. Lewelling and J. D. Stevens flooded the county with literature in denunciation of me." He lost the election.

When U'Ren addressed the Milwaukie Grange in 1907, Sophronia and J. D. Stevens heckled him.

In 1908 U'Ren ran for office again, this time for the U.S. Senate, as a Republican. But as soon as he announced his candidacy Sophronia and J. D. Stevens resumed their public denunciations of him. He withdrew from the race a few weeks after entering it.

While making his living as a lawyer, U'Ren continued his work as a lobbyist for democratic reforms. Through his leadership, the people of Oregon passed the Direct Primary Bill in 1904. Now they, rather than the party machines, could choose their nominees for office. And by writing into the Direct Primary Bill that candidates for the legislature might pledge themselves to vote for or against the people's choice for U.S. senators, he introduced to Oregon the practice of choosing U.S. senators by popular election.

In the following years, the I. & R. worked its magic. Under U'Ren's leadership, initiatives were passed to extend the I. & R. to cities, to give municipalities complete home rule, and to make it easier for the legislature to refer constitutional measures to the people (with a half vote instead of a two-thirds vote of both houses). The "recall" initiative let the people discharge any state official and choose a successor by a special election. Another successful initiative made the people's choice of U.S. senators mandatory, and yet another required proportional representation, so that each legislator had to be elected by a roughly equal number of voters.

U'Ren never managed to get a single-tax law passed. He was defeated in other ways, too. He tried to abolish the state senate in favor of a unicameral legislature, and failed. He ran twice more for the legislature, and lost. But Oregonians still remember him for the democratic reforms he won—reforms that together are known as the Oregon System.

The Lewellings—Seth, Sophronia, and Alfred—deserve much credit for helping U'Ren on his way. "They worked faithfully and devotedly and we all contributed what money we could afford," U'Ren told the *Oregonian* in 1908. "No finer men every lived than Seth Lewelling and Alfred Lewelling."

Seth has received special praise, from at least one historian, for his role in the passage of the I. & R. "Too great credit cannot be given Seth Lewelling, the one man who had the means to finance such an undertaking. . . . Probably at the beginning of all such reforms there is usually such a man as Seth Lewelling, an enthusiast who is willing to mortgage his property to the last dollar in order to succeed."

Sophronia died on August 2, 1928. She was buried alongside Seth.

Chapter 13
Afterwards

> Oregon has won more medals . . . for her fine fruits than any other state in the Union, and the fame of several varieties of Pacific Coast fruits has spread to the remotest corners of the earth.
>
> —*Morning Oregonian*, February 4, 1907

In the end, what did the Lewelllings leave us?

The brothers' horticultural gifts were many. Although Henderson wasn't the first to bring grafted trees to Oregon, he planted the territory's first grafted orchard, and with the help of his brothers and William Meek he furiously propagated and marketed his trees until commercial as well as homestead orchards, bearing big, sweet fruits in great variety, dotted the whole Willamette Valley and spread into Washington and beyond. The brothers provided some of the first apples, pears, and cherries to fruit-starved California gold miners. As Californians began to plant their own grafted orchards, the Lewellings supplied trees, from Seth's nursery in Oregon, from the little nursery Seth and John planted at Illinoistown, from Henderson's nursery at Fruit Vale, and from John's at San Lorenzo. John made red currants a popular California crop. Seth developed the first cherries that could withstand rough shipping, including a variety that home and commercial growers still cherish today. John and Meek, for a time, grew most of California's cherries. John developed an almond variety that became an orchard standard. And through his role in the St. Helena Vinicultural Club John was fundamental to the development of today's West Coast wine industry.

The Lewellings' story is a gift in itself. Henderson's adventures are most memorable, for his heroism in bringing a wagonload of trees to Oregon and for his hubris in trying to start a Harmonial Brotherhood colony in Central America. Other parts of the brothers' story are more touching than sensational. The Lewellings weren't industrialists of the land; they were gardeners. They grew various crops, not just one, for home consumption as well as for sale. In a sense, the world was the Lewelling's garden, because they didn't just cultivate plants; they cultivated people. They shared their skills as well as their scions not only with family members and friends but with every interested farmer who came their way. They worked to improve farming and the farming life through horticultural societies and fairs, through the Grange and the Farmers' Alliance, and through political organizing. They cultivated children by supporting schools, and they cultivated themselves through books, lectures, and night classes. They cultivated community through Quaker meetings, Spiritualist circles, public service, and cooperative ventures of various kinds. Because of their honesty, kindness, and pacifism, theirs is a kinder, gentler story of westward expansion.

Like other radical Quakers, Henderson and John, in Iowa, agitated against slavery and provided refuge and transport to runaways. Seth probably participated in the same work in Indiana. On leaving the Eastern states, the Lewellings rejected religious rites and rules and left others to finish the work of freeing the slaves. Still, the brothers remained visionaries. They took up new causes, including the fight against monopoly capitalism and the struggles for women's rights and the democratic process. We have Seth to thank, in part, for Oregon's system of direct democracy. We should also remember him, with every bite of a Bing cherry, for his lifelong stand against racial hatred.

I set out to see what I could of the Lewelling legacy.

The Places

Milwaukie, Oregon, has its own municipal government, but to the casual visitor the city seems inseparable from the rest of the Portland metropolis. Much of Henderson's land claim is now the ultra-exclusive Waverley Country Club, but in 1955 twenty-eight trees from the original orchard still survived on adjacent residential parcels. One of the trees, a then still very prolific Gloria Mundi, produced apples averaging a pound and a quarter in weight. One of the apples measured more than sixteen inches around and weighed more than two pounds. (Those trees have almost certainly since died.)

In 1940, Seth Lewelling's house was razed to make way for a gas station. A seventy-five-year-old flowering peach tree, which Anson Burlingame had sent as a seedling from China, was uprooted and transplanted to the rear of a new Milwaukie city hall. The tree survived for decades there, until it was finally cut down in 1987.

But locals remember Seth Lewelling—more so than they do Henderson, who, after all, lived in the area for only six years or so. Up Johnson Creek from the Waverley Country Club is the neighborhood called Lewelling, built on town lots that Seth bought as an investment, and within the Lewelling neighborhood is the Seth Lewelling Elementary School.

Thanks to Oregon's laws protecting farmland, agriculture still thrives in Clackamas County. Commercial fruit-tree culture has mostly moved beyond the Cascades, but the county has berry farms, filbert orchards, and thousands of small home orchards with apples, pears, cherries, and peaches. Clackamas County Community College has a fruit arboretum, operated by the Home Orchard Education Center, and near Molalla is Joanie Cooper's Temperate Orchard Conservancy, with several thousand cultivars of apple and other fruits. On the conservancy's list of available scions is Seth's Sweet Alice apple. Perhaps Seth is a hazily remembered inspiration for today's enthusiastic home fruit growers, throughout the Willamette Valley and especially in Clackamas County.

Little sign of Henderson remains in Oakland, California. Not long after Governor Weller bought Fruit Vale, he sold it to a man named Hugh Dimond, an Irish-born liquor dealer. After Dimond's death, in 1896, the canyon became "a famous picnic ground and a gathering-place . . . for all the artists and sketching clubs within a radius of twenty miles." Sadly, the house Henderson built was partially destroyed by fire in 1913. Four years later, the Dimond family sold the last twelve acres to the city of Oakland. At some point the house was razed, and the land became Dimond Park.

In 1923, Reverend Franklin Rhoda and the Fruitvale Women's Club proposed moving one of Henderson's original apple trees from Fruitvale Avenue to Dimond Park as a memorial to the area's first horticulturist. But transplanting such a big, old tree must have proved too difficult. Instead, in February 1924 the Fruitvale Women's Club planted three young redwood trees in Dimond Park, in memory of Henderson, the famous plant breeder Luther Burbank, and a prominent conservationist named May Crocker. Five of Henderson's descendants—two granddaughters, a great-granddaughter, a grandniece, and a great-grandnephew—attended the ceremony, and Franklin Rhoda told Henderson's story to the crowd. Henderson's tree, according to the newspaper account, was planted on what had been his house site.

When I visited Dimond Park, I could easily imagine where the house had been. The magnificent oak that had stood beside the house was gone. But side by side were two conifers, a redwood and another tall tree that I couldn't immediately identify. In their shade, dozens of people practiced tai chi. Had the redwood been planted by the women's club? I scratched around the base of each tree but found no sign of a marker. Henderson seemed to have been forgotten at Dimond Park. But, then, he lived here only about five years.

At Mountain View Cemetery, in the Oakland Hills, Henderson's grave is now marked by a large granite stone. Henderson's name is at the top, with the words "FATHER PACIFIC HORTICULTURE" just below. I suspect that Franklin Rhoda had the stone engraved and installed.

Listed further below are the names of Henderson's relatives buried in the same plot: his daughter Hannah, her husband William Bradbury, and her daughter (with Walter Wood), Charlotte Lynch, as well as Henderson's daughter Rachel, her husband Henry Wilson, and Rachel's daughter (with Seth Eddy) Della Bidwell. Pearlie Wilson, who has a separate headstone, died in 1872, so Henderson must have been preparing for his own death well in advance of his fatal heart attack. I am somehow comforted to know that two of his daughters and their families stayed close to the notorious free lover until the end.

I'd never heard of San Lorenzo before I started researching the Lewellings. Nobody I knew in California had heard of it. There is the San Lorenzo Valley in the Santa Cruz Mountains, yes, but a town of San Lorenzo?

This unincorporated burg is just one bedroom community among many in the sea of pavement and little houses that lines the east side of the bay. After big farms like Eli's and Meek's were divided into smaller farms, the smaller farms were divided again, during World War II, for workers' housing. San Lorenzo's first "village"—1,329 houses—was built in eight months in 1944. Now San Lorenzo and surrounding towns have no orchards, no farms at all. The yards are generally too small for more than one tree, and many have none. Thirty-eight percent of the residents are Latino, immigrants or children of immigrants.

The San Lorenzo Pioneer Cemetery is bordered by a freeway on one side and a highway on another. The cemetery is fenced, the gate kept locked to keep out campers and vandals. A sign informs visitors of a renovation project in progress, but headstones are missing and broken, and large shrubs grow in the paths. My husband and I walked through a person-size gap in the fence to see the Lewelling and Meek plots. When the county employee assigned to let us in arrived, he said we could have been arrested for entering the cemetery before he unlocked the gate.

While we walked among the plots, a man reached his arm through the fence and gently waved around his cell phone. He had a spirit-finding app, he said. As we looked at his phone two gauzy bubbles appeared over John's and Elvy's graves. Suddenly the bubbles transformed themselves into skeletons. They were spirits, said the man. I asked why they had appeared over these two graves. Sometimes spirits come out because they don't get enough flowers or visitors, the man said. I hadn't thought to bring flowers. Maybe I should have brought fruit?

We drove to Meek Park via Lewelling Boulevard, formerly Main Street; the road was renamed after Eli's death. To reach the mansion we crossed a footbridge over what a sign identified as San Lorenzo Creek. I was glad for the sign, because without it I might not have recognized the smooth concrete chute, its walls covered with colorful graffiti, as a creek at all. I looked closer: Down the center of the chute ran a narrow, shallow trough bearing a trickle of water. This was the creek that, once upon a time, had annually flooded and fertilized all the surrounding land.

The Hayward Area Recreation and Park District operates Meek's mansion and its grounds as a public park and wedding venue. We couldn't go into the house, but we admired the exterior and wandered around the lovely grounds. We saw a walnut tree and a few fruit trees, a symbolic mini-orchard.

St. Helena is still a small town, with many nineteenth-century buildings still in use. We found John's stone winery on Spring Street, though we struggled to see the walls through the ivy that covers them. The Winegrowers' Hall was long gone, but on Church Street by the railroad was the bonded warehouse, its midsection now occupied by a wine-storage company—for consumers, not producers.

Surrounding the town and covering nearly all of the Napa Valley are commercial vineyards. Members of the St. Helena Vinicultural Club might be shocked at the success of their long-ago efforts. But the path to the present wasn't at all straightforward.

Not long after John's death, Harvy Lewelling and other winegrowers tore out vines infested with phylloxera. Some replanted their vineyards with grafted vines. Then came Prohibition—actually not such a dry time for Napa Valley winegrowers, who could still ship grapes for home wine making (many vines were grafted with sturdy shipping varieties, though they made inferior wine). After the repeal of Prohibition, the California wine industry recovered slowly, not only because of the Depression but also because Americans had lost interest in fine wine after gaining a taste for soda pop. During World War II, prunes and walnuts were important Napa Valley crops, grown mainly for shipping overseas.

Under Harvy's ownership, the Lewellings' St. Helena ranch endured hard times. The price of a box of pears fell by 50 percent from September 1892 to October 1894, and half the plum trees in California were cut down. But the ranch also produced table grapes, apricots, and citrus, and this diversity proved advantageous. When Eli died, in 1926, Harvy inherited the lucrative San Lorenzo farm, whose even more diverse products included avocados, asparagus, olives, figs, and peonies. Harvy ran the San Lorenzo farm for a few years, until Alameda County bought it, in 1930, to produce food for the county poor farm and hospital. This and other real-estate deals, including the sale of the first parcel John bought in Napa Valley, helped support what remained of the St. Helena farm.

Harvy was wealthy enough to let a hired crew run the farm while he kept busy with other things. He succeeded John as a director of the Grangers' Bank of California and as president of the Bank of St. Helena (he kept the latter position for twenty-five years, without drawing a salary). He became a director of the St. Helena Vinicultural Association, as the former club was called by 1889. A natural mechanic, Harvy invented an almond sheller and an animal-pen watering system and, with a friend, built the county's first automobile. He installed a gas plant at his home and later supplanted it with the first private electrical unit on the Pacific coast. He also organized a telephone exchange and a gas company, bred fancy chickens, and practiced photography.

Westering emigrants' fecundity generally dwindled when they reached the Pacific shores, and the Lewellings were no exception. Of Henderson's eleven children, only the first and third, Alfred and Asenath, produced big families (Alfred had nine children, Asenath eleven). The younger among the second generation generally married late and had few offspring. Seth Lewelling had six children and only two grandchildren. John outdid Seth: he had eight children and seven grandchildren, Sarah's three and Harvy's four.

The most remarkable thing about the St. Helena Lewellings is that they have kept much of their land and continued to farm it. In 1923 Harvy gave three of his children, Ethel, Lester, and Raymond, twenty acres each (the fourth child, Mabel, worked as a schoolteacher). The siblings grew prunes and walnuts, and Ethel and her husband, Albert Taplin, raised turkeys in their walnut orchard. In 1939 Harvy died and left all his land, about four hundred acres, to Raymond. Raymond sold some of the land but held on to most of it. He had no children, and Ethel and Lester had only one child each: Ethel had a son, Ken Taplin, and Lester had a daughter, Janice Wight. When Raymond died, in 1987, he left the remaining properties (including the bonded warehouse) not to Ken and Janice but in trust to their children. Ken and Janice each had three. At this writing, the cousins still share ownership.

There are no almond, prune, walnut, apricot, or cherry orchards on the Lewelling land now; all of it is in wine grapes. Janice's son Doug manages the family vineyard along with five hundred more acres of Napa Valley vineyard. Most of the grapes are sold, but a portion of the vineyard supplies the family's own three wineries: Lewelling Vineyards, Taplin Cellars, and Hayfork. Doug and his two brothers, Dave and Alan, run Lewelling Vineyards with help from Doug's daughter, Haley, who is now winemaker for both Lewelling and Hayfork, her own label. Bill and Stephen Taplin operate Taplin Cellars with another sixth-generation family member, Adam Taplin. Since Bill and Stephen's sister, Melinda Taplin, has passed on, this means that all of the fifth-generation Lewellings, as well as two from the sixth generation, are still involved with the family farm.

No one has lived in John Lewelling's house for a long time. But it still stands, in fairly good condition. Inside, the nineteenth-century furnishings remain, including a huge dining table with a surprisingly large number of chairs around it. I didn't count them, but they must number at least sixteen, perhaps twenty or more. Everyday meals must have been like parties for the Lewellings.

Local legislation has motivated winegrowers to keep their land as farmland. In 1968, Napa County created the Napa Valley Agricultural Preserve, the first such set of zoning laws in the country. More than forty-seven thousand acres are now protected in perpetuity through conservation agreements between landowners and the Land Trust of Napa County. This success may have inspired locals to fight—and win--against a plan to build a freeway up the valley.

The land trust has kept the Napa Valley pretty and productive, but it hasn't kept other families on the land. Most of the Napa Valley wineries are owned by large corporations. In fact, the Lewelling descendants are the only family in the area that have continued farming their land since the early days of the Napa Valley wine business. There is something special about this family.

I must mention here also John's other grandchildren, the Kings—or, at least, the one who made his mark in farming, Lewis Leroy. Born to John and Elvy's daughter Sarah at Mission San José, he, too, is part of the Lewelling legacy. He and his wife raised fruit in San Lorenzo before moving to Roseville, twenty miles northeast of Sacramento, in 1890. There they established an estate called Cherry Glen, with eleven thousand fruit trees—cherries, peaches, apricots, plums, almonds, and figs. On a separate forty-acre parcel, Lewis grew table grapes. Many streets in Roseville still bear the names of King family members.

Few other Lewelling descendants were farmers or ranchers. Don Llewellyn, Seth's only child to survive him, had no chance to take over the Milwaukie Nursery. Instead, he enjoyed a long career as Milwaukie's fire chief.

At least one of Henderson's grandchildren carried on with westward expansion—except that he went east. In 1904, Alfred's youngest son, Seth Patterson Luelling, moved with his family over the Cascades and claimed 160 acres north of Madras under the Homestead Act of 1862. The family started a new Luelling lineage in Central Oregon, where some of Seth Patterson Luelling's descendants are still farming—although they can't profitably grow tree fruit in the high desert.

The Lewellings' horticultural influence extended far beyond their family. There were all the people they taught, collaborated with, or inspired, including William Meek, Enos Mendenhall, Ralph Geer, Joseph Lambert, Henry Miller, Ezra Meeker, Franklin Rhoda, members of the St. Helena Vinicultural Club and horticultural societies, exhibitors and attendees at horticultural fairs, and hundreds of hired workers. And these men in turn taught, collaborated with, and inspired many others in the art and science of horticulture. In addition, John Lewelling contributed greatly to the development of the Napa Valley wine industry through his work on the bonded warehouse, the Viticultural Hall, the Bank of St. Helena, and his efforts to combat phylloxera.

The Fruits

The Lewellings also left us their fruits, the ones Henderson brought to Oregon and the ones Seth and John developed.

Henderson brought us the Royal Ann (formerly Napoleon), long the queen among "blush" cherries, although in recently decades it has been largely replaced by the very similar Rainier. Prone to browning, Royal Ann is the cherry for which the faux maraschino process was developed, using brine and dye and flavoring but no maraschino liqueur or alcohol of any kind. I think the cherry is much nicer fresh from the tree.

Few of the apples Henderson brought from Iowa and New York remain popular among commercial farmers today. Exceptions are Gravenstein and Newtown Pippin, but even these are mostly grown for local consumption (and Martinelli's cider). Many of the old varieties lacked resistance to scab and other diseases, and when commercial orchardists acquired modern cold-storage equipment they lost interest in apples that would keep well all winter in cool as well as cold conditions. But the old varieties are treasured by fruit enthusiasts, who still grow many of them in home orchards.

Among the pears Henderson brought from Iowa and New York, only Barlett has retained its popularity. Because the trees come into bearing early, because the fruits are big and pretty and fragrant, and because the pears are equally suitable for eating fresh, drying, and canning, Bartlett was becoming California's dominant pear variety as early as the 1850s. It is still the most popular commercial pear in the United States.

Neither Seth's Black Republican cherry nor John's Lewelling's Prolific almond remain popular, but both were both widely planted for decades. With its excellent shipping qualities, the Black Republican had an essential role in the advancement of California's and Oregon's cherry industries. Lewelling's Prolific was long a standard variety in California's almond industry. Seth's Bing, happily, is still the standard among sweet black cherries, both in commercial Pacific coast orchards and in home gardens.

Other Lewelling fruits are hard to find. The fruit grower H. M. Williamson wrote that Seth's Golden Prune was "superior to any one of the remarkable prunes originated by the great California wizard of horticulture, Burbank," but that "the variety has never received the attention and thorough testing which the intrinsic merit of the fruit justifies." By 1914 the plum had to be "chased down, both historically and culturally." Finding it physically, today, seems nearly impossible. Lost also are Seth's Luelling grape and Mother's Favorite pear, and the Sweet Alice apple is very rare. I haven't found even the names of Seth's rhubarb and gooseberry introductions. John's Lewelling's Prolific grape seems to be lost, too.

Perhaps those varieties that are lost will be found, and will be found worth growing again. Since the Black Republican cherry was placed on the Slow Food Ark of Taste, an international catalog of endangered foods, several nurseries have begun selling Black Republican trees. Although Lewelling's Prolific almond is no longer commercially grown, Doug Wight found one tree and had it propagated. Lewelling's Prolific almond is now growing in my front yard in Lebanon, Oregon.

Appendix 1

TREE FRUITS HENDERSON BROUGHT FROM IOWA TO OREGON

Summer apples: **Early Harvest,**Early Pennoch, Golden Sweet, Red Astrachan, Summer Bellflower, Summer Pearmain, Sweet June, Gravenstein

Autumn apples: **Blue Pearmain, **Drap d'Or, *Golden Sweet, King of Tompkins County, Rambo, Red Cheek Pippin, Seek-No-Further, **Vandevere

Winter apples: Baldwin, Esopus Spitzenberg, Fall Beauty, Golden Russet, Jenneting (or Junating, or Joanneting) Lady, Northern Spy, *Pound Pippin, **Swaar, Tulpehocken, **Waxen, White Pearmain, Winesap, Yellow Bellflower, Yellow Newtown Pippin

Summer pears: Bartlett, Early Butter

Autumn pears: Fall Butter, Flemish, **Louise Bonne de Jersey, *Marie-Louise, Seckel

Winter pear: *Moon's, **Pound, Winter Nelis

Crabapple: Siberian

Quince: Orange

Cherries: Black Heart, Black Tartarian, Kentish, May Duke, Royal Ann (Napoleon)

Peaches: Crawford's Early, Crawford's Late, Golden Cling

Plum: *Greengage, *Jefferson, *Smith's Orleans, *Washington

---

*Varieties named in an Oregon *Weekly Times* article (August 28, 1851) but omitted from a list that Alfred provided the historian George Himes.

**Varieties named by Joseph Lambert in a memo at the Oregon Historical Society. Lambert would have judged according to which trees appeared oldest when he took over the orchard. He may have been wrong about the apples Drap d'Or, Early Harvest' and Swaar and the pears Louise Bonne and Pound, since these were all varieties Henderson brought back from New York in 1852.

Appendix 2

APPLES AND PEARS HENDERSON BROUGHT FROM NEW YORK

According to Seth's diary of 1850 to 1853, Henderson brought back the grafted fruit trees listed below. After each I've indicated its certain or likely place of origin.

In an article in the *Willamette Farmer* (December 29, 1876), Henry Miller mentioned other apple varieties that he believed Henderson brought from the East: Glass (from North Carolina, "the apple I believe to be the best cider apple of all"); Alexander (from Russia), Carolina June, Summer Queen (probably from New Jersey), Tulpehocken (Pennsylvania), Green Sweeting (United States), Michael Henry (New Jersey), Winter Queen (United States), and Milam (Virginia or Kentucky).

According to Miller, Mother was "an excellent fruit, but sickly tree," and Pumpkin Sweet was a prolific "pig-apple" that won awards but didn't deserve them.

APPLES

Canada Reinette (Canada)
Drap d'Or (France)
Early Harvest (North America?)
Fameuse (Canada?)
Haisley (probably Hawley, New York)
Lyman (Large) Summer (Connecticut)
Lyman's Pumpkin Sweet (Connecticut)
Melon (New York)
Mother (Massachusetts)
Northern Spy (New York)
Peck's Pleasant (Rhode Island?)
Porter (Massachusetts)
Red Astrachan (Russia)

Rhode Island Greening (Connecticut)
Roxbury Russet (Massachusetts)
Seek-No-Further (Ohio)
Spice Sweet (Massachusetts)
Summer Scarlet Pearmain (United States?)
Swaar (New York)
Sweet Bow/Sweet Bough/Early Bough (North America)
Twenty Ounce (Northeastern United States)
Williams Favorite (Massachusetts)

PEARS

Beurré d'Aremberg (France)
Beurré Gris d'Hiver (France)
Columbia (North America)
Dearborn's Seedling (Massachusetts)
Dix (Massachusetts)
Duchesse d'Angoulême (France)
Easter Beurré (Belgium)
Flemish Beauty (Belgium)
Frederick of Wurtemberg (Belgium)
Joséphine de Malines (France)
Louise Bonne de Jersey (France)
Osband's Summer (New York)
Pound (England)
Seckel (Pennsylvania)
Stevens' Genesee (New York)
Swan's Orange (New York)
Triomphe de Jodoigne (Belgium)
Tyson (Pennsylvania)
Urbaniste (France)

Notes

CHAPTER 1: Leaving Carolina

7 **Daniel Boone's Wilderness Road**: Daniel Boone, too, was raised a Quaker.

At least four hundred Quaker families: Diamond, 105.

9 **he was Anglican**: Diamond, 17.

Meshack owned 480 acres: Diamond, 26.

10 **they may even have distilled some of the cider**: Enos Mendenhall, born into a Guilford County family of Friends in 1822, wrote that his father kept a barrel of peach brandy under the bed. Enos Mendenhall to John Mendenhall, February 2, 1873.

12 **Anne Jessop, a Quaker minister**: North Carolina Encyclopedia, accessed February 12, 2021, https://www.ncpedia.org/biography/jessup-ann. Anne Jessop's first name was sometimes spelled *Ann*, and her last name *Jessup*. The story of Anne Jessop and her fruit trees came originally from Addison Coffin's "Early Settlement of Friends in North Carolina: Traditions and Reminiscences," in *Southern Friend* 5 (1983): 27–38.

North Carolina Quakers took about twenty: Diamond, 41. Diamond quotes Addison Coffin, "Early Settlement of Friends in North Carolina," in *Southern Friend* 5 (1983).

Henderson . . . learned to graft: Diamond, 19.

13 **The landscape was fragile**: Daniels, 407–408.

. . . the sheriff had three hundred foreclosures: Heiss 1957, 294.

14 **anyone liberating a slave had to post a bond**: Hilty, 33. The county court could reduce the bond requirement for freeing a slave. Five hundred dollars was a more common amount than $1,000, and securities were accepted.

the Yearly Meeting required their doing so: For the Quakers, the word *meeting* took the place of ecclesiastical terms such as *church, parish, congregation*, and *diocese*. It was also used to indicate a system of temporal and territorial governance. So, the yearly meeting ruled over the quarterly meeting, which in turn ruled over the monthly meeting. The history of the North

Carolina Yearly Meeting's restrictions regarding slavery is detailed in Weeks, 208–209, 216–217, and Hilty, 20–38.

15 **Freeing these Black people without removing them**: In 1797, the Yearly Meeting complained in a petition to Congress in 1797 that 134 Black people its members had freed had been sold back into slavery. Lindley, 66–67.

Meshack Lewelling joined the Back Creek Meeting: Diamond, 47.

set up a school for Black children: Diamond, 50.

he contracted with a slave-owning neighbor: Diamond, 50–51.

1819 Meshack joined a committee of elders: Diamond, 48.

16 **the population of Randolph County**: Diamond, 54.

they had found nothing in the laws: Weeks, 258. Actually, Black settlement in Ohio had been illegal since 1804, but the law wasn't enforced (Hilty, 96).

Owen A. Garretson: Garretson.

Reports from various North Carolina meetings: Hilty, 66–67.

Rarely did a family travel alone: Hinshaw, 141.

17 **By 1821, it is estimated, at least twenty thousand Friends**: Elliott, 82.

18 **the Friends, like other Americans . . . bred profusely**: The U.S. birth rate was declining by the end of the eighteenth century, and among Quakers in New York, New Jersey, and Pennsylvania it was actually lower than in the general population. Still, in 1800 the U.S. birth rate, at seven children per women, was higher than that of any European country. And North Carolina Friends were known for their unusually large families. Wells.

19 **"the Jerusalem of Quakerism"**: Addison Coffin, 55–56.

the Walking Purchase of 1737: Thomas Penn fooled the Delaware by claiming to have found a lost treaty for a tract of land that extended as far as a man could walk in a day and a half. He then hired three very fast walkers—or, actually, runners—to cover twice the distance the Delaware had anticipated. The tribe lost 1,200 square miles of land.

21 **another settler had spent two days cutting his way**: Ballenger.

22 **Jane gave birth to her seventh child**: Heiss 1972, 161.

CHAPTER 2: Sweet Home Indiana

23 **soil "that needed only to be tickled with a hoe"**: Fox, 28.

required settlers to plant orchards immediately. Henris, 222. Lands leased for schools in Ohio had to be planted with 100 apple trees. Knepper, 58.

a family would be eating well: These trees were "standard," or full-size. Today's dwarf and semi-dwarf fruit trees come into bearing much sooner.

24 **the first sawmill wasn't built in the area until 1836.** Diamond, 104.

25 **"the principal circulating medium."**: Pleas, 19.

no more than five hundred residents: Pleas, 19.

Mary and her husband bought an adjacent claim: Diamond, 185.

Meshack and . . . Henry, were denounced: Heiss 1972, 192.

26 **Some Lenape tribal members lingered**: *History of Henry County*, 253.

Friends monitored the tribes' well-being: Buys, 81–100.

among the Shawnee and other native peoples: Buys, 94.

her husband, Tom Newby: Tom Newby had been disowned by the Friends in North Carolina after he shot a neighbor's cow.

27 **Asiatic cholera, a fast killer:** Altonen.

Fifteen of 150 residents . . . died in the epidemic: *History of Henry County*, 438.

Henry County's official surveyor. Diamond, 106.

The money the boys earned: Mayhill. In the records of land sales Meshack's name was sometimes recorded as Luallen rather than Lewelling.

Henry, Henderson, and John had already married: Heiss 1972, 192.

28 **Elizabeth was "a very pretty woman"**: Jane Harriet Luelling.

Henderson's farm was a few miles north: Diamond, 103.

have three children by her: The youngest of those children, James H. Lewelling, would work for Seth in the Milwaukie Nursery in the 1880s. *Statesman Journal* (Salem, OR), March 8, 1935.

Fruit trees . . . were planted there: Dunn, 117; *History of Henry County*, 82.

29 **annual meeting of the Ohio Pomological Society**: Ohio Pomological Society, 46–77; Coxe 1817, Coxe 1810, 31. The last is a collection of captioned colored plates that were excluded from Coxe's book.

"an innovation upon the works of nature." Ohio Pomological Society, 46–47.

30 **One of Silas Wharton's associates in Wayne County**: Esthaven, 5, 21.

farmers often drove as far away as fifty miles: Votaw, 272.

31 **[Hampton] refused to buy products of slave labor**: Votaw, 277.

"Nearly all the earliest nurserymen were members": Fox, 466.

eighteen nurseries in Indiana. Beecher, 189.

joined with Henry Ward Beecher: Beecher, then a Congregationalist minister in Indianapolis, became editor of the *Indiana Farmer and Gardener* soon after the first meeting of the Indiana Horticultural Society.

Other Quaker farmers contributed: Ohio Pomological Society, 52.

31 **the Never Fail apple**: In the 1950s Never Fail would become a parent of Fuji, which is now produced in greater quantity than any other apple in the world.

32 **to found the Duck Creek Monthly Meeting**: Dorrel and Hamm. Other sources give the date of the founding of the meeting as 1823, but I think they are wrong.

he refused either to join the militia: Diamond, 104–105.

Meshack and Jane were appointed: Heiss 1972, 192.

"supervisor of the road": Diamond, 104.

"Elias Hicks is as good a man as Jesus Christ": Dorrel and Hamm.

33 **Hicksites created their own parallel system**: By 1829, a third of the approximately ninety-five thousand Friends in the United States and Europe had become Hicksites. Buys, 35–36.

Seth Hinshaw: There have been many Friends named Seth Hinshaw. The one who comes up most often in Internet searches is Seth B. Hinshaw, a twentieth-century Quaker historian. Another Seth Hinshaw, a farmer, moved to the Greensboro area just a few years after the Seth Hinshaw discussed here. The biographies of these two Seth Hinshaws are often confused.

Hinshaw's house "was the meeting place": Addison Coffin, 63–64. Mesmerism was Franz Mesmer's theory of animal magnetism, which maintained that all living things possessed an invisible natural force that could have physical effects, including healing. *Grahamism* refers to Sylvester Graham, who advocated an extremely bland vegetarian diet with abundant whole grains, and daily bathing (an eccentric practice in the nineteenth century). Seth Lewelling, his wife, and Henderson Luelling would later adopt the Graham diet or something close to it. Fourierism, or Associationism, was the French intellectual Charles Fourier's philosophy of utopian socialism; Henderson would later adopt a philosophy of this sort, too.

Greensboro's Liberty Hall: The townspeople of Greensboro built Liberty Hall in 1843, apparently for the purpose of holding such meetings. The meetings gave Greensboro a reputation as a hotbed of abolitionism.

mentoring young William Lewelling: Garretson, 551.

Lorenzo Dow . . . circuit rider: Price, 39–73.

adopted his middle name: Lorenzo Dow was preaching widely long before William Lewelling was born, but because middle names were unusual in the early nineteenth century I suspect that William Lewelling adopted his in early adulthood. William Lewelling so admired Lorenzo Dow that he named his youngest son Lorenzo Dow Lewelling. Lorenzo Dow Lewelling would become a Populist governor of Kansas.

34 **New Garden, a short distance north**: New Garden was renamed Newport in 1834 and Fountain City in 1878.

Friends lent Black people land: Opper, 58.

"the prejudice against a colored population": Hamm, Beckman, Florio, Giles, and Hopper, 21.

slave states were burdening Indiana: Buys, 104.

a more appropriate spiritual home: Methodists of the period had an emotional, demonstrative style of worship that sharply contrasted with the Friends' meetings, which were often conducted entirely in silence—although racism among the Methodists led in 1816 to the formation of a new denomination, the African Methodist Episcopal (AME) Church. Peter and Millie Winslow, the first Black landowners in Henry County, deeded a half-acre of their land for an AME church in 1844, after their son Daniel Winslow became a circuit rider for the denomination.

35 **Levi and Catherine Coffin . . . took in fugitive slaves**: Levi Coffin, 113.

Black migrants sent to Haiti in 1826: Opper, 47, 53–54.

36 **"unrighteous work of expatriation."** Buys, 106.

protested to Congress the proposed annexation of Texas: Buys, 110.

Conservative Friends began speaking out: Buys, 111.

Friends should stop joining outside associations. Buys, 112–113.

Resurrection was spiritual, not physical: R. M. Jones 1921, 518–519. The dispute wasn't merely theological. The literalists were followers of Joseph John Gurney, an eloquent and erudite Quaker minister from England who traveled through North America in 1837. Although Gurney was an ardent opponent of slavery, some questioned his friendship with Henry Clay, a slaveholding politician who had promoted both war with Britain in 1812 and the Missouri Compromise, which foiled efforts to prohibit slavery's expansion. Clay was far from a favorite of the radical Friends, and his taint probably rubbed off on Gurney.

38 **Henderson and Elizabeth waited:** L. T. Jones 1914.

Henry County, Iowa. Whereas Henry County, Indiana, was named for Patrick Henry, the Founding Father from Virginia who fought for religious liberty, Henry County, Iowa, was named for a general in the Blackhawk War, James Dougherty Henry.

CHAPTER 3: Radical Quakers on the Prairie

39 **drove a team of young mares instead of oxen**: Jane Harriet Luelling; "Llewellyn Researcher."

Eastern red cedar: *Juniperus virginiana* has become invasive in its native territory, but when the Lewellings arrived in Iowa it was well controlled by prairie fires and so grew mainly on the limestone bluffs along the rivers.

41 **throngs of New Yorkers visited**: Prince, ii.

41 **received a certificate of transfer**: Heiss 1972, 304.

"the proprietors are in the constant habit": Prince, iii.

the Lewellings offered forty-five varieties: *Hawkeye and Iowa Patriot*, February 4, 1841.

"those who feel an interest in the nursery business": *Hawkeye and Iowa Patriot*, October 8, 1840, and February 4, 1841.

42 **their monthly meeting had to be canceled**: Jones 1911, 5.

David Diamond: 155–156.

43 **a technique popular at the time**: Diamond, 115–116; Phoenix, 280–282.

the Lewellings could advertise: *Hawkeye and Iowa Patriot*, October 8, 1840.

the trunks of some fruit trees split: Diamond, 160.

44 **"almost every homestead"**: Garretson 1929, 551.

William considered himself primarily a minister: Minister, farmer, and horticulturist were the occupations that William, John, and Henderson, respectively, would identify as their own when they joined the Liberty Party in 1843. Diamond, 150.

when he died, in 1847: *Llewellyn Traces* 5.

his father made a total of fourteen trips east: Alfred Luelling to Ralph C. Greer.

45 **"the effluvia from the decaying sod"**: Baldwin, 157; Kellum.

Henderson became the meeting's first overseer: Diamond, 167.

One hundred eighty-five children . . . attended Friends' schools: Jones 1914.

46 **"the largest and most commodious"**: Jones 1911, 42.

Begun in 1842 and completed by 1845: National Register of Historic Places.

like many a Quaker meetinghouse: In a meetinghouse, one door was for men, and the other for women, because the room was divided down the middle for men's and women's business meetings.

All three of the brothers had sufficient funds to invest in real estate. Diamond, 147.

give away a small parcel to a widow: Diamond, 160.

47 **stories of slave rescues in the Salem area**: Some of these stories are collected in Garretson 1924, and most of those concern Owen Garretson's father, Joel Garretson, a close friend of Henderson Lewelling. Other stories of slave rescues are in Jones 1911.

the Beehive: Leeper 2007c.

they were said to enter Friends' stables: Jones 1911, 41.

Iowa's first legislature: Iowa won its own territorial status in 1838, after becoming part of Michigan Territory in 1834 and Wisconsin Territory in 1836.

49 ***Free Labor Advocate*:** May 8, 1841; April 16, 1842; November 26, 1844.

The group presented the governor: Dykstra 1993, 37.

would oppose any candidate: Dykstra 1993, 35.

50 **Turner had led his parishioners**: Dykstra 1993, 29.

Quaker women led the formation: Clauser-Roemer.

the Wayne County Free Produce Association: The American Free Produce Association, at first called the Western Free Produce Society, formed the same year. It eventually fizzled out, because, for Americans in the 1840s, doing without slave-made goods was as hard as doing without Chinese-made goods is for Americans today. Nueremberger, 48–51.

51 **the Salem Monthly Meeting of Anti-Slavery Friends.** Leeper 2007a.

censured the anti-slavery radicals: Salem Monthly Meeting Minutes.

Aaron Street Jr., who had joined his father: Leeper 2007b.

52 **territory-wide meeting**: Dykstra 1982; *Western Citizen*, November 23, 1843; December 28, 1843; and January 18, 1844.

53 **Congress was besieged with . . . anti-war petitions**: Carpenter, 357.

London Yearly meeting sent a delegation: This story is told at length in Jones 1914, 137–144.

Lately he had read newspaper accounts: Alfred Luelling to John Minto.

54 **"It makes no difference how much"**: Garretson 1929.

he used the oxen to break new prairie: Alfred Luelling to Ralph C. Greer.

Henderson and Elizabeth ended up selling: Diamond, 180–181.

In the summer of 1846 Henderson was pleased to learn: Alfred Luelling to John Minto.

Oregon's provisional government had banned slavery: *Except* as a punishment for crime. Also, the provisional government limited suffrage to "every free male descendant of a white man."

legislature had banned the settlement of free Black people: This was in part a reaction to the Cockstock Affair, in which a dispute involving two Black settlers had resulted in the death of a Wasco man and two white men. Fears arose that Blacks might incite violence among Indians, especially after a false rumor spread that one of the Black men, married to a native woman, had threatened to incite his wife's people to "a great interracial war."

CHAPTER 4: The Traveling Nursery

55 **Alfred Luelling, described his father's preparations**: Alfred's account of the Lewellings' journey is in his letter to Ralph C. Geer.

Robert Avery, who had a fruit-tree nursery: Williamson, 104; Wragg.

56 **In 1848 he was a "vegitearian or Grahamite":** Diamond, 289.

Nathan and Rebecca Hockett and their four children: Except where indicated, the Hockett's Overland Trail story comes from William A. Hockett's accounts.

Enos Mendenhall: William Hockett (1909) remembered that Enos brought along a wife, but I haven't been able to verify this. If he did, she died along the trail, probably early in the journey.

Spicer Teas: *Rogue Digger.*

57 **Thomas Hockett had been disowned in 1843**: Jones 1911, 22.

The Fishers had been Anti-Slavery Friends: Salem Monthly Meeting Minutes.

they took a one-hundred-thirty-mile detour: This is according to an account William Hockett wrote at age seventy-six with help from his father's letters. In another account, which William wrote five years earlier, the crossing was upriver, at what would become Brownville, Nebraska. Hockett 1909; Hockett 1914.

a St. Joseph newspaper editor estimated: Dary, 168.

he had seven wagons: Olson, 7.

58 **a train of about 114 wagons**: Dary, 177.

Ralph Geer: Geer.

a miller who brought along two granite millstones: Carraway.

59 **turn over their collection of fruit seeds**: Carraway; Olson, 55.

the overland journey "was a long picnic": Cosgrove.

Spicer Teas, would die soon after arriving: Hockett 1914. If Enos Mendenhall really brought along a wife, the total deaths among the Salem emigrants were six.

60 **John Fisher was buried**: A week later another emigrant train found Fisher's grave dug up. Apparently, Indians had done this to take his clothing. Some emigrants disguised graves as well as they could, instead of marking them, so the bodies would be left alone. Diamond, 210.

Eighty to one hundred people attended: Hockett 1914, 762.

sleeping and cooking with the Hocketts: Mills.

Henderson took better care of the trees: J. H. Luelling, 14.

writings of Sylvester Graham: Graham, 47.

61 **"forty mounted Pawnees"**: Cosgrove, 259.

62 **"They were notorious boasters"**: Cosgrove, 260.

The Bonsers bragged: Carraway.

Bonsers had to ransom their prize racehorse: Thompson.

petting an ox: Mendenhall, 5.

63 **family camped near a large band of Indians**: J. H. Luelling, 14.

the Great Spirit lived in trees: J. H. Luelling, 14.

Bonser company reached the North Platte crossing: Morgan, 138–139.

64 **William Barlow, in 1845, had "dumped on the ground"**: Barlow. Led by his father, Samuel, William Barlow's party avoided the trip down the Columbia by blazing a trail around Mount Hood, which Samuel developed the next year into the Barlow Road. If William had brought his trees, it is doubtful they would have survived, since the party left its wagons in the mountains through the winter.

65 **Barlow did save a small sack of apple seeds**: Duruz 1941, 93.

On August 11: This is the date of Angeline's death as her mother reported it to her parents. It may be wrong; Rachel Fisher's dates often conflict with those of other emigrants.

66 **the Raynor company brought measles**: The emigrants didn't bring measles from the States; they caught it from Indians. Walla Walla and Cayuse men had caught the disease while on a horse-trading expedition to California and brought it home with them. Boyle.

On August 19: This is the date of Nathan Hockett's death as reported by James Raynor, who performed the burial service. Other accounts give various dates. Raynor.

"black measles": Hockett 1914.

67 **Whitman had tried . . . to convince Henry Davis**: Carraway.

the Lewellings were much impressed: They might have been less favorably impressed had they heard what Whitman had said to Ralph Geer's company some weeks before. Whitman complimented Geer for punching an Indian who had tried to persuade Geer's wife to give him her turkey wing (feathered, not cooked), and the missionary praised another man for whipping the Indian. "If more men would do likewise, instead of giving them presents for their impudence and theft," Geer remembered Whitman saying, "it would be better for all concerned." Geer.

68 **a teaching job at Waiilatpu**: Raynor.

69 **how Ralph Geer lost Joel Palmer's fruit trees**: Diamond, 241.

"It looks like starvation": Smith.

large enough for forty dismantled wagons: Edwards, 146.

69 **potatoes, onions, and peas bought from Indians**: Smith; Edwards, 164.

71 **nothing could be found of them but a grease spot**:" Hastings.

Elizabeth Smith: All of Elizabeth Smith's observations come from her letter to Pauline Foster and Cynthia Ames.

Bonser cleverly stabilized the boats: Thompson.

72 **The Lewelling and Bonser boats finally reached Fort Vancouver**: J. H. Luelling, 8.

The palisade alone was 220 yards long: Fort Vancouver in the 1830s and 1840s is described in Gibson, 33–35.

his distant cousin Isaac Mills: Mendenhall, 4.

Rachel Fisher to Isaac and Charity's twenty-one-year-old son: Rachel Fisher Mills would lose five more children, but five would grow to adulthood in Oregon. Unlike her Mills and Mendenhall relations on the West Coast, she would for the rest of her forty-six years practice "plainness in dress and address," despite her isolation from other Friends. Alfred Luelling would write her obituary. Holmes; A. Luelling 1870.

73 **Tom found the family a home on the Tualatin Plains**: Shortly after the Hocketts moved out of Portland, Tom disappeared to join the war against the Cayuse, a reaction to the Whitman massacre. Later he returned only to say goodbye; he was going to St. Louis to join the army. The children found shelter and work in three separate households, and Rachel became a substitute mother to Jesse, who was still a toddler. The next year ten-year-old William Hockett, only recently off crutches, joined a cattle drive to California to feed the gold miners. He returned to Iowa in 1851. His brother Solomon also returned to Iowa. Only Rachel and Jesse would remain in Oregon, and Rachel would die young, at twenty-five. Hockett 1914; Raynor.

a bigger, better cabin: This cabin belonged to James John, an 1841 settler who became locally famous for such kindnesses.

captives of the Cayuse. A month later, the Hudson's Bay Company ransomed all the captives, at the company's own cost.

CHAPTER 5: Webfeet

74 **malaria . . . would be yet:** Cook, 309.

Lot sought a site where he could build a sawmill: Olson, 8.

75 **paid him off with Iowa store goods**: A. Luelling to R. Geer.

76 **"lay in great heaps over the ground". . .** A. Luelling to R. Geer.

"with ax and fire plied almost day and night": A. Luelling to R. Geer.

"Among the trees were": Duruz 1941, 91; Lewelling 1896; *Oregon Weekly*, August 28, 1851.

77 **only one small Clackamas village remained**: Gray, 304.

local Indians were annoying. *Oregonian*, June 7, 1903.

minor depredations elsewhere: Victor, 224, 225.

they were instead battling the measles: Boyd, 26–28.

sign a treaty ceding all their land: A prior treaty, signed in 1851, was never ratified.

78 **Lewelling orchard was a novelty**: In a letter at the Oregon Historical Society, Nathaniel Wyeth claimed to have planted and grafted fruit trees at Fort William on Sauvie Island in 1834, but hostility from both the local Indians and the Hudson's Bay Company ensured that his venture failed within a year.

***Rubus ursinus*—**: *R. ursinus* eventually became a parent of the loganberry, the boysenberry, and the marionberry.

an oft-told story: Cardwell 1906, 28–29. The "Old Apple Tree," possibly planted by Aemilius Simpson, a cousin of Governor-in-Chief George Simpson, stood in what had been the Employee Village at Fort Vancouver until its death in 2020. Cromwell.

John Minto noted a 'Mission' grapevine: *Statesman Journal* (Salem), May 12, 1895.

the original site of Jason Lee's Methodist mission: *Daily Oregon Statesman*, March 4, 1904. Now Willamette Mission State Park, the mission site is on the Willamette River north of Salem.

apple trees . . . were bearing so heavily: Gibson, 33–34.

they were expensive—$5 each: Settlemier, 94.

Joseph Gervais: Lake, 8.

79 **The Iowa Anti-Slavery Society's fifth and last annual meeting**: Dykstra 1993, 73.

80 **the little town of Bonaparte, Iowa.** At first they called the town Meek's Mill.

divorced his first wife for "insanity": Hinckley, 72; Van Buren County, Iowa, District Court Case 916, District Court Record B, April, 1844, 424–425.

her father wrapped her in a handkerchief: Hinckley, 72.

Lysander Stone: Wood, 981. Traveling with Meek and Stone may have been Alexander Jackson Poe, a brother of Meek's first wife. Like Stone, Poe reported that he reached the Willamette Valley in 1847 by way of the Barlow Road.

He took about twenty: A. Luelling to R. Geer.

carried them through on the Barlow Road. Wood, 981.

81 **Meek had also brought seeds**: Oregon State Board of Horticulture, 12. No historical sources say Henderson brought seeds, but his failure to do so would be hard to explain.

threw their claims together: Olson, 34.

"no young girl over the age of twelve": Thompson.

Jane Harriet Luelling: One of Alfred's daughters, Jane was born fourteen years after Mary's death but became a keeper of Luelling family stories. J. H. Luelling.

Wills and his son would soon build: Dimon, 8.

82 **"stout, robust, energetic, sober men"**: Burnett, 255.

The Oregonians scouted out a new trail: Peter Burnett led the company; Thomas McKay piloted it. Joel Palmer and Lindsay Applegate were two of the other five men who, with William Meek, scouted out the route from Klamath Lake. Burnett, who would become California's first governor, is remembered for his efforts to ban Black people from both Oregon and California, to force California Indians into servitude, and to end immigration from China. Burnett, 252–272; A. Luelling to R. Geer.

83 **the Oregon City newspaper editor**: *Oregon Spectator*, October 12, 1848. The *Spectator*, incidentally, had shut its doors for more than a month after its printers left for California.

84 **in 1849 fifty or more docked there**: Peterson del Mar, 77.

whether slavery would be permitted: In September 1849 the territorial legislature proscribed Black immigration, but that law was rescinded in 1854. Washington Territory would break off from Oregon Territory in 1853.

the first big red apple: Cardwell 1891, 12–13.

He acquired seedling trees: Ralph Geer; T. T. Geer, 94. Geer's house and some of the trees he planted still stand. They can be visited at the educational farm now called Geercrest, just south of Silverton in the Waldo Hills.

85 **other millers, for whom he would serve as agent.** Olson, 8.

"They build schoolhouses": Olson, 77.

86 **a "Mr. Pugh."** Lewelling 1896. The seller was probably either John Martin Pugh or William Porter Pugh, two brothers who emigrated from Indiana in 1845 before settling near the present town of Keizer in Marion County. Either "Mr. Pugh" had made a trip back to the Eastern states since 1845, or else the seeds were five years old when Henderson and Meek bought them. In any case, a good proportion of the seeds proved viable. Bancroft, 526.

he went out . . . to take soundings: Dimon, 11.

Henderson, Alfred, and Meek all filed claims: Exact boundaries would be established only after a federal employee surveyed the land. In August of 1851 Henderson, Alfred, Meek, and other landowners submitted a petition pleading for the surveying to be done so they could fence their parcels, because "our range is fast consumeing by stock pastured upon us." The survey was finally completed in May 1852.

87 **Oliver Nixon . . . described the Luelling family**: Diamond, 273.

completed their sawmill. According to Olson (34, 44, 48), Henderson and Meek also built a grist mill and, with W. P. Doland and Charles Hopkins, formed the Milwaukie Milling Company, which would eventually operate the grist mill and several sawmills. But I have found no other evidence that Henderson and Meek had any mills besides a single sawmill.

89 **Newtown Pippin**: Albany *Democrat*, August 19, 1906.

Andrew Jackson Davis Meek: It's doubtful that Meek chose the name; he seems to have had no religious or spiritual affiliation beyond freemasonry.

90 **"Spiritualism is Quakerism enlarged"**: Stebbins, 134.

"The world will hail with delight": Davis, 675–676.

91 **"a warm breathing passed over my face"**: Doyle, 21.

allowing . . . Rachel to have an accordion: S. Lewelling Diary.

92 **Henderson took the negative position.** Olson, 54.

"the principles instilled": Unsigned and undated letter at the Milwaukie Museum, probably written by Alfred's daughter Jane Harriet Luelling.

CHAPTER 6: Family Reunion

93 **Seth kept a diary**: Most of the diary is available as a typed transcript at the University of Oregon (Seth Lewelling Diary). The transcript is not entirely accurate. At the Oregon Historical Society is much of the original diary, but its early pages are almost entirely illegible (Seth Lewelling Papers). Except where indicated, the details of Seth's journey are from one or the other of these two sources.

95 **Enos missed Iowa**: Mendenhall 1853.

some of their mutual acquaintances: Mendenhall 1850.

96 **"the first hotel of the place"**: *History of Placer County*, 356.

97 **as much as three ounces in three hours' time**: *History of Placer County*, 356.

two Illinoistown storekeepers hired fifty a day: *History of Placer County*, 355.

"**. . . scalps on exhibit.**" *History of Placer County*, 357–359.

"I have taken in . . . about $300": Mendenhall 1850.

98 **Elihu, Thomas C., and Isaac Frazier**: Mendenhall 1850. The Fraziers had been among the defendants in *Ruel Daggs vs. Elihu Frazier et al.*, in which all of the accused were found guilty of violating the 1793 Fugitive Slave

Law. But because they had liquidated their assets before the jury rendered its verdict, Ruel Daggs never received any compensation. The full story of Ruel Daggs and his slaves is too long to relate here, but it features Henderson's stone house, in front of which Salem's justice of the peace faced the slavecatchers. The Ruel Daggs saga is fully told in Dykstra 1993.

98 —**songs about love, loss, and loneliness.** The songs include "The Carrier Dove," by Daniel Johnson and John Newland Moffitt, 1841; "Thou Reignest in This Bosom," by William Dressler; and "De Floating Scow ob Ole Virginia," a minstrel song transcribed into standard English.

99 **Frederick Morse, died**: Olson 16, 17, 84. Morse's headstone is now in the Milwaukie Museum.

100 **"quite a lot" of fruit seeds**: Lewelling 1896.

John . . . also brought seeds: Napa County *Reporter*, February 25, 1881.

ten to twelve thousand one-year-old apple trees: I am not sure who the supplier was. Several other emigrant families were entering the nursery business, with seedling trees for either cider or rootstock.

101 **(he must have meant grouse)**: The Chinese ring-necked pheasant was not introduced to Oregon until 1882. From Oregon it gradually spread across the country.

103 **Mission San José had hundreds of grafted pear trees**: Brown; Wickson 1888, 504, 505.

James A. Griffith, went to Oregon: *St. Helena Star*, April 13, 1883.

W. H. Nash and R. L. Kilburn: The nursery was probably Ellwanger-Barry of Rochester. The cultivars included Rhode Island Greening, Roxbury Russet, Winesap, Red Romanite, and Esopus Spitzenburg apples; Bartlett and Seckel pears; and Black Tartarian and Napoleon Bigarreau cherries. Wickson, 46.

The Russians at Fort Ross: Stainbrook.

The scions were said to have come from Monterey: When the expedition led by Jean-François de la Perouse reached Monterey in 1786, the French gave the Spanish seeds for planting. Perhaps they also left some of their "small forest" of living trees, at least some of which were grafted. La Perouse, 7.

Other grafted-fruit orchards were planted: *Oakland Tribune*, February 26, 1939.

104 **"the fruit shipping capital of America"**: The Grace Hubley Foundation, accessed September 15, 2022, https://www.gracehubleyfoundation.org.

relics of old orchards. The Felix Gillet Institute, situated near Grass Valley, searches out these old trees and attempts to identify the cultivars.

105 **Illinoistown was not on their way.** Enos and Emily Mendenhall leave the story at this point, so I will sum up the rest of their lives: When the Gold Rush slowed, Enos bought a sawmill four miles from Illinoistown. He invested in the first transcontinental railroad, which would begin its ascent of the Sierra Nevada a stone's throw from Illinoistown, but somehow he was cheated out of his share (Mendenhall 1873). Still, he profited from the proximity of his mill to Camp 20, a construction base for the Central Pacific Railroad. When Camp 20 morphed into the new town of Colfax, the Mendenhalls built a large hotel there, the Pioneer House. It opened in 1865. After the Civil War, business slackened, so Enos packed up his gold and apple saplings and went to San Diego County, where he and his three sons eventually developed a cattle ranch of more than twelve thousand acres on Palomar Mountain. Emily stayed in Colfax, to run the hotel and serve as midwife and nurse to the community. In 1874, a fire burned down the hotel along with most of the town, and Emily retired with her daughters to Napa County, where she resided near John Lewelling and his family. Although Emily lived until 1921, she never moved to San Diego County. She said she was tired of pioneering.

CHAPTER 7: Land of the Big Red Apple

106 **John and Seth's trip**: The details of Seth's activities in this chapter are from his diary.

107 **Ephraim was reported to be dead:** Breck, 33–34.

109 **"My last day's work at it"**: Lewelling 1896.

110 **an affidavit**: Himes, 96. Judge Pratt had presided over the trial of the Cayuse reputedly responsible for the Waiilatpu massacre.

111 **Bayard Taylor**: Taylor, 13.

113 **Henderson had Downing personally point out**: Cardwell March 1906, 36. The Newtown Pippin—usually called simply Pippin, although that name can refer to any seedling apple—became the chief product of Watsonville, California, the chief ingredient of Martinelli cider, and the apple I ate every day through the winter as a child. Squat, intensely fragrant, with tart, dense flesh and russeting around the stem, it was always grass-green, never yellow.

Ralph Geer was soon producing: Down, 233.

Alfred Stanton would advertise: *Oregon Argus*, November 29, 1856.

P. W. Gillette had brought grafted trees: Cardwell 1900, 179.

John W. Ladd, of Howell Prairie: Down, 233.

114 **Ralph Geer advertised**: *Weekly Oregon Statesman*, May 25, 1852.

116 **purple-fruited "double-bearing" raspberry**: *Daily Alta California*, December 18, 1852.

fourteen men were kept grafting: Lewelling 1893, 243.

116 **Joseph Lambert**: Dimon, 15, 23.

117 **branch nurseries**: Lewelling 1893, 243.

extended their lands to the south: Dimon, 17.

Jane, two months short of fourteen years: The minimum age of marriage for females under Oregon's provisional laws was fourteen years, but the law was apparently unenforced during this transitional period. In December of 1853 the territorial legislature would raise the minimum to fifteen years.

118 **witnessed George's transactions**: Dimon, 13, 15.

advertised in the *Oregon Weekly Times*: Olson, 54.

he signed a deed of sale to his stone house: Diamond, 292.

". . . **Milwaukie Nursery, H. & S. Luelling, Proprietors.**" *Oregon Weekly Times*, November 26, 1853.

bore 240 pounds: Lewelling 1893, 243.

119 **in boxes bound with strap iron**: Cardwell March 1906, 37.

"Very little of it sold for less than $1 per pound"... Lewelling 1893, 244.

they realized $500. *California Farmer*, July 11, 1862.

CHAPTER 8: Stretching South

120 **"old floating coffin S. S. Lewis"**: *Pacific Rural Press*, January 5, 1884.

The potatoes gave out in three days: Grant, 58.

121 **"beautiful as an oats field in the prairie."** Enos Mendenhall to Jacob Mendenhall, May 1, 1853.

122 **Rancho Ex-Mission San José**: Elias Beard didn't acquire a "perfected" title to the land until 1865. Guinn, 1024.

"more than 180 acres of potatoes": According to one witness, "the size of these potatoes was something marvelous. It was common to find some of three pounds weight, and frequently those weighing from three to five pounds." Wood, 846.

350 mature trees: James Reed, the Donner Party member who was exiled from the group after he killed another man, spent the summer of 1847 at the mission, reunited with his family. When a ship captain came in search of hides, tallow, and wine—products the padres and their Indian workers had provided in the past—Reed had the bright idea to dry the mission's pears, which were ready to harvest by the wagonload. The dried pears were probably the first fruit exported from California, and they were a hit among Hawaiians. *Oakland Tribune*, February 26, 1939.

A single tree yielded: Guinn, 1024–1025.

123 **Elias offered to let John plant**: *Overland Monthly*, August 1885.

123 **seedling trees available for John**: A possible source of rootstock was A. H. Myers, who established his Pioneer Nursery in Alameda in 1852, a year before John established his nursery at Mission San José.

listed cherries among the mission fruits: Capron, 111. Capron may have been referring to the native Catalina or hollyleaf cherry, *Prunus ilicifolia*, whose fruits are edible but mostly pit.

The orchard included 300 cherry trees: *California Farmer*, October 19, 1855.

124 **Captain Whalley . . . to visit Eastern nurseries**: Halley, 110; *Pacific Rural Press*, January 5, 1884; *Overland Monthly*, August 1885.

Sales of currants: *Overland Monthly*, August 1885. Currants and gooseberries are now little known in the United States, because the federal government banned them from 1911 to 1966, and some states banned them for even longer. The bans were intended to protect five-needle pines, alternate hosts for a rust disease.

John planted new apple varieties: *California Farmer*, Sept. 16, 1859. Red June is probably the same as Carolina June, and Carolina may have been brought to Indiana by Addison Coffin. Bussey, vol.2, 35.

In 1855 John's orchard included: *California Farmer*, October 19, 1855.

distinguished by its breadth. *California Farmer*, October 19, 1855.

125 **He ended up buying several adjacent parcels**: Rhoda, Luelling Portfolio.

126 **an oak tree said to be "the largest but one"**: *San Francisco Call*, April 13, 1896.

Franklin Rhoda: Rhoda, Henderson Luelling Portfolio.

more than sixteen times what he had paid for it. If Huerstel swindled Peralta, he wasn't the only person to do so. Peralta ended up losing nearly all of his eleven thousand acres.

Alfred and Mary bought 217 acres: *Daily Alta California*, September 18, 1860.

Henderson sold his half: Dimon, 16.

Henry Eddy, for $15,000: In 1866 Henry Eddy sold the land to Reverend John Sellwood, with the stipulation that he, Henry, could erect a six-foot-high dam on the creek and convey the water through the land to what would become the Standard Mill. This land, combined with Sellwood's own donation land claim, would eventually become the town of Sellwood, which was incorporated into Portland in 1893.

127 **Henderson would continue as a partner**: Dimon, 16.

Betsey Ann Eddy Countryman: Her name was also spelled *Betsy*.

Eliza: Eliza would move to New York along with Henry and Jane in the 1870s. She would marry Isaac A. Wood, serve as state president of the

Women's Christian Temperance Union, change her first name to Elizabeth, and finally move to Burbank, California.

127 **Hannah**: Hannah would marry Walter G. Wood three years later.

Fruit Vale Fourth of July celebration: Halley, 129.

her daughter Theresa's obituary: *Oakland Tribune*, March 9, 1911.

128 **couldn't remember seeing an apple**: Settlemeir, 99.

he felt like a criminal. Miller.

They sold six hundred to eight hundred apples: Miller.

"**Shylock had his day**": *Oregonian*, August 5, 1854.

129 **"Five dollars was sometimes paid for a single apple"**: Minto.

they were found to be damaged by heat: *California Farmer*, July 11, 1862.

"the receipts from Oregon": July 11, 1862. Cardwell (June 1906) cites very different figures. According to him, Oregon shipped 6,000 bushels in 1855 and 20,000 boxes in 1856. The size of a box hadn't yet been standardized, but it probably held forty to forty-five pounds, whereas a bushel holds about sixty pounds.

Pears, peaches, and plums: Lewelling 1893.

a box of Esopus Spitzenberg apples: Cardwell June 1906.

the major part of the winter [fruit] supply: Wadsworth, 477.

a two-story, ventilated fruit house: Wadsworth, 478–479.

130 **"Neat, Light, Cheap"**: *American Agriculturalist*, January 1864, 153.

forty thousand feet of lumber: *Sacramento Daily Union*, July 18, 1859.

Elisha would patent his own fruit-box design: *Sacramento Bee*, October 26, 1871. U.S. patent number 01197776 A.

"nearly all the fruit raised in Oregon": Guinn, 1303.

Meek "netted $45,000": Halley, 556.

131 **the Oregon and California Railroad Company**: Olson, 29.

Seth presented the editor: October 21, 1854.

132 **he added a branch nursery**: *Oregon Weekly Times*, October 21, 1854.

Hugh had worked for Seth: Pattison, 191.

Seth also planted his own orchard: *Daily National Democrat* (Marysville), October 27, 1860.

several strawberry varieties: Lewelling 1893. Strawberries grew popular much more quickly in California, where Alameda County produced 250 tons of them in 1860. Rhoda, 1874.

Oregon's first Italian prune orchard. Cardwell June 1906, 42.

132 **a German plum**: According to Cardwell (June 1906, 41–42), this "native of the Rhine, propagated from the seed, and cultivated more extensively in

Germany and over the continent of Europe than any other fruit, is the 'butter' and the condiment of the peasantry and a principal source of revenue." The German plum is also known as the Quetsche.

134 **He also bought a legitimate title**: *Pacific Rural Press*, January 5, 1884. Castro's compulsive gambling, combined with the necessity of paying for lawsuits against squatters, eventually resulted in the complete loss of his rancho. He fled to Chile and died there.

fifty thousand one- to two-year-old fruit trees: *California Farmer*, November 6, 1857.

a consignment on the steamship *Oregon*. *Daily Alta California*, September 12, 1858. Seth probably recorded the sale in his 1858 diary, but that diary has not survived.

59,374 grafted trees: California State Agricultural Society 1859, 263; California State Agricultural Society 1860, 101, 102; *California Farmer*, April 1, 1859.

cherries did "much better": *Daily Alta California*, September 16, 1860.

forty-eight acres of orchard: *Daily Alta California*, September 16, 1860.

"every variety of fruit and berry": *Pacific Rural Press*, September 29, 1877, *Daily Alta California*, May 15, 1882.

135 **supplied other, smaller nurseries.** *Daily Alta California*, December 10, 1858.

among the forty-six richest persons: Halley, 144.

With sixteen acres in orchard: *Daily Alta California*, September 18, 1860.

time to take on civic responsibilities. Halley, 144, 145.

136 **the society opened rooms in Sacramento**: *California Farmer*, June 7, 1855.

"plates of Seckle pears": Los Angeles *Star*, October 27, 1855.

the society sent a visiting committee: *Pacific Rural Press*, January 5, 1907.

Henderson and Alfred were both founding members. Williamson 1905b.

a delegate to the State Agricultural Society Convention. *Daily Alta California*, October 10, 1860.

Seth Luelling would also play a role: *Weekly Oregon Statesman*, August 30, 1859; Himes 1907, 333; California State Agricultural Society 1860, 469, 180. Seth was to have represented Oregon at the Pacific Rail Convention, the first convention aimed at establishing a transcontinental railroad, but he was at the fair in Sacramento throughout the rail convention in San Francisco. *Sacramento Daily Union*, September 23, 1859. Presumably Seth's wines were made from American grapes. They were a joint creation with A. Stanborn, probably a neighbor or farmhand.

137 **Seth visited the Puget Sound**: Seth Lewelling Papers; California State Agricultural Society 1860, 438.

137 **Seth visited Henderson and John**: Seth Lewelling Papers.

"a large number of horticulturalists": *Los Angeles Star*, Jan. 24, 1857.

John presented apples: S. L. Price, 91–94; *Sacramento Daily Union*, September 30, 1857.

active member of the horticultural society. *Sacramento Daily Union*, April 19, 1858; *Daily Alta California*, April 15, 1859.

John exhibited again: *Sacramento Daily Union*, October 6, 1858; *California Farmer*, October 8, 1858, and September, 16, 1859.

138 **"Preserved Meats and Vegetables, Pickles, Etc."** Mechanics' Institute, 1859.

The district held its first fair: The advent of the Bay District Fair caused the California Horticultural Society to stop holding fairs. San Francisco simply couldn't support two such fairs each year. *Daily Alta California*, April 12, 1860.

Henderson was vice president: *Sacramento Daily Union*, September 16, 1858; Halley, 130. Henderson's election was mentioned in the newspaper but omitted from Halley's account.

Alfred became a vice president: *Sacramento Bee*, June 22, 1860.

The Alameda County Agricultural Society held fairs: *Sacramento Daily Union*, October 8, 1859 (the same issue that reported the departure of the free lovers); *Sacramento Daily Union*, October 7,1859, and June 9, 1860; *Daily Alta California*, June 7, 1860.

the San Francisco Bay District Agricultural Society: *Sacramento Daily Union*, March 24, 1860; *Daily Alta California*, October 11, 1860; *California Farmer*, Oct. 12, 1860.

the best seedling almond. *Daily Alta California*, October 11, 1860; Milo Nelson Wood, 91.

139 **a new kind of association**: *Oakland Tribune*, February 26, 1939; *Pacific Rural Press*, November 18, 1916.

crowded with articles on fruit-growing: Williamson, 1905b.

a committee "to examine fruits": *Oregon Statesman*, October 18, 1859.

the Multnomah County Agricultural Society. Cardwell June 1906, 158.

The Fruit Growers' Association of Oregon: Himes 1907, 334.

CHAPTER 9: Folly and Glory

141 **a store to sell Spiritualist newspapers**: Buescher, 26.

Nelson J. Underwood: Buescher, 25.

"a middle-aged, benevolent-looking man": Buescher, 49.

Tyler's past. Buescher, 49-52.

143 **free lovers were advocates**: Davis 1881.

Spiritualists usually forswore it. Hardinge, 233.

the main events seem clear. Most of the quotations in this section are from the *Sacramento Daily Union*, May 19, 1860. The story was based on one first published in the *San Francisco Times*. Still extant articles on the attempted Harmonial Brotherhood colony are in the *San Joaquin Republican* (May 31, 1859; May 19, 1860; and September 20, 1860), the *Marysville Daily National Democrat* (May 19, 1860, and October 14, 1859), the *Oregon Statesman* (August 30, 1859), and the *Sacramento Daily Union* (October 8, 1859, and September 18, 1860). The story is also told in Buescher, 53–55.

144 **Levi, Albert, and Oregon**: According to Rhoda (Henderson Luelling Portfolio), Eliza Ann and Rachel were also on the trip, along with Levi and Albert (he did not mention Oregon). But newspaper accounts mention only sons.

Tyler's wife: *Sacramento Daily Union*, September 18, 1860.

the company included ten men: *Sacramento Daily Union*, Sept. 18, 1860.

the girl showed the court a vial of strychnine: Buescher, 53.

"The principal food": *Sacramento Daily Union*, May 18, 1860.

145 **sixty miles up a river.** This was probably the Coco River, which forms the border between Honduras and Nicaragua, although newspaper articles refer to the Como River.

"These radical reformers": *Sacramento Daily Union*, May 19, 1860.

healthy German girls: Buescher, 54.

Tyler and his wife "had seceded": *Sacramento Daily Union*, May 19, 1860.

"pestilent doctrine" of free love. *San Joaquin Republican*, May 19, 1860.

146 **Albert would be living with Asenath**: Albert worked for John Bozarth even after Asenath's death, in 1874, and until his own death, in 1883. He was married, shortly before Asenath died, in a triple ceremony with two of her children. When he died he left a wife and two children (a third child had died in infancy).

Henderson Luelling was her first husband. *Oakland Tribune*, March 9, 1911.

he was a storekeeper in Brooklyn: *Great Register of Alameda County*, 1866.

working as a merchant in San Francisco. *Great Register of San Francisco*, 1868.

147 **Henderson the elder was calling himself**: *Great Register of Alameda County*, 1866.

Meek had visited California: According to Seth's 1854 diary, Meek left July 15 and returned August 6.

147 **letter to Fidelia Stone**: Dimon, 17.

148 **he offered his share in the farm**: His share was half of his, Henderson's, and Alfred and Mary's claims, minus forty-two acres sold to Seth in 1857, ten acres sold to Hector Campbell in 1854, and two acres for the graveyard.

149 **eight years to repay the loan.** Because profits were decreasing for Oregon fruit growers, Miller and Lambert started a nursery for seeds, bulbs, and rare plants and trees, such as ginkgoes. Henry Miller also imported Oregon's first Italian prune trees, from which Seth would start the state's first Italian prune orchard. In 1870 Miller moved to Portland, where he ran a flower shop and ornamental nursery. Lambert continued to manage the Milwaukie orchard. In the mid-1870s he introduced the Lambert cherry, from a seedling rootstock that overtook the grafted cutting. Trained by the Luellings in horticulture, Lambert would become Seth's respected colleague in the fruit business and his competitor in horticultural fairs.

Meek arranged with a local bank: Dimon, 18.

Meek bought 400 acres to start: Halley, 555. The land had been part of San Lorenzo Baja, the rancho of Barbara Soto, Guillermo Castro's sister.

150 **in 1864 he would have 4,200 cherry trees**: Halley, 555.

He would have sixty to seventy-five horses: Baker, 183.

"More than three fourths of all the cherries": Rhoda 1874, 465.

151 **among the first farmers to ship cherries**: Baker, 181.

plants he bought from Seth Luelling. In 1873, according to his diary, Seth sold Meek poplar, coral bark maple, ash, buckeye, larch, dogwood, sugar maple, beech, mulberry, ironwood, and elm trees, and Carolina allspice and huckleberry shrubs.

CHAPTER 10: Seth

153 **the surviving diaries**: The diaries in the Oregon Historical Society collection are from 1854, 1859, 1860, 1862 to 1873, and 1875 to 1878.

154 **Seth planted filberts**: Schuster (99) and others have conjectured that the Luellings were the first, or among the first, to introduce to Oregon the filbert—the European hazelnut, or *Corylus avellana*—which they supposedly imported from England and Austria. If Henderson brought filbert trees to Oregon, he probably obtained them not from Europe but in New York (A. J. Downing was selling seven varieties of filberts in 1845, and Ellwanger and Barry listed two varieties, red and white, in their 1860 catalog). But filberts weren't included in Seth's lists of plants that Henderson brought from the East Coast. Seth probably got filbert nuts or suckers from his friend and neighbor Henry Miller, who imported filberts to Oregon in 1855 (*Willamette Farmer*, February 2, 1877). Seth listed "large English" filberts in his 1870 catalog (Schuster, 100).

155 **the state had 338 hives**: *Oregon Argus*, August 7, 1858. The paper noted that Meek and Eddy had 25 of those hives, but I suspect they were actually Seth's.

156 **John's orchard was under two feet of water**: *Oakland Tribune*, April 9, 1853.

famous for its pure white flour. Olson, 45. Joseph Kellogg invented a machine for separating the edible seeds of blue-pod (farewell-to-spring, or *Clarkia amoena*) from the wheat.

Sweet Alice apple: Sweet Alice is in a fruit list at the back of Seth's 1866 diary, so that is probably the year he first sold the variety.

Mrs. Butler: Emma Hardinge described Mrs. Butler as displaying "gifts of mediumship in the direction of test, trance, and clairvoyance, not excelled by any in America. . . . . She was generally influenced by the spirit of a poor boy calling himself 'Jack,' who, it seemed had lived a few years on earth, a friendless, homeless, vagabond life." Hardinge, 479.

157 **"I estimate the number of Spiritualists at about one-fifth of the population"**: Hardinge, 479–480.

C. A. Reed, another Salem Spiritualist: Hardinge, 480.

158 **a severely restricted diet.** *Willamette Farmer*, November 3, 1876; *Sunday Oregonian*, February 20, 1910. The latter article was written by Eugene Thorpe, who had joined Willie in anti-Spiritualist and pro-temperance activities.

Seth had once raised his own wheat: *Daily Alta California*, November 26, 1866.

160 **Seth bought a "bathing tub" . . . for $211**: The price of the tub is from the *Oregon Sunday Journal*, March 31, 1940. The *Journal* said he bought the tub in 1859, but the date must be wrong, unless Seth waited nine years to assemble the bathtub.

161 **Andrew Eddy**: Andrew had remained in Oregon with his father when Rachel moved to the Bay Area. After the divorce, Seth Eddy married George Grimes's widow, Marietta Miller Grimes.

Seth was canning whole fruit: By 1870 home canning was routine for many American families. Jars of various types were made for the purpose, with glass or metal caps and rubber sealing rings, and farm magazines provided detailed instructions.

Seth would buy them a piano: *Oregon Sunday Journal*, March 31, 1940.

162 **California had nearly forty professional nurseries.** *Pacific Rural Press*, November 18, 1916.

"California sent us apples": Cardwell March 1906, 38.

162 **Henry Miller believed that the list**: *Willamette Farmer*, December 29, 1876.

George Walling's seedling Late Peach Plum: *Willamette Farmer*, February 2, 1877. Seth and George Walling of Oswego, frequently bought trees from one another. Whichever cultivar Seth's trees were, most of them were killed by a late frost in 1873.

163 **he didn't know the parentage.** *Oregonian*, July 25, 1870; Wickson, 282.

***Portland Daily Bulletin* described the big, sweet new cherry**: Reprinted in *San Francisco Examiner*, August 17, 1870.

Seth sent a pound of the cherries: Ellison, 330, 332.

164 **more money from the Black Republican**: Lewelling 1893.

John, however, was not entirely impressed: *Pacific Rural Press*, September 20, 1879.

165 **Oregon's first statewide Republican convention**: *Oregon Argus*, February 21, 1857.

The exclusion clause: The clause was invalidated by the Fourteenth Amendment to the U.S. Constitution in 1868 but remained on the books until 1926.

166 **direct primary election**: W. C. Woodward September 1911, 227.

adopted the Republican Party's: W. C. Woodward September 1911, 235.

firmly renounced abolitionism. W. C. Woodward September 1911, 250.

Thomas Dryer: W. C. Woodward September 1911, 259.

Milwaukie's Grant Club: *Oregon City Enterprise*, February 29, 1868. Hector Campbell chaired the club.

167 **Florence Olson Ledding, later explained**: *Oregon Sunday Journal*, March 31, 1940; McClintock, June 1967, 167.

also probably a seedling of Black Eagle: Wickson, 282.

a "colored man," John "Setin": The man's name was probably Seton or Seaton. Seth never mentioned him again in his surviving diaries.

twelve-year-old Black runaway: The boy's name was John Hicklin, and he may have been fleeing poverty, an abusive stepfather, or both. *Morning Oregonian*, July 19, 1885.

168 **"a most valuable acquisition"**: *Northwest Horticulturist*, January 1898, 146; Hines, 498.

Golden Prune. Williamson 1916, 21; Bailey, 17.

four hundred pounds per tree. *Pacific Rural Press*, April 11, 1914.

They grew well in California: *Pacific Rural Press*, April 14, 1914.

Seth's other creations: *Northwest Horticulturalist*, January 1898.

bought at least one subscription: Seth Lewelling Papers.

he took leadership roles: In 1870 and 1878 Seth was elected to the finance committee of the State Agricultural Society; in 1870 and 1871 he was chief marshal of the state fair pavilion; and in 1879 and 1880 he served as president of the society. *State Rights Democrat* (Albany), January 28 and December 20, 1870; *Eugene City Guard*, December 14, 1878; *Willamette Farmer* September 12, 1879, and June 18, 1880.

169 **he trained Ezra Meeker**: *Oregonian*, February 18, 1940.

J. M. Ogle, of Puyallup Nursery: Seth Lewelling Papers.

he would . . . graft the tops together: *Oregonian*, June 7, 1903. Other horticulturists were doing this sort of grafting, too. You can see it in the 1878 illustration of Eli's farm in San Lorenzo.

trees that bore several kinds of fruit: *Northwest Horticulturalist*, January 1898.

"stingiest man": Ledding.

fruit dryer: *Willamette Farmer*, May 23, 1884.

shipping cherries to California. August 5, 1871.

a five-foot branch of a Royal Ann: July 30, 1871.

170 **ban on work on Sunday.** Seth quoted someone, probably an employee, in his 1877 diary: "There is Mr Luelling he is a good moral man he helps the Poor & is a good man every way a side from that I don't think that is verry good he will work Sundays & every thing of that kind."

Spiritualists other than Andrew Jackson Davis. The writers were S. J. Finney, Datus Kelley, and Warren Chase.

New Era Spiritualist camp: McClintock 1967, 201. The camp is still operating, as New Era Church. The property includes a hotel built in 1890.

secretary of the camp. *Willamette Farmer*, June 23, 1882.

171 **the stage mediums**: Hardinge, 480. In public "tests," mediums would prove they knew personal information about strangers. The audience was to believe that the information came from spirits.

W. E. Jones, a Portland merchant: "Specialities: Books on Spiritualistic, Theosophic, Freethought, Political, Social and Sexiologic Subjects." Seth Lewelling Papers.

172 **included two of Henderson's grandchildren**: *Oregon Daily Journal*, June 30, 1937.

an officer for both the Oddfellows and the Good Templars: *Washington Independent*, July 1, 1875, and July 22, 1875.

172 **Mary Harlan**: Mary was from San Ramon, California.

he took a case to trial: *Washington Independent*, June 17, 1875.

172 **Willie continued his straight-laced activities**: *Oregon City Enterprise*, January 31 and April 11, 1878; *New Northwest*, May 11, 1877.

lectures to expose Spiritualism: *Oregon City Enterprise* March 22 and March 29, 1877. They may have got no further on the lecture circuit than Salem. I found no more announcements nor any reviews of their presentations.

173 **he gave the opening address**: *Oregonian*, October 20, 1877.

a special journal just for the trip: Seth Lewelling Papers.

Henry Charles Wilson. Their daughter, Pearl, had died at about two years old in 1872. She was buried in the plot reserved for her grandfather.

Rubie Rosella Cadwell: Reichelt, 110.

174 **descendants of Caleb Rich**: *San Jose Mercury*, December 27, 1883.

Through Caleb's will: To his widow's distress, Caleb left $10,000 in money and lands at his death to a group of San Jose Spiritualists, for the support of the "Harmonial Philosophy or Science of the Soul." His will specified that "no part of the funds shall ever go to the support of the Bible or the creeds derived therefrom, it having become such a tax and burthen on the world. The main object shall be to investigate in every practical way the capabilities and science of the soul." *San Jose Mercury*, August 11, September 2, and September 4, 1883.

Mr. Shortridge: This may have been Elias Shortridge, a Church of Christ minister and father of Clara Shortridge Foltz, who won the right of women to attend law school in California.

175 **Seth saw, for the first time, the woolly aphid**: Lewelling 1892.

Indicted for embezzlement: *Morning Times* (Oakland), September 14, 1878; *Daily Alta California*, February 2 and 18, 1879. Soon after securing his freedom, O. C. married Emily Jane Norris, of San Ramon. For a time he ran the Norris family ranch, which produced wheat, barley, and hogs. He later moved to Fresno, where he managed hotels. His son Oregon Columbia eventually changed his last name to Llewellyn. *Martinez News-Gazette*, November 21, 1896; *Stockton Evening Mail*, May 4, 1896; *Fresno Morning Republican*, June 29, 1912; *Alameda Daily Argus*, July 1, 1912.

176 **Henderson was lying dead**: *San Jose Daily Herald*, December 28 and December 30, 1878.

Willard Harvey . . . drowned: *Oregon City Enterprise*, December 29, 1911.

Willie died: *Oregonian*, August 29, 1879. *Willamette Farmer*, September 12, 1879. Mary Harlan Luelling moved to the Bay Area with Lorin Leroy when he was six. He grew up to become a civil engineer in Oakland. Mary did not remarry. At some point both she and her son changed their last name to Llewellyn.

Seth decided to sell off all his nursery stock: *Oregonian*, April 9, 1902.

Alfred's daughter Annie died: *San Francisco Examiner*, October 2, 1886.

"highly esteemed pioneer": *Daily Morning Times* (San Jose), December 28, 1880.

177 **stores closed for the day**: Hayward Area Historical Society.

"one of the best pieces of land": *Oakland Tribune*, January 6, 1883.

Seth arrived in California: *Oakland Tribune*, February 26, 1883.

Smith & Luelling's: *Livermore Herald*, January 10, 1884. Perhaps Seth had concluded that Oregon Champion, a cultivar from Salem, was superior to the gooseberry he had bred himself.

CHAPTER 11: John

178 **John planted 500 apple trees**: Menefee, 355.

German Prune: *Napa Reporter*, April 7, 1882.

179 **John's apples were mainly the Golden Russet**: *Record Union* (Sacramento), October 7, 1882.

apricots . . . were being canned and bottled: *Los Angeles Evening Star*, September 17, 1880.

180 **John planted 1,600 almond trees and 50,000 vines**: Menafee, 355.

one of two principal almond growers: *St. Helena Star*, April 27, 1877.

he raised ten thousand pounds of them: *St. Helena Star*, September 28, 1877.

springs would provide plentiful water: Menefee, 355; S. L. Price, 42; *Pacific Rural Press*, April 6, 1878.

including running water and a cistern: S. L. Price, 30, 42. The water system John designed is still functional today.

181 **John designed the area around the house**: S. L. Price, 36, 48; *St. Helena Star*, September 3, 1880.

among the most beautiful in the valley: *St. Helena Star*, October 27, 1882.

he paid as much as a thousand dollars: S. L. Price, 32.

John continued to develop the property: *St. Helena Star*, November 25, 1881, and April 4, 1879.

183 **"Prospects in California"**: *Sacramento Daily Union*, June 7, 1862.

County committee on credentials: *Daily Alta California*, August 2, 1868.

Board of Forest Commissioners: *Sacramento Daily Union*, February 14, 1872.

183 **he died of tuberculosis**: *Sacramento Daily Union*, May 7, 1872. The spring—Adams Springs—would later be developed as a resort, but Elisha probably slept there in a tent.

offered the land for sale: *Alameda Daily Argus*, July 3, 1882.

"**. . . the largest apple orchard in the county**": *Oakland Tribune*, October 5, 1885.

185 **John was elected Worthy Master**: August 15, 1874.

John and his family took active roles: *Petaluma Weekly Argus*, December 17, 1875; *St. Helena Star*, January 7, 1876 and January 27, 1883; *Sacramento Daily Union*, August 30, 1879; *Pacific Rural Press*, June 26, 1875 and October 14, 1876. The Grangers' Bank was situated in the Grangers' Building in San Francisco, on the northeast corner of California and Davis streets. On the same floor was the California Farmers' Mutual Fire Insurance Association. Upstairs were the state Grange headquarters.

186 **the Bank of St. Helena**: *St. Helena Star*, July 21, 1882.

drying grapes into raisins: *St. Helena Star*, October 27, 1876.

187 **Malaga**: Malaga is also known as White Muscat of Alexandria.

shipped to Chicago Flame Tokay: *St. Helena Star*, September 23, 1881.

wine from cherries: *Daily Alta California*, September 16, 1860.

Frank Stock, of San José: Pinney, 265.

George B. Crane: *St. Helena Star*, May 18, 1885.

Charles Krug: Palmer, 509.

188 **brought back cuttings of 380 grape varieties**: Haraszthy, 24.

to make wine from his own grapes: Palmer, 509. Krug's wife, Carolina Bale, was a granddaughter of María Isidora Vallejo.

sold under foreign labels: *St. Helena Star*, December 24, 1880; Sullivan, 64.

St. Helena winegrowers: *St. Helena Star*, December 23, 1875.

189 **his own wine cellar**: *St. Helena Star*, May 27, 1875; June 24, 1875; September 1, 1876; September 15, 1876. The stone building still stands, at 1635 Spring Street.

gave new growers cuttings: *Weekly Calistogian*, January 1, 1879.

worked with the State Viticultural Commission: Palmer, 204.

Other members asked his opinion: *St. Helena Star*, April 29, 1876; June 18, 1880; July 2, 1880; July 14, 1880; February 25, 1881; and September 2, 1881.

order from a Philadelphia merchant: Sullivan, 62.

winegrowers produced nearly one million gallons: *Weekly Calistogian*, January 1, 1879.

lobbied the U.S. Congress: Palmer, 204. *St. Helena Star*, March 12, 1880.

190 **a committee to write a bill**: *St. Helena Star*, February 17, 1883.

a bonded warehouse: Palmer, 205; *St. Helena Star*, May 17, 1878; July 19, 1878; September 20, 1878; and June 12, 1883; State of California Historic Resources Inventory.

St. Helena Viticultural Hall: *St. Helena Star*, February 20, 1880; March 18, 1880; April 2, 1880; August 13, 20, and 29, 1880.

191 **initially been planted in 1832**: The first Buena Vista vines were planted by an indigenous man on his Mexican land grant. Haraszthy, 24.

appointed John and two other men: *Napa Valley Register*, September 16, 1880.

192 **infected vines at J. C. Weinberger's**: *St. Helena Star*, February 25, 1881, and March 11, 1881.

Henry Crabb had begun experimenting: Sullivan, 61.

he demonstrated to the group: *St. Helena Star*, March 16, 1883.

Nestor DeGouy: *St. Helena Star*, June 2, October 27, and December 15, 1882; *Napa Register*, July 20, 1883. Nestor was presumably of French origin; his wife advertised in the *Star*, on June 27, 1879, as a "French Dress Maker (Lately arrived from San Francisco)."

the revival of the California Horticultural Society: *Napa Valley Register*, September 24, 1879, and November 7, 1879. The California Horticultural Society was born a third time in 1932 and has sustained itself ever since.

"he had never seen a better season": *Napa County Reporter*, June 1, 1883.

picking five hundred pounds of apricots: *St. Helena Star*, July 27, 1883.

he was sick: *Pacific Rural Press*, January 12, 1884.

193 **a marble bust of himself**: *Napa County Reporter*, September 29, 1883. The bust was the work of Marion Wells, a prominent sculptor who taught with Virgil Williams in the San Francisco Design School, and the column was sculpted by Camellis Young. S. L. Price, 37.

harvested ten tons of almonds: *Napa County Reporter*, October 12, 1883. At this time other Napa Valley farmers were uprooting their almond trees in favor of vines, which were better suited to the climate.

his own grape cultivar: *St. Helena Star*, October 30, 1883; *Pacific Rural Press*, November 17, 1883.

194 **John died at a half hour after midnight**: *St. Helena Star*, January 27, 1883.

his body was carried by train: *Pacific Rural Press*, January 5, 1884.

194 **"a sterling good man"**: *Pacific Rural Press*, December 29, 1883.

his superior judgment: *Pacific Rural Press*, January 12, 1884.

194 **California producers won twenty-one medals**: Sullivan, 94.

195 **the ruined vineyards of St. Helena**: *St. Helena Star*, January 8, 1892.

1906 earthquake: *St. Helena Star*, June 8, 1906.

John Allyn wrote the *St. Helena Star*: December 31, 1883.

CHAPTER 12: Pests and Politics

196 **James R. Cardwell remembered**: June 1906, 156.

The enemies were various: For Seth, phylloxera was never a concern. As far as anyone could tell, neither Henderson nor anyone else had brought it into Oregon. The insect wasn't discovered in the state until 1955. It was found in a commercial vineyard only in 1990, when Oregon was finally experiencing its own wine boom.

"the Apple Blight": *Willamette Farmer*, September 12, 1879, and June 18, 1880. Although the September article was headed "Northwestern Horticultural Society" and the June article "State Horticultural Society," I believe that in both cases the journalist was writing about the Oregon State Agricultural Society. The Oregon State Horticultural Society didn't form until 1885.

Seth himself opined: Although he may have been unfamiliar with apple scab, Seth knew about fungal diseases of plants and ways to treat them. In 1865, for example, he bought potassium carbonite, a fungicide.

197 **sales of fruit trees gradually increased**: McClintock 1952.

177 local Granges in Oregon: McClintock, September 1967, 200.

198 **organization was too conservative**: McClintock, September 1967, 200.

Rachel Fisher: Rachel would die in 1868.

a "Spanish ram": *Oregon Statesman*, September 21, 1863.

local and statewide civic affairs: *Oregon Weekly Statesman*, January 12, 1870; *State Rights Democrat*, January 19, 1872; *Willamette Farmer*, February 15, 1873; November 20, 1874; and December 10, 1879; *Eugene City Guard*, December 14, 1878; *Oregon City Enterprise*, October 10, 1873; *Forest Grove Independent*, January 10, 1874; and *Washington Independent*, June 10, 1875.

Alfred and his family moved: William Mills had moved to the town of Clackamas, five miles southeast of Milwaukie, in 1873.

to host Abigail Scott Duniway: *New Northwest*, June 3, 1880.

Multnomah Grange met there twice: *Willamette Farmer*, March 7, 1884; March 21, 1884; May 30, 1884; October 31, 1884.

199 **Alfred and Mary moved back**: In Milwaukie Alfred became a notary public and established Milwaukie's first circulating library, in the law office of Thomas Lakin.

a statewide Spiritualists' organization: *Daily Reporter* (McMinnville), November 3, 1886. Alfred also served as secretary of the New Era Spiritualist camp, near Canby, in 1882. *Willamette Farmer*, June 23, 1882.

"the boys have shivereed them every night": Dimon, 34.

fellow reformers and intellectuals: McClintock 1967, 201.

201 **more than three-quarters of California's farmworkers**: Arreola, 7.

Many Chinese farmers came with horticultural expertise: "Many white farmers were taught valuable lessons in intensive farming by the Chinese. . . . They were among the first to show the practicability of irrigation. . . . While the white man plowed and sowed and then sat down to wait for rain, the Chinese dug and planted and supplied his vegetation from artificial sources of water." Baker, 181.

202 **one accidentally set fire to a fence**: *St. Helena Star*, July 29, 1875.

To two of them he gave a place to sleep: He noted in his diary that one of the men would require "a bland diet"—a good thing, since that is exactly what the Lewellings would provide.

chittum bark: Seth called chittum "Bear Berry," but he didn't mean kinnikinnick. Also known as *cascara sagrada* or *Rhamnus purshiana*, chittum was an indispensable laxative, of which Seth was a wholesaler as well as a gatherer.

stayed with the Luellings: In 1880, according to the U.S. Census, four laborers lived with Seth and Clarissa, from Oregon, New York, Denmark, and China. Sit Ah Bing and Sit Ah Fay lived in an outbuilding.

In a Federal Writers' Project interview: Ledding.

203 **Anson Burlingame . . . who had visited Seth in 1859**: Burlingame was in Oregon in 1859 because his parents, Joel and Freelove Angell Burlingame, lived in Linn County, just east of today's Lyons on Fox Prairie (also known as Fox Valley). Joel was a delegate to the national Republican convention that nominated Abraham Lincoln in 1860. The peach tree Anson sent would stand beside Seth's house for seventy-five years.

They did indeed work cheap: *Willamette Farmer*, February 4, 1881.

204 **refused to take jobs at the Salem woolen mills**: *Albany Register*, May 21, 1870.

thanks to Harvey Scott: Wong, 44–45.

broke up a Chinese woodcutters' camp: *Portland Tribune*, December 10, 2020.

205 **Bing was "fast supplanting its parent"**: Williamson 1905, 105–106.

206 **"ignorant, illiterate, lazy"**: Olson, 74.

Alliance met at Seth's house: McClintock, September 1967, 201–202.

207 **"brought to the Lewellings young men"**: McClintock, September 1967, 203.

first Single Tax Conference: Joseph Fels Fund Commission, 21. Henry George's followers live on today; along country roads in the Willamette Valley, I still occasionally see signs bearing the words *Single Tax*.

208 **U'Ren later remembered**: R. C. Woodward, 153.

U'Ren pretended to come under the influence: *Morning Oregonian*, March 9, 1908.

209 **"I read the book through"**: R. C. Woodward, 6–7.

Milwaukie Farmers' Alliance decided to organize: *Oregon Daily Journal*, April 10, 1921. *Oregon Daily Journal*, April 10, 1921.

They asked the state executive committee: Gaston, 565.

210 **"the same men held offices in both groups"**: McClintock, September 1967, 205.

J. D. Stevens was later described: *Oregon City Enterprise*, March 22, 1907.

elect a Populist presidential elector: The voters, not the parties, chose representatives to the Electoral College.

Seth invited U'Ren to become a partner: McClintock, September 1967, 204.

"There was no sale for nursery stock": Duruz 1941, 95.

nor would he agree to U'Ren's leaving the partnership: *Morning Oregonian*, March 9, 1908.

gave U'Ren a share in all the family's taxable property: Seth Lewelling Papers.

fruit-tree-planting boom: Williamson, 292–293.

212 **Alfred joined like-minded men**: *Oregon Courier*, March 20, 1891.

an indebtedness against the property: *Morning Oregonian*, March 9, 1908.

closed the nursery at Canby: McClintock, September 1967, 204.

U'ren had the authority to sign Seth's name: *Morning Oregonian*, March 9, 1908.

213 **They prepared fifty thousand pamphlets**: McClintock, September 1967, 208; Olson, 74.

Sophronia . . . claimed. . . . U'Ren countered: *Morning Oregonian*, March 9 and 10, 1908.

Not all the founding members were considered radicals: *Oregon Courier*, January 26, 1894. Among the founding members of the Milwaukie Grange were four Starkweathers and two Sellwoods, whose names today's Portlanders know well.

first, among Oregon Granges to endorse the reforms: *Oregon Daily Journal*, April 10, 1921.

J. D. Stevens walked all over Clackamas County: McClintock, September 1967, 208.

214 **"to punish the members who had broken their pledges"**: Steffens, 305.

215 **"Moses that was to lead the people of the state"**: *Morning Oregonian*, March 9, 1908.

the house in Milwaukie and twenty-two acres: *Morning Oregonian*, March 9, 1908.

216 **U'Ren moved out of the Lewelling home**: *Morning Oregonian*, March 9, 1908.

Sophronia filed an affidavit: *Oregon City Enterprise*, May 20, 1898.

formal charges against U'Ren: R. C. Woodward, 48.

hit each other in the face: R. C. Woodward, 50.

"Mrs. Lewelling and J. D. Stevens flooded the county": *Morning Oregonian*, March 10, 1908.

Sophronia and J. D. Stevens heckled him: *Oregon City Enterprise*, December 29, 1911; *Morning Oregonian*, March 18, 1907.

217 **"No finer men every lived"**: *Morning Oregonian*, March 9 and 10, 1908.

Seth has received special praise: Olson, 75.

CHAPTER 13: Afterwards

219 **still very prolific Gloria Mundi**: *Oregon Journal*, October 23, 1955.

A seventy-five-year-old flowering peach tree . . . was uprooted and transplanted: *Oregonian*, March 30, 1940.

220 **"a famous picnic ground"**: *San Francisco Call*, April 13, 1896.

the house . . . was partially destroyed by fire: *San Francisco Call*, July 3, 1913.

proposed moving one of Henderson's original apple trees: *San Francisco Chronicle*, September 16, 1923; *Oakland Tribune*, January 20, 1923.

Fruitvale Women's Club planted three young redwood trees: *Oakland Tribune*, February 22, 1924.

223 **price of a box of pears fell**: J. S. Smith, 108.

The ranch also produced table grapes, apricots, citrus: *St. Helena Star*, July 28, 1884, and October 4, 1889; *Napa Weekly Journal*, January 14, 1886 and January 27, 1887.

223 **San Lorenzo farm, whose even more diverse products**: S. L. Price, 118.

Alameda County bought it, in 1930: S. L. Price, 120.

223 **sale of the first parcel John bought in Napa Valley**: S. L. Price, 113–114.

director of the Grangers' Bank of California: *St. Helena Star*, July 28, 1884.

director of the St. Helena Vinicultural Association: *St. Helena Star*, July 26, 1889.

about four hundred acres, to Raymond: S. L. Price, 122.

227 **Seth's Golden Prune was "superior"**: Williamson 1902, 105.

the plum had to be "chased down": *Pacific Rural Press*, April 11, 1914

Bibliography

Altonen, Brian Lee. "Asiatic Cholera and Dysentery on the Oregon Trail: A Historical Medical Geography Study." PhD diss., Portland State University, 2000.

Arreola, Daniel D. "The Chinese Role in the Making of the Early Cultural Landscape of the Sacramento-San Joaquin Delta." *California Geographer* 15 (Fall 1975): 1–15.

Bailey, G. E. *A Manual of Prune Culture in Idaho and the Northwest.* Chicago: Rand, McNally, 1896.

Baker, Joseph Eugene. *Past and Present of Alameda County, California.* Vol. 1. Chicago: S. J. Clarke, 1914.

Baldwin, Elmer. *History of LaSalle County.* Chicago: Rand, McNally, 1877.

Ballanger, Nathan H. "The Early Quakers of Henry County, Indiana." Paper read before Henry County Historical Society, 1890. Accessed February 15, 2021, http://www.hcgs.net/quakers.html.

Barlow, William. "Reminiscences of Seventy Years." *Oregon Historical Society Quarterly* 13 (September 1912): 276–278.

Beecher, Henry Ward. "Indianapolis in 1843: A Henry Ward Beecher Letter." *Indiana Quarterly Magazine of History* 3 (December 1907): 189–193.

Boyd, Robert T. "Pacific Northwest Measles Epidemic of 1847–1848." *Anthropology Faculty Publications and Presentations* 147 (Spring 1994). Accessed February 14, 2022, https://pdxscholar.library.pdx.edu/anth_fac/147.

Breck, Ruth Allendorf, ed. *The Eddy Family in America, Supplement 1968.* Middleboro, MA: Eddy Family Association, 1968.

Britten, Emma Hardinge. *American Spiritualism: A Twenty Years' Record of the Communion between Earth and the World of Spirits.* 4th ed. New York: Emma Hardinge Britten, 1872.

Brown, Tom. "Gardens of the California Missions." *Pacific Horticulture.* Accessed October 29, 2023, https://pacifichorticulture.org/articles/gardens-of-the-california-missions/.

Buescher, John Benedict. "The Miner's Dream: Magicians and Mystagogues in Gold Rush California." 2020. Accessed October 28, 2023, http://iapsop.com/jbb/2020__buescher___the_miners_dream.pdf.

Burnett, Peter H. *Recollections and Opinions of an Old Pioneer.* New York: D. Appleton, 1880.

Bussey, Daniel J. *The Illustrated History of Apples in the United States and Canada*. Mount Horeb, WI: Jak Kaw Press, 2016.

Buys, John William. "Quakers in Indiana in the Nineteenth Century." PhD diss., University of Florida, 1973.

California State Agricultural Society. *Transactions of the California State Agricultural Society during the Year 1858*. Sacramento: John O'Meara, State Printer, 1859.

———. *Transactions of the State Agricultural Society during the Year 1859*. Sacramento: C. T. Botts, State Printer, 1860.

Cantor, Geoffrey. "Quakers and Science: An Overview." *Quaker Religious Thought* 99 (2003), article 10.

Capron, Elisha Smith. *History of California, from Its Discovery to the Present Time*. Boston: John P. Jewett, 1854.

Cardwell, James Robert. "President's Report." In *First Biennial Report of the Oregon State Board of Horticulture*. Salem, OR: Frank C. Baker, State Printer, 1893.

———. "A Dear School: A Trifling Circumstance and Its Results." In *Sixth Biennial Report of the Board of Horticulture*, 179–183. Salem, OR: W. H. Leeds, 1900.

———. "Early Horticultural Days in Oregon." *Proceedings and Papers of the Twenty-fourth Annual Meeting of the Oregon State Horticultural Society*. December 7–8, 1909.

———. "The First Fruits of the Land: A Brief History of Early Horticulture in Oregon, Part 1." *Quarterly of the Oregon Historical Society* 7 (March 1906): 28–51.

———. "The First Fruits of the Land: A Brief History of Early Horticulture in Oregon, Part 2." *Quarterly of the Oregon Historical Society* 7 (June 1906): 151–162.

Carpenter, Daniel. *Democracy by Petition: Popular Politics in Transformation, 1790–1870*. Cambridge, MA: Harvard University Press, 2021.

Carr, Ezra S. *The Patrons of Husbandry on the Pacific Coast*. San Francisco: A. L. Bancroft, 1875.

Carraway, Ann. "A Travel Log of 1847 as Told by Martha Bonser Armstrong." Accessed January 23, 2022, http://www.oregonpioneers.com/BonserFamily.htm.

Clauser-Roemar, Kendra. "Tho' We Are Deprived of the Privilege of Suffrage: The Henry County Female Anti-Slavery Society Records, 1841–1849." Master's thesis, Indiana University, 2009.

Coffin, Addison. *Life and Travels of Addison Coffin: Written by Himself*. Cleveland: William G. Hubbard, 1897.

Coffin, Levi. *Reminiscences of Levi Coffin: The Reputed President of the Underground Railroad*. 2nd ed. Cincinnati: Robert Clarke, 1880.

Cook, S. F. "The Epidemic of 1830–1833 in California and Oregon." *University of California Publications in Archaeology and Ethnology* 43, no. 3 (1955): 303–326.

Cosgrove, Hugh. "Reminiscences of Hugh Cosgrove." *Quarterly of the Oregon Historical Society* 1 (September 1900): 253–269.

Coxe, William. A *View of the Cultivation of Fruit Trees and the Management of Orchards and Cider*. Philadelphia: M. Carey and Son, 1817.

——. Manuscript, 1810–31. U.S. Department of Agriculture National Agricultural Library Botany Collections, Beltsville, MD.

Cromwell, Robert J. A *Short History of the "Old Apple Tree," Located in the Old Apple Tree Park, Vancouver National Historic Reserve, Vancouver, Washington, Compiled From Various Historical Sources.*" Northwest Cultural Resources Institute Short Report No. 34. Vancouver, WA: Fort Vancouver National Historic Site, 2010.

Daniels, R. B. "Soil Erosion and Degradation in the Southern Piedmont of the USA." In *Land Transformation in Agriculture*, ed. M. G. Wolman and F. G. A. Fournier, 407–428. New York: John Wiley and Sons, 1987.

Dary, David. *The Oregon Trail: An American Saga*. New York: Knopf, 2004.

Davis, Andrew Jackson. *Principles of Nature, Her Divine Revelations, and a Voice to Mankind*. New York: S. S. Lyon and William Fishbough, 1847.

——. *The Genesis and Ethics of Conjugal Love*. Boston: Colby & Rich, 1881.

Delp, Robert W. "A Spiritualist in Connecticut: Andrew Jackson Davis, the Hartford Years, 1850–1854." *New England Quarterly* 53 (September 1980): 345–362.

Diamond, David. "Migrations: Henderson Luelling and the Cultivated Apple." PhD diss. University of Northern Arizona, 2004.

Dimon, Elizabeth F. *'Twas Many Years Since: 100 Years in the Waverley Area, 1847–1947*. Milwaukie, OR: E. F. Dimon, 1981.

Dorrel, Ruth, and Thomas D. Hamm. "Duck Creek Monthly Meeting Births and Deaths (Henry County)." Indiana Historical Society Press, 2008. Accessed April 6, 2021, https://indianahistory.org.

Down, Robert Horace. A *History of the Silverton Country*. Portland: Berncliff Press, 1926.

Downing, Andrew Jackson. "A Few Words on Fruit Culture." *Horticulturalist* 6 (July 1851): 297–299.

——. *The Fruits and Fruit-Trees of America*. New York: John Wiley & Son, 1869.

Downing, Charles. *Selected Fruits: From Downing's Fruits and Fruit-Trees of America*. New York: John Wiley & Son, 1871.

Doyle, Arthur Conan. *The History of Spiritualism*. Vol. 1. New York, George H. Doran, 1926.

Dunn, Jacob Piatt. *Indiana: A Redemption from Slavery*. Boston and New York: Houghton, Mifflin, 1888.

Duruz, Willis Pierre. "Notes on the Early History of Horticulture in Oregon: With Special Reference to Fruit-Tree Nurseries." *Agricultural History* 15 (April 1941): 84–97.

———. *Principles of Nursery Management*. New York: A. T. De La Mare, 1950.

Dykstra, Robert R. *Bright Radical Star: Black Freedom and White Supremacy on the Hawkeye Frontier*. Cambridge, MA: Harvard University Press, 1993.

———. "White Men, Black Laws." *Annals of Iowa* 46 (Fall 1982): 403–440.

Edward, G. Thomas. "The Oregon Trail in the Columbia Gorge, 1843–1855: The Final Ordeal." *Oregon Historical Quarterly* 97 (Summer 1996): 134–175.

Elliott, Errol T. *Quakers on the American Frontier: A History of the Westward Migrations, Settlements, and Developments of Friends on the American Continent*. Richmond, IN: Friends United Press, 1969.

Ellis, William. *The Compleat Cyderman: or, the Present Practice of Raising Plantations of the Best Cyder Apple and Pear-Trees, with the Improvement of Their Excellent Juices*. London: R. Baldwin, 1754.

Ellison, Joseph W. "The Beginnings of the Apple Industry in Oregon." *Agricultural History* 11 (October 1937): 322–343.

Esthaven, C. R. "By Boat from Indiana: How the Pioneer Fruit Trees Came to the 'Far West.'" *Fruit Grower and Farmer* 26 (November 1, 1915): 5, 21.

Fisher, Rachel. "Letters from a Quaker Woman: Rachel Fisher." In *Covered Wagon Women*, ed. Kenneth L. Holmes, 97–108. Glendale, CA: Arthur H. Clark, 1983.

Fox, Henry Clay, ed. *Memoirs of Wayne County and the City of Richmond, Indiana*. Vol. I. Madison, WI: Western Historical Association, 1912.

Garretson, Owen A. "The Lewelling Family—Pioneers." *Iowa Journal of History and Politics* 27 (October 1929): 548–563.

Gaston, Joseph. *The Centennial History of Oregon, 1811–1912*. Vol. I. Chicago: S. J. Clark, 1912.

———. "Travelling on the Underground Railroad in Iowa." *Iowa Journal of History and Politics* 22 (July 1924): 418–453.

Geer, Ralph C. "Occasional Address for the Year 1847." In *Transactions of the Ninth Annual Re-union of the Oregon Pioneer Association for 1879*, 32–42. Salem, OR: E. M. Waite, 1880.

Geer, T. T. "Response to Address of Welcome." In *Proceedings and Papers of the Twenty-fourth Annual Meeting of the Oregon State Horticultural Society, December 7-8, 1909*, 94–95. Portland: Oregon State Horticultural Society, 1909.

Gibson, James R. *Farming the Frontier: The Agricultural Opening of the Oregon Country, 1786–1846*. Seattle: University of Washington Press, 1985.

Graham, Sylvester. *A Lecture on Epidemic Diseases Generally, and Particularly the Spasmodic Cholera*. New York: Mahlon Day, 1833.

Grant, H. Roger. *Transportation and the American People*. Bloomington: Indiana University Press, 2019.

Gray, W. H. *A History of Oregon, 1792–1849*. Portland: Harris and Holman, 1870.

Guinn, J. M. *History of the State of California and Biographical Record of Coast Counties, California*. Chicago: Chapman Publishing, 1904.

Halley, William. *The Centennial Year Book of Alameda County, California*. Oakland: William Halley, 1876.

Hamm, Thomas D., April Beckman, Marissa Florio, Kirsti Giles, and Marie Hopper. "A Great and Good People: Midwestern Quakers and the Struggle Against Slavery." *Indiana Magazine of History* 100 (March 2004): 3–25.

Hamm, Thomas D., David Dittmer, Chenda Fruchter, Ann Giordano, Janice Mathews, and Ellen D. Swain. "Moral Choices: Two Indiana Quaker Communities and the Abolitionist Movement." *Indiana Magazine of History* 87 (June 1991): 117–154.

Haraszthy, Arpad. "Wine-Making in California." *Harper's New Monthly Magazine*, June 1864.

Hardinge, Emma. *Modern American Spiritualism: A Twenty Years' Record of the Communion Between Earth and the World of Spirits*. 4th ed. New York: Emma Hardinge, 1870.

Hastings, Loren B. "Diary of Loren B. Hastings, a Pioneer of 1847." In *Transactions of the Fifty-first Annual Reunion of the Oregon Pioneer Association for 1923*, 12–26. Portland: F. W. Baltes, 1926.

Hayward Area Historical Society. *Cherryland, California: A History of the William MeekFamily*. Videorecording. https://www.haywardareahistory.org/william-meek-family-history.

Hedrick, U. P. *The Pears of New York*. Albany, NY: New York Department of Agriculture, 1921.

Heiss, Willard C., ed. *Abstracts of the Records of the Society of Friends in Indiana*. Pt. 4. Indianapolis: Indiana Historical Society, 1972.

Henris, John. "Apples Abound: Farmers, Orchards, and the Cultural Landscapes of Agrarian Reform, 1820–1860." PhD diss. University of Akron, 2009.

Hilty, Hiram H. *Toward Freedom for All: North Carolina Quakers and Slavery*. Richmond, IN: Friends United Press, 1984.

Himes, George H. "Historical Sketch of the Society." *Proceedings and Papers of the Twenty-fourth Annual Meeting of the Oregon State Horticultural Society, December 7–8, 1909*, 95–98. Oregon State Horticultural Society.

——. "History of Organization of Oregon State Agricultural Society." *Quarterly of the Oregon Historical Society* 8 (December 1907): 317–352.

Hinckley, Edith Parker. *Frank Hinckley: California Engineer and Rancher, 1838–1890*. Claremont, CA: Saunders Press, 1946.

Hines, H. K. *An Illustrated History of the State of Oregon*. Chicago: Lewis Publishing Company, 1893.

Hinshaw, Seth B. *The Carolina Quaker Experience*. Greensboro: North Carolina Friends Historical Society, 1984.

History of Henry County, Indiana, Together with Sketches of Its Cities, Villages and Towns. Chicago: Inter-State Publishing, 1884.

History of Placer County, California, with Illustrations and Biographical Sketches of Its Prominent Men and Pioneers. Oakland: Thompson & West, 1882.

History of Wayne County, Indiana, Together with Sketches of Its Cities, Village and Town Vol. II. Chicago: Inter-State Publishing, 1884.

Hockett, William A. "William Albert Hockett son of Rebecca Mills and Nathan H. Hockett." 1909. In *Hocketts on the Move: The Hoggat/Hockett Family in America*, ed. Sarah Myrtle Osborne and Theodore Edison Perkins, 749–58. Pleasant Garden, NC: S. M. Osborne, 1982.

———. "Experiences of W. A. Hockett on the Oregon Trail 1847." 1914. In Osborne and Perkins, *Hocketts on the Move*, 759–768.

Indiana Horticultural Society. *Annual Report of the Indiana Horticultural Society.* Indianapolis: R. J. Bright, 1872.

Jones, Louis Thomas. "Salem: The Pioneer Quaker Community of Iowa." Master's thesis, University of Kansas, 1911.

———. "The Quakers of Iowa." PhD diss. State University of Iowa, 1914.

Jones, Rufus M. *The Quakers in the American Colonies.* London: Macmillan, 1911.

———. *The Later Periods of Quakerism.* Vol. 1. London: Macmillan, 1921.

Joseph Fels Fund Commission. *Single Tax Conference.* Cincinnati: Joseph Fels Fund Commission, 1911.

Kellum, Rachel. "Reminiscence of the Settling of Iowa." Accessed November 9, 2021, http://freepages.rootsweb.com/~jeanlee/genealogy/rachelkellumarticles.htm.

Kerrigan, William. *Johnny Appleseed and the American Orchard: A Cultural History.* Baltimore: Johns Hopkins University Press, 2012.

Knepper, George W. *The Official Ohio Lands Book.* Columbus, OH: State Auditor, 2002.

Lake, E. R. *The Apple in Oregon.* Bulletin No. 81. Corvallis: Oregon Agricultural Experiment Station, 1904.

La Perouse, Jean-François de Galaup. *The Journals of Jean-François de la Perouse, 1741–1788.* Berkeley: Heyday Books, 1989.

Ledding, Florence Olson (Mrs. Herman Ledding). Interview by Sara B. Wrenn, Milwaukie, Oregon, January 30, 1939. Library of Congress Folklore Project, Life Histories, 1936–39. MSS55715:BOX A729.

Leeper, Jean. "Anti-Slavery Monthly Meeting, Salem, Iowa." 2007a. Accessed October 9, 2021, https://sites.rootsweb.com/~ialqm/Anti-SlaveryMeeting.html.

———. "Ownership of the Lewelling Quaker Museum." 2007b. Accessed October 9, 2021, https://sites.rootweb.com/~ialqm/lewellinghouseowners.htm.

———. "Beehive." 2007c. Accessed October 23, 2022, https://sites.rootsweb.com/~ialqm/beehive.com.

Lewelling, Seth. Diary, March 23, 1850–April 26, 1853. Special Collections and Archives, University of Oregon Libraries, Eugene, Oregon.

Lewelling, Seth. Papers, 1854–1915. MSS 23. Oregon Historical Society. Portland, Oregon.

———. "Horticulture in Early Days." In *The Second Biennial Report of the Oregon State Board of Horticulture to the Legislative* Assembly, Seventeenth Regular Session, *1893*, 242–245. Portland: Oregon State Board of Horticulture, 1893.

Lindley, Harlow. "Quakers in the Old Northwest." In *Proceedings of the Mississippi Historical Association for the Year 1911–1912*, ed. Benjamin F. Shambaugh. Vol. 5. Cedar Rapids, IA: Torch Press, 1912, 60–72.

"The Llewellyn Researcher." Accessed October 2, 2023, https://llewellyn-genealogy.ghost.io/.

Llewellyn Traces 5 (December 1993).

Luelling, Alfred. Letter to editor. *Willamette Farmer*, March 26, 1870.

———. Letter to Fidelia Meek. March 3, 1889. In Jane Harriet Luelling and Ellen Luelling Givens, *Luelling, Lewelling, Llewellyn-Campbell: Family History and Genealogy*, 1929, 10–14.

———. Letter to John Minto. January 27, 1884. In Luelling and Luelling Givens, *Luelling, Lewelling, Llewellyn-Campbell*, 1–2.

———. Letter to Ralph Geer. April 20, 1879. In Luelling and Luelling Givens, *Luelling, Lewelling, Llewellyn-Campbell*, 2–9.

Luelling, Jane Harriet. "Bringing the 'Traveling Nursery' Across the Plains in 1847: Compiled from Letters Written by Alfred Luelling and Others Interested in the History of the Luelling Family." In Luelling and Luelling Givens, *Luelling, Lewelling, Llewellyn-Campbell*, 1–17.

Marciel, Doris, and the Hayward Area Historical Society. *San Lorenzo*. Charlestown, SC: Arcadia Publishing, 2006.

McClintock, Thomas C. "The Luelling Family" (1952). Typescript. Valley Library, Oregon State University.

———. "Henderson Luelling and Seth Lewelling, Pioneers of Horticulture in Oregon." *Oregon Historical Society Quarterly* 68 (June 1967): 153–174.

———. "Seth Lewelling, William S. U-Ren and the Birth of the Oregon Progressive Movement." *Oregon Historical Society Quarterly* 68 (September 1967) 196–220.

Mayhill, R. Thomas. *Land Entry Atlas of Henry County, Indiana 1821–1849*. Knightstown, IN: The Bookmark, n.d.

McLagen, Elizabeth. *A Peculiar Paradise: A History of Blacks in Oregon, 1788–1940*. 2nd ed. Corvallis: Oregon State University Press, 2022.

Mechanics' Institute. *Report of the Industrial Exhibition: 1859*. San Francisco: Mechanics' Institute, 1859.

Mendenhall, Enos. Letter to Jacob Mendenhall. October 13, 1850. Typescript at the Colfax Area Historical Society, Colfax, California.

———. Letter to Jacob Mendenhall. May 1, 1853. Typescript at the Colfax Area Historical Society, Colfax, California.

———. Letter to John Mendenhall. February 2, 1873. Typescript at the Colfax Area Historical Society, Colfax, California.

Mendenhall, Sylvester Charles and Esther Annie I. Mendenhall Wright. *History of Geneology* [sic] *of the Family of Enos Thomas and Rachel Emily (Mills) Mendenhall of California*. Escondido, CA: 1961.

Menefee, C. A. *Historical and Descriptive Sketch Book of Napa, Sonoma, Lake, and Mendocino*. Napa, CA: Reporter Pub. House, 1873.

Miller, Arthur. "Reminiscences." In *Proceedings and Papers of the Twenty-fourth Annual Meeting of the Oregon State Horticultural Society, December 7–8, 1909*, 104–105. Portland: Oregon State Horticultural Society, 1909.

Minto, John. "Early Horticulture in Oregon." In *Fifth Biennial Report of the Board of Horticulture*, 172–175. Salem, OR: W. H. Leeds, State Printer, 1898.

Morgan, Dale L. "The Mormon Ferry on the North Platte: The Journal of William A. Empey, May 7–August 4, 1847." *Annals of Wyoming* 21 (July–October 1949): 111–167.

Napa Valley Historical Society. Lewelling Family Audiotape, no. 25. October 27, 1980.

National Register of Historic Places nomination for the Lewelling, Henderson and Elizabeth (Presnel), House, July 20, 2007, https://npgallery.nps.gov/NRHP/GetAsset/NRHP/82002620_text.

North Carolina Yearly Meeting. *A Narrative of Some of the Proceedings of North Carolina Yearly Meeting on the Subject of Slavery within Its Limits*. Greensborough, NC: 1848.

Nuermberger, Ruth Ketring. *The Free Produce Movement: A Quaker Protest Against Slavery*. Durham, NC: Duke University Press, 1942.

Ohio Pomological Society. *Transactions of the Ohio Pomological Society: Ninth Session*. Columbus: Follett, Foster, 1859.

Olson, Charles Oluf. *The History of Milwaukie, Oregon*. Milwaukie, OR: Milwaukie Historical Society, 1965.

Opper, Peter Kent. "North Carolina Quakers: Reluctant Slaveholders." *North Carolina Historical Review* 54 (January 1975): 37–58.

Oregon State Board of Horticulture. *First Biennial Report of the Oregon State Board of Horticulture*. Portland: A. Anderson, 1891.

Osborne, Sarah Myrtle, and Theodore Edison Perkins. *Hocketts on the Move: The Hoggatt/Hockett Family in America*. Pleasant Garden, NC: S. M. Osborne, 1982.

Owen, Robert Dale. *The Debatable Land between This World and the Next*. New York: Carleton, 1872.

Palmer, Lyman L. *History of Napa and Lake Counties, California*. San Francisco: Slocum, Bowen, 1881.

Pattison, Anna. "Miss Anna Pattison: From an Interview." In *Told by the Pioneers: Reminiscences of Pioneer Life in Washington*, 191–192. Vol. 1. Olympia: Washington Pioneer Project, 1937.

Peterson del Mar, David. *Oregon's Promise: An Interpretive History.* Corvallis: Oregon State University Press, 2003.

Phoenix, F. K. "Root Grafting." *Horticulturist and Journal of Rural Art and Rural Taste* 1 (December 1846): 280–282.

Pinney, Thomas. *A History of Wine in America: From the Beginnings to Prohibition.* Berkeley: University of California Press, 1989.

Pleas, Elwood. *Henry County; Past and Present: A Brief History of the County from 1821 to 1871.* New Castle, IN: Pleas Brothers, 1871.

Price, R. N. *Holston Methodism: From Its Origin to the Present Time.* Vol. 2. Nashville: Smith & Lamar, 1912.

Price, Sandra Leland. "The Lewellings: A Microhistory of Family Farming and Agricultural Development in California, 1850–2010." Master's thesis. Sonoma State University, 2011.

Prince, William. *Catalogue of Fruit and Ornamental Trees and Plants, Bulbous Flower Roots, Green-house Plants, &c. &c.* New York: T. and J. Swords, 1822.

Raynor, James O. *Journal of a Tour from Iowa to Oregon April 1847.* Mss. 158. Oregon Historical Society. Portland, Oregon.

Reichelt, Marie Ward. *History of Deerfield, Illinois.* Deerfield, IL: Glenview Press, 1988.

Republican Party of Oregon. *A Record of the Republican Party in the State of Oregon.* Portland: Register Publishing Company, 1896.

Rhoda, Franklin. "Cherry Culture in California." *Appendix to Journals of Senate and Assembly of the Twentieth Session of the Legislature of the State of California.* Vol.6. Sacramento: State Printer, 1874.

——. Material Relating to Henderson W. Luelling. Portfolio. Bancroft Library, University of California, Berkeley.

Rogue Digger. Medford, OR: Rogue Valley Genealogical Society, 1997.

Salem Monthly Meeting Minutes. Transcribed by Jean Leeper and Lewis Savage, 2007. Accessed October 9, 2021, https://sites.rootsweb.com/~ialqm/documents/SALEMMMMINUTESfrom1841SeparatistMeeting.pdf.

Schuster, C. E. "Notes on the History of Nut Production in the Pacific Northwest." In *Thirty-Sixth Annual Report of the Oregon State Horticultural Society*, 99–103. Portland: Oregon State Horticultural Society, 1944.

Settlemier, J. H. "Sixty Years of Nursery Business in Oregon." In *Oregon State Horticultural Society Proceedings*, 99–100. Portland: Oregon State Horticultural Society, 1910.

Smith, Elizabeth. Letter to Mrs. Pauline Foster and Mrs. Cynthia Ames. May 25, 1848. In T. T. Geer, *Fifty Years in Oregon: Experiences, Observations, and Commentaries upon Men, Measures, and Customs in Pioneer Days and Later Times*, 132–138. New York: Neale Publishing Company, 1912.

Smith, Jane S. *The Garden of Invention: Luther Burbank and the Business of Breeding Plants*. New York: Penguin Press, 2009.

Smith, Clarence L. and Wallace W. Elliott. *Illustrations of Napa County, California, with Historical Sketch*. Oakland, CA: Smith and Elliott, 1878.

Soulé, Frank, John H. Gihon, and James Nisbet. *The Annals of San Francisco*. 1855. Berkeley: Berkeley Hills Books, 1999.

Stainbrook, Lynda S. "Fort Ross Orchards: Historical Survey, Present Conditions and Restoration Recommendations" (manuscript). California Department of Parks and Recreation, 1979. Ross Conservancy Library, http://www.fortross.org/lib.html.

Stebbins, Giles B. *Upward Steps of Seventy Years*. New York: United States Book Company, 1890.

Steele, R. J., James P. Bull, and F. I. Houston. *Directory of the County of Placer for the Year 1861*. San Francisco: R. J. Steele, James P. Bull, and F. I. Houston, 1861.

Steffens, Lincoln. *Upbuilders*. New York: Doubleday, Page, 1909.

Sullivan, Charles L. *Napa Wine: A History from Mission Days to Present*. 2nd ed. San Francisco: Wine Appreciation Guild, 2008.

Swaim, H. H., ed. *Transactions of the Indiana Horticultural Society for the Year 1922*. Indianapolis: State Printing and Binding, 1923.

Taylor, Bayard. *Eldorado, or Adventures in the Path of Empire*. New York: Knopf, 1949.

Thompson, Roger Knowles. "John Bonser." Retrieved February 4, 2022, from http://www.orgenweb.org/bios/bonser-john-1.html.

Thompson and West. *Official Historical Atlas Map of Alameda County, California*. Oakland: Thompson and West, 1878.

Thornbrough, Emma Lou. *The Negro in Indiana before 1900: A Study of Minority*. Bloomington: Indiana University Press, 1993.

Thornburg, Thomas, to Henry Thornburg. In "An Early Quaker Letter from North Carolina," ed. Willard C. Heiss. *North Carolinian: A Quarterly Journal of Genealogy and History* 3 (June 1957): 293.

Victor, Frances Fuller. *The Early Indian Wars of Oregon*. Salem, OR: Frank C. Baker, State Printer, 1894.

Votaw, Anna M. "Andrew Hampton, Pioneer Nurseryman of Indiana." In *Transactions of the Indiana Horticultural Society for the Year 1908*, ed. W. B. Flick, 270–278. Indianapolis: State Printing and Binding, 1909.

Wadsworth, W. *The California Culturist: A Journal of Agriculture, Horticulture, Mechanism and Mining*. Vol. 1: June 1858–May 1859. San Francisco: Towne & Bacon, 1859.

Walske, Steven C., and Richard C. Frajola. *Mails of the Westward Expansion, 1803 to 1861*. Western Cover Society, 2015.

Weeks, Stephen B. *Southern Quakers and Slavery: A Study in Institutional History*. Baltimore: Johns Hopkins Press, 1896.

Weiner, Dana Elizabeth. "Racial Radicals: Antislavery Activism in the Old Northwest, 1830–1861." PhD diss. Northwestern University, 2007.

Wells, Robert V. "Family Size and Fertility Control in Eighteenth-Century America: A Study of Quaker Families." *Population Studies* 25, no. 1 (1971): 73–82.

Wickson, Edward James. "California Mission Fruits." *Overland Monthly*, May 1888, 501–505.

——. *The California Fruits and How to Grow Them*. 10th ed. San Francisco: Pacific Rural Press, 1889.

Williamson, H. M. "Henderson Luelling and Seth Lewelling, Pioneers of Horticulture in Oregon." In *Eighth Biennial Report of the Board of Horticulture of the State of Oregon*, 103–106. Salem, OR: J. H. Whitney, 1905a.

——. "Beginning and Growth of Nursery Business in Oregon." In *Eighth Biennial Report of the Board of Horticulture of the State of Oregon*, 291–293. 1905b.

——. "Early History of the Prune Industry in Oregon." *Proceedings of the Thirtieth Annual Meeting of the Oregon State Horticultural Society*, 19–27. Seventh Annual Report, 1915. Portland, Oregon: Metropolitan Printing Company, 1916.

Wilson, Hattie (Rachel) Luelling. Letter to Franklin Rhoda. August 24, 1915. Material Related to Henderson W. Luelling. Portfolio. Bancroft Library, University of California, Berkeley.

Wong, Marie Rose. *Sweet Cakes, Long Journey: The Chinatowns of Portland, Oregon*. Seattle: University of Washington Press, 2004.

Wood, M. W. *History of Alameda County, California*. Oakland, CA: M. W. Wood, 1883.

Wood, Milo Nelson. *Almond Varieties in the United States*. USDA Bulletin No. 1892. Washington, DC: U.S. Government Printing Office, 1925.

Woodward, Robert Charles. "William Simon U'Ren: In an Age of Protest." Master's thesis, University of Oregon, 1956.

Woodward, Walter Carleton. "The Rise and Early History of Political Parties in Oregon—IV." *Quarterly of the Oregon Historical Society* 12 (September 1911): 225–241, 243, 245–263.

Woodward, Walter Carleton. "The Rise and Early History of Political Parties in Oregon—V." *Quarterly of the Oregon Historical Society* 12 (December 1911): 301–350.

Wragg, W. J. "Pioneers in Iowa Horticulture." *American Fruits* 23 (March 1916): 62.

Acknowledgments

This project has taught me that archivists are among the nicest people in the world. I am especially grateful to Diane Curry of the Hayward Area Historical Society, Mariam Hansen of the St. Helena Historical Society, Roger Staab of the Colfax Area Historical Society, Dave Helman and Jean Leeper of the Luelling Quaker Museum, Greg Hemer of the Milwaukie Historical Society, Rachel Lilley of the Special Collections and Archives Research Center at Oregon State University, Kathy Stroud and Lauren Goss of Knight Library at the University of Oregon, and Nikki Koehlert of the Oregon Historical Society. Others who have helped with my research are Steve Harrison of Henderson County, North Carolina; Peter Strom of Colfax, California; Amanda Van Lanen, professor of history at Lewis-Clark State College; Barbara Mahoney, a longtime specialist in Oregon history; Kim Hummer, former research leader for the National Clonal Germplasm Repository in Corvallis, Oregon; Jim Labbe, who shared his research on Oregon's abolitionists; and Doug and Dave Wight, John Lewelling's descendants in St. Helena, California.

I am also thankful for the scholars who preceded me in researching the Lewellings and whose writings are refreshingly reliable: David Diamond, who wrote his dissertation on Henderson Luelling from his birth until his move to California; Sandra Leland Price, whose thesis concerns John Lewelling's Napa Valley farm; and John Benedict Buescher, who wrote about Henderson and his nemesis, E. S. Tyler, in *The Miner's Dream.*

I am grateful, too, to the staff of Oregon State University Press—especially my editor, Kim Hogeland—and to my copy editor, Ryan Schumacher.

I am indebted to my daughter, Rebecca Waterhouse, for her lovely maps. And I owe the most thanks of all to my husband, who read drafts of my chapters, accompanied me on research trips, patiently listened to all my Lewelling stories, and kept me well fed when I was too preoccupied to cook.

Index